❖ Advance Praise for *Writing to Make a Difference* ❖

"*Writing to Make a Difference* is a great balance of both instructional and interactive tips, tools, and exercises for those who want to effectively communicate the difference they are making in the world. This book helps to lower the barrier for organizations that desire to tell their story in a way that captures both head and heart."

Alandra L. Washington, Deputy Director, W.K. Kellogg Foundation

"Dalya Massachi's clear, helpful, and well-organized book should be on the shelf of every non-profit administrator, community organizer, and advocate. There is literally nothing else of its kind on the market. It is the *Elements of Style* for the grassroots fundraising and marketing world."

Leif Wellington Haase, Director, California Program, New America Foundation

"If you think your work is important, if you feel you have a message to deliver, if you have people that need help to understand how this is done — this is the book. Massachi is fresh, direct, professional and insightful, and is the perfect guide and a tremendous coach."

Jeff Hamaoui, CEO, Origo Inc. and social investment and enterprise specialist

"The Achilles' heel of many programs is the poor quality of the writing describing what the organization does. Now, Dalya Massachi has drilled down to all that is important about good writing. I recommend this book for those of us who write regularly, and for those of us who don't write because we don't think we can."

Kim Klein, author, *Reliable Fundraising in Unreliable Times*

"This is an outstanding work, one of the best I have read in the genre, and of possible use in university public relations and organizational communication courses. The writing lessons are succinct, the methods to convey them effective, and the style itself an example of professional brilliance. I recommend *Writing to Make a Difference* because I know that it will."

Dr. Michael Bugeja, Director, School of Journalism and Communication at Iowa State University and author, *Interpersonal Divide: The Search for Community in a Technological Age*

"For a manager, this book is a no-brainer. It's fast, concise, clear, and focused. For a team member, this book is the end to "preachy" communications training and the beginning of a new way of looking at the words you use and the impact you want them to have."

"I highly recommend this book to anyone who is studying, wants to work in, or is working in the not-for-profit environment. Writing is an essential skill for fundraising activities, and Massachi's book provides the techniques to build this skillset."

"I can now dispense with a whole shelf of books that partially address my needs in favor of one that was actually written for those of us working in grassroots and community settings."

"*Writing to Make a Difference* is an essential work for community improvement organizations, nonprofits, and value-based groups. Massachi offers practical advice and real-world scenarios in an accessible format, rich in illustrations and asides. Useful for experienced fundraisers as well as novices."

"*Writing to Make a Difference* is a guide for turning a socially committed person into a wordsmith who can spark the sensibilities and move the imagination."

"This book places you at the center of the craft of writing for social change and public benefit. While writing and re-writing require work, the long haul should be as fun as Massachi makes it."

"Massachi's voice sounds real and helpful. Her breadth of examples is remarkable—learn how dozens of organizations like your own write stirring messages. She also includes one of the best treatments I've seen of cross-cultural communication and how to recognize and avoid exclusionary language."

"This book is a must-have for anyone on the front lines of nonprofit development or communications. It's a rich source of tips and tools for everyone from the struggling beginner to the experienced writer. Dalya Massachi both explains and demonstrates how to write with technique as well as heart."

Ilona Bray, author, *Effective Fundraising for Nonprofits*

"I love this book -- it's a real contribution to the nonprofit management literature! [It guides us] to find our writing voice and help our audiences care more about our missions. This should be a reference on the desk of every nonprofit organization staff that has responsibility for writing."

Denice R. Hinden, PhD, ACC, President, Managance Consulting & Coaching

"Whether we write a little or a lot, few of us have the talent and hard-earned wisdom of Dalya Massachi. Now she lavishly shares that talent and wisdom in this book, with practicality and power. Her results-oriented approach to writing is unique and refreshing!"

Tess Reynolds, CEO, New Door Ventures

"Inspired and inspiring. I can't think of anyone who could not derive great benefit from this book…It is a great example of "walking the talk"—offering a model of all its lessons. I'll be recommending this book to all my clients."

Deborah Pruitt, Ph.D., Founder and Principal, Group Alchemy Consulting

"This is it: a straightforward, no muck, comprehensive compendium of facts, examples, and exercises to test the waters, build the boat, and take sail. This is one book I would recommend to every member of my team."

Johnson Hor, Esq., Board Member, Art Endowment, Inspire to Do, Lawyers' Club of San Francisco

"This book is as friendly as the *For Dummies*® books, but with much more depth. It feels almost as if Massachi wrote it just for me! The book is very well-designed and, of course, exceptionally well-written. I'd give it a 10 out of 10!"

Lori Warren, former Communications Director,
Insight Center for Community Economic Development

"With easy-to-implement techniques, *Writing to Make a Difference* brings to light how individuals can expand upon their current writing abilities to create powerful communications. I highly recommend this book to anyone connected with the nonprofit sector."

Lynne Norton, Marketing Manager, OpportunityKnocks.org

"I've watched Dalya Massachi succeed by taking her own advice. In the process, she has built a compelling framework for the craft of public-interest writing, and a powerful skill set for helping community activists. Take this walk with her!"

Melissa Everett, Ph.D., author,
Making a Living While Making a Difference: Conscious Careers for an Era of Interdependence

"Organizations and activists wanting to create a peaceful and equitable world need to communicate their ideas and vision clearly. This book gives simple-to-follow guidance on how to do this, in a world that is overloaded with jargon and complexity. A valuable resource for writers of all levels."

Sarah Hobson, Executive Director, New Field Foundation

"Nonprofit professionals must write concisely, yet with passion. This new resource provides the tips and examples all will find beneficial to support best our organizational missions."

SueAnn Strom, Vice President, Academic Partnerships, American Humanics

"This book is an excellent, comprehensive resource. Young people and seasoned professionals alike will find useful information on writing in a way that *will* make a difference."

Elaine Leibsohn, Vice President, America's Promise Alliance

"*Writing to Make a Difference* provides a good grounding for anyone who wants to influence or engage others toward any message, both inside and outside the organization."

Judith Wilson, M.C.C., executive coach and co-author,
Coaching Skills for Nonprofit Managers and Leaders

Writing to Make a Difference:
25 Powerful Techniques to
Boost Your Community Impact

By Dalya F. Massachi

First Edition

Writing
FOR COMMUNITY SUCCESS

Berkeley, CA

PUBLISHED BY WRITING FOR COMMUNITY SUCCESS
POST OFFICE BOX 5607, BERKELEY, CA 94705
www.dfmassachi.net

Bulk orders of this book are available at a discount; please contact the publisher.

Book design and illustrations: Sharon Constant/Visible Ink
Cartoons: Copyright Mark Litzler
Author photo: Copyright J. Daniel Sawyer
ISBN: 978-0-9788836-0-7
Library of Congress Control Number: 2006933986

Printed and bound in the United States of America
FIRST EDITION

Publisher's Cataloging-in-Publication Data
Massachi, Dalya F.
    Writing to make a difference : 25 powerful techniques
to boost your community impact / by Dalya F. Massachi.
-- 1st ed.
    p. cm.
    Includes bibliographical references and index.
    LCCN 2006933986
    ISBN-13: 978-0-9788836-0-7 (pbk.)
    ISBN-10: 0-9788836-0-8 (pbk.)
    ISBN-13: 978-0-9788836-1-4 (e-book)
    ISBN-10: 0-9788836-1-6 (e-book)
    1. Business writing. 2. Nonprofit organizations.
    3. Social service. 4. Schools.   I. Title.
    HF5718.3.M37 2011   808'.06665
                    QBI10-600024

About the Author

Dalya F. Massachi has been an avid writer—and reader—since learning to hold a pencil. Her first Letter to the Editor, about prayer in public schools, was published in her hometown (Charlotte, NC) newspaper when she was only twelve. She has been writing about social issues ever since.

Dalya has committed herself to sharing her writing skills and passion for social change with a wide variety of organizations and individuals across the country. For more than seventeen years she has worked as a trainer, writing coach, editor, consultant, journalist, and activist, primarily focusing on fund development and communications. Dalya has crafted countless successful marketing pieces, grant proposals, news articles, and columns. In addition, she has been involved with the production of several books (as co-editor, contributor, or copyeditor) and has produced a number of websites and radio pieces. Dalya currently pens "The Writer's Block" column on OpportunityKnocks.org.

Since 2001, Dalya has taught writing techniques to nearly 2,000 workshop, online seminar, and college course participants. Many professionals and volunteers have come to her for one-on-one writing coaching.

From 2000-2004, Dalya served as Founding Director of BAIDO: San Francisco Bay Area International Development Organizations. She recently sat on the advisory board of the Social Sector Leadership Certificate Program at John F. Kennedy University. Dalya has worked and/or studied in Central America, Africa, Israel, the United Kingdom, and several regions of the U.S. She holds an M.A. in Communication & International Development and a B.A. in International Studies. Since 2004 she has appeared in several editions of *Marquis Who's Who.*

You can learn more about Dalya's company, Writing for Community Success, at the end of this book.

To Mom, Dad, David, and Deborah.
You enrich my life beyond words.

Acknowledgments

Writing this book has been quite an adventure! I have learned an incredible amount both about writing and about myself. Much of that growth has been due to the fantastic people who have helped me along the way. Books are always collaborative in nature, and this one has proven to be a prime example. Let me begin to thank the many people who have contributed.

First, I have to thank the nearly 1500 participants in my writing workshops across the country and online since 2001, my wide range of one-on-one coaching clients, and scores of professionals in organizations I have been honored to work with. I am especially indebted to the Boston and San Francisco Bay Area public-interest communities, with whom I have worked especially closely. All of these wonderful people have offered me their insights, information, thoughts, and questions.

My friends and family — across the country — have listened patiently to my mishaps, given advice, lent or gifted me money, cheered me on, and otherwise supported me through this experience. And that has truly made all the difference.

A few people in particular need to be singled out:

- J. Daniel Sawyer was my Writing Buddy Extraordinaire, and offered a seemingly endless supply of help, encouragement, and laughs.

- Asher Davison, who appeared at just the right time, served as my excellent copyeditor and showed me how wonderful it can be to work with someone to help put the final polish on my "baby."

- Sharon Constant's graphic design and illustration expertise, and extremely supportive friendship, have meant a lot to me.

- Mark Litzler generously responded to my cold email request for some of his cartoons for this book. While many of his pieces have appeared in well-known publications, such as *The Chronicle of Philanthropy* and *The Harvard Business Review*, Mark was happy to open his portfolio to this first-time book author.

- Heather Cassell has, in a kind and supportive way, helped me get this book out to the people who can most benefit from it.

- Stephen Grettenberg saw me through various laptop crises and other computer-related challenges.

- Kenneth McGee, Michael R. Brown, Lynne Kehoe, my Women's Circle, and Korey Wong were there for me as good friends and checked up on me (as a writer and a person) frequently.

- Sandra Phillips, J. Robert Cox, Melissa Everett, Michael Bugeja, Josep Rota, Irma Herrera, and Sarah Hobson have, at different times in my writing life, served as strong, personable, successful mentors.

Since the beginning of my book-writing process I have sought feedback, and my community has been terrifically forthcoming. More than 80 people from my e-newsletter list lent me their ideas in my initial online survey of potential readers. Their input was invaluable, as I aimed to find out more about what people want and need to know as they go about *writing to make a difference*. Four other individuals reviewed early drafts and I am very grateful to them: Susan Belgard, Maureen Lopes, Katherine Ross, and Melissa Luke.

As I got closer to publication, many outstanding colleagues and friends stepped forward to offer their thoughts, immeasurably improving the final product. They included:

Alyssa Nickell, Ana-Marie Jones, Anne Perrick, Bill Coy, Bill Huddleston, Chris McKenna, Deborah Massachi, Deborah Pruitt, Diane de Lara, Fred Setterberg, Ilona Bray, Jane Scurich, Janet Camerena, Jeffery Obser, Jessica Hamburger, John Tobey, Kari Gray, Margaret Okuzumi, Marina DiCerbo, Martin Witte, Pam Swan, Pamela Hawley, Patricia Pellicena, Paulette Traverso, Randolphe Belle, Rose Diamond, Sarah Backes-Diaz, Seth Schneider, Shalini Nataraj, Stephen Cataldo, and Susan Marchionna.

My final book production team emerged from the ether to help me complete the last leg of the journey: Erin McReynolds, Beth DeLashmutt-Poore, and Daniel Lazo.

I extend my special thanks to the following organizations and individuals for granting me permission to print or reprint their original work. They, of course, retain all applicable copyrights: ahajokes.com, Center for Assessment and Policy Development, Josh Kahn of Humanized Productions, Insight Center for Community Economic Development, SPIN Project, Michael Barger of Walls of Hope School of Art & Open Studio, Janet Lockhart, Susan M. Shaw, and Bill Coy.

Last but not least, I have to mention the various spots that served as my research touchpoints and quiet writing spaces. I found my second home in libraries, especially the Berkeley Public Library, cafes, and cyberspace. Without them this book would not exist.

Contents

Preface

This is the book I wish had been around when I first started as a writer. In time, as I improved and needed deeper guidance, I probably would have re-read it more than once. Many of the tips I provide here are personal lessons learned through trial and error — or by picking up pointers along the way.

My journey started at a very young age. I remember writing poems, short stories, and letters as early as first grade. I relished the smooth motions of cursive and delighted in new words and phrases. When I was eight my family moved from upstate New York to North Carolina, and I turned to the written page to mourn the loss of my first home and friends.

By middle school my writing had turned into more than just a personal outlet. My political consciousness was starting to develop, and I wrote Letters to the Editor of my city's newspaper — and they got published. I wrote articles on a range of topics in my school's newsletter. My supportive parents sent me to summer writing programs to nurture my growing interest.

A MAJOR BUMP IN THE ROAD

But at age 13, a serious bicycle accident landed me in the hospital for eight weeks with a head injury. I lost everything. I could not walk, talk, feed myself, control my hands. My writing life was all but forgotten.

My father, however, was not about to give up on me. He knew that my writing self was trapped in there somewhere. As soon as I could hold a pen and put it to paper, there in my bed at the rehab hospital, he gave me a writing assignment. In my wobbly but marginally legible scrawl, I was to record the name of every person who entered my room: each doctor, nurse, family member, and friend.

It was a taxing effort. I thought I could not handle it. After all, I had just been through a life-threatening trauma. What value could a visitor list hold?

More than I knew.

As the long, drawn-out days turned into interminable weeks, the shaky lines formed into recognizable letters. The *o*'s got rounder and the *t*'s taller. As my doctors and therapists looked on, I was not the only one amazed.

And then a crucial moment imprinted itself on my memory. For weeks I had yearned to enjoy the outdoors — to be free of the antiseptic environment of the hospital, to feel the wind against my face and fresh air in my lungs.

A large window looked out from my room onto … nothing in particular. But that did not matter; it let in the natural light. It was so bright outside, so inviting, so clear that there was much to experience in the wider world.

That special day I wrote a poem entitled *Sunshine*. It was only a few lines. And that day I cried tears of joy, not pain. Though I could barely walk and my speech was slow and garbled, I could still write!

BOUNCING BACK

Soon afterward, when I was on my feet again, I plunged back in. I entered essay contests all through high school. I wrote regularly for the kids' page of the local newspaper. And at my high school paper, I grew from features reporter into co-editor-in-chief. I published poems in the school literary magazine and was asked to contribute to an article for a national teen magazine.

In college my love for writing expressed itself mostly in my research papers. As part of my campus activism, I wrote articles for several student publications.

After graduation I was determined to pursue my passion for writing in the public-interest sector. I found jobs as an editorial consultant for a small nonprofit, an ESL tutor, and a secretary at a university. I started freelancing for local, national, and even international newspapers, magazines, newsletters, etc. I got a part-time job in the fund-raising department of a civil rights law firm, which—along with my work on women's and peace issues — introduced me to the world of donor work and grantwriting. During graduate school in Ohio, I landed a gig at the *Columbus Dispatch*, for which I wrote more than a dozen opinion columns on cross-cultural and gender issues.

I have concentrated on fundraising and marketing writing—with a journalistic touch — ever since.

MY WORK WITH CLIENTS

For more than seventeen years, I have answered the call from community-benefit organizations — and individuals — to advance their ***writing to make a difference***. Using the essential information I share in this book, as writer and editor, I have helped my clients to:

- Implement strategic plans
- Build long-term relationships with readers
- Reach new and varied audiences
- Attract investments
- Inspire press and online coverage
- Educate and motivate constituencies
- Boost their writing efficiency
- Spice up important documents

- Land jobs and promotions

- Solve persistent writing problems

- Tap their creative potential

- Avoid misinterpretation, mixed messages, and embarrassing or costly errors

- Work with their colleagues to improve written materials

While this work has been interesting and rewarding—even fun—I know it is only part of the whole picture. You see, I am not content with always being the one to fix up, clean up, or punch up documents. Sure, it is an ego boost to help make my clients' documents the best they can be. But to *really* contribute to my community in the long run, I have to pass on my knowledge and empower others to improve their own writing.

In addition, as an outside consultant, I can only ever know so much about any given organization. Insiders have a much better sense of day-to-day issues and how the organization addresses them. While my clients often appreciate my editorial perspective, I need their in-depth knowledge to create documents that work.

All of this leads me to seek to share my insights and techniques in a way that builds the internal capacity of people like my clients and students. In addition, I would love to touch the lives of many more than I could ever hope to meet in person.

So while I continue to craft messages and tidy up language for my clients, my not-so-hidden agenda is always to build their own writing abilities and confidence. Ultimately, their dependence on me will diminish (or even end). And that is how it should be.

This is one of the ways I can "pay it forward," a concept popularized by the 2000 film of that title. I have been blessed with an amazing amount of support from family, friends, and mentors. I have been given many outstanding experiences, both in the U.S. and abroad. Now it is my turn to repay my debt—not back, but forward—to people who can use my help as they go about ***writing to make a difference.***

THE NEXT STEP

While writing this book, I found myself going through much of the process I recommend here. That is, I examined the essence of how this book can benefit and engage my specific readers (as described in Part I) and went on to use the 25 techniques I offer in Parts II-IV. I also used many of the Recommended Resources I list at the end of the book.

You are holding the results right now. So what you waiting for? Dig in!

Introduction

By picking up this book, you have shown that you are in tune with some key facts.

You know that strong writing skills are critical if you want to make a difference in your community — your neighborhood, your country, the world.

You also know you win credibility with great writing and lose it with poor writing. You realize that not only *what* but *how* you write makes a lasting impression. And you understand that your published materials say a lot about you—and your organization — when you are not around.

You know that in the marketplace of ideas, those who can write well are seen as the "experts" at much more than putting words on a page. (Note that the words "author" and "authority" come from the same Latin root!)

Writing is also an invaluable tool to help you think more clearly about your work and what it means to you and your community. This process often spells the difference between spouting off a half-baked idea and promoting a coherent thought, plan, or message.

Check out almost any job description for work in the public interest and you will find at least a passing reference to the need for good writing skills, offline or online. Writing well will help you succeed in fundraising, marketing, public education, advocacy, project management, etc. We are talking about applications virtually anywhere you go. (Appendix 1 lists twenty of the most common document types you may be asked to write.)

WHO SHOULD READ THIS BOOK?

This book is for you if:

- ◉ You are just beginning to write for a social-benefit organization or project (as a staff member, board member, or volunteer), and you need useful tools and examples to get started and keep moving;

- ◉ Your organization is developing a social-benefit component to its work and you are interested in integrating that perspective into your writing;

- ◉ As a student or instructor in a community-oriented discipline, you are seeking a book that teaches how to effectively reach out to constituents;

- ◉ You are a bit rusty and need some refreshers to get back up to speed;

- ◉ You already write well but feel that you could tighten things up a bit with a distilled package of reminders;

- ◉ You often work with inexperienced marketing or fundraising writers, and you would like to provide them with some concise and targeted advice.

What if you really do not have the time (or the inclination) to do all of your own writing? This book will help you provide the feedback your collaborators need to help you create powerful pieces.

WHO IS *"WRITING TO MAKE A DIFFERENCE"*?

Books like this often focus exclusively on people involved with nonprofit organizations or classic social movements. While I have been part of such groups since childhood, I now aim to expand our notion of what it can look like to "make a difference." The world is changing, and many for-profit businesses are developing more environmentally sustainable and socially responsible ways to work. Legions of government agencies and educational institutions are also moving in this direction.

In light of this, I have chosen to include in this book all of the components of what is becoming known as the "social sector." This includes nonprofit organizations to be sure, but also extends to many other groups and entities seeking to achieve a social benefit.

These organizations go by a variety of names, including: social enterprises, green or progressive businesses, community education institutions, social ventures, public-benefit corporations, and cause-related marketing programs. They also may form as special community outreach departments of larger organizations.

These entities might directly offer goods or services for conscious consumers, or focus on research, policy advocacy, infrastructure improvement, or other strategies.

And I cannot forget the untold numbers of individual entrepreneurs, artists, activists, and concerned citizens who may not officially affiliate with any organization or group, but seek to make a difference on their own.

You will notice that I use adjectives such as "socially responsible," "mission-driven," "community-benefit," "community-oriented," "public-interest," "values-based," and "public-benefit" to describe the organizations or efforts that you, my readers, are involved in. All of these terms connote perspectives and motivations, and each elicits a different idea of what you might try to convey to your readers.

But regardless of the specific organizational context, all community-oriented writing projects are variations on a common theme: marketing for the public good. That is, building awareness, developing relationships, raising funds, advocating for positive social change, and marking our progress. We are offering our readers the opportunity to be part of something larger than themselves.

AND WHAT MAKES *WRITING TO MAKE A DIFFERENCE* DISTINCT?

When you write in support of a cause or on behalf of a public-benefit organization, you need to have a wide range of readers in mind. You might be targeting clients, donors, investors, volunteers, colleagues, the press, or others with a specific interest in your work. You know they are busy and want brief, easy-to-read, highly relevant pieces. They have diverse needs and concerns—you have to speak directly to those motivations.

In school, you learned to write for the specific tastes and preferences of your teachers or professors. You may have even learned to pad your writing to reach minimum page number requirements. And you may have used certain words to impress your instructors. But in the world of work, your readers are not people to whom you will bid goodbye at the end of the term.

Instead, you want to establish and nurture lasting relationships. Your readers need to hear from you regularly—and not just when you are asking for a donation, a purchase, or an investment.

The good news is that lessons learned from other types of writing will still come in handy.

You can take cues from the conventional business world, with its focus on branding, customer benefits, and market research. The rigor of research-based academic writing will help you make your case with solid evidence. The world of creative writing and great literature can inspire you to bring your words to life and paint pictures in your readers' minds. And journalistic writing can remind you to cover the main elements of your most pressing news. Even letters you write to family or friends, or entries you make in your private journal, can help you develop your writer's voice and express your personal style.

But when you are ***writing to make a difference*** in your community, remember that:

1. Your bottom line is not purely profit for your shareholders—or personal self-expression or intellectual curiosity. You are also aiming to educate your readers and promote a product, service, or concept with an eye toward widespread social or environmental benefit: often called the "triple bottom line."

2. You and your readers share an interest in and concern with what might be called "idealistic" concepts, such as social mission, values, beliefs, and sustained commitment. You are basing your choices on a vision that appeals to both the head and the heart. It is your job as a writer to inspire your readers to move from those ideals to a readiness to act.

3. You are often dealing with unpopular, poorly understood, or below-the-radar issues that may not enjoy the mainstream spotlight. Your writing

will require you to find ways to collaborate with your readers and engage in meaningful conversations that lead to community solutions.

4. You are not seeking to impress your readers with fancy words or lengthy diatribes. Your aim is to inform, persuade, inspire, and motivate (maybe even entertain) — and then wrap it up.

HOW DOES THIS BOOK FIT IN?

This book aims to help you make sure your readers would describe your work with the four basic Cs:

Clear

Concise

Compelling

Correct

and the four bonus Cs:

Creative

Colorful

Catchy

Clever

I will help you contextualize and integrate writing lessons from many places so that you can immediately apply them to your community-oriented work.

Over the years, from various positions in the field, people have told me of their need for some guidance in their everyday writing tasks. They have wanted concise advice on specific writing assignments that: introduce their work, share information, update their community, raise money, relate to online readers, reach the press, keep their organization running smoothly, etc. They also have sought solid insight into the core leadership skill of writing to encourage public engagement.

Virtually everyone working in the public interest — advancing a solution to a social problem — has to do some writing at some point. The better you can do that, the deeper and broader your impact will be. Your organization may produce great work or come up with outstanding ideas, but if you present your achievements or thoughts poorly they will not get very far.

You may be like I am and love committing words to paper (refer to the Preface for more on my personal writing story). If so, you are always on the lookout for new ways to bring your writing to life.

Or, you may never have intended to become a writer at all. You may be one of the many people who got into this field for other important reasons: an interest and passion concerning a certain issue, an urge to give something back to your community, a perspective you want to share, etc.

Either way, you probably do not have a pile of extra cash lying around to hire outside writing consultants. Neither do you have time to waste producing ineffective written pieces. Learning to write more efficiently and confidently makes the most sense.

All of this means that people like you can benefit from a brief go-to resource that encapsulates the most essential and relevant pointers about ***writing to make a difference***. If that guide could also show how writing can be fun and easy to improve, all the better.

I believe this book is that guide.

You do not always need to rely on the designated "writers" to express what you think or feel. Think about it: You are working to expand the life options of people in your community. Why limit your own by saying that you "can't write"? While you may continue to feel some anxiety concerning your writing skills, good advice and lots of practice will go a long way.

WHAT CAN YOU EXPECT?

Writing is a craft: part art and creativity, part sweat and technicalities. And, as in woodworking, sewing, or ceramics, you have to hone your skills over time. This book offers you lots of food for thought, but the proof is in the practice. The more you apply the suggested techniques, the more natural they will become, and the more your writing will improve. The idea is to focus on what you are already doing right and build on that.

Most of us have not paid much attention to writing advice since grade school. Really — I understand. It kind of took a backseat. But this need not condemn you to plodding through old textbooks aimed at children. Instead, let me bring you up-to-date on some of the most relevant pointers for socially responsible organizations.

In this book I cover 25 interrelated writing techniques, many of which enhance each other when used in tandem. But you can improve your writing by applying just one or two. If you find yourself getting a bit overwhelmed or short on time, pace yourself and try different ones on different occasions.

Experience and experimentation will tell you when various techniques are most appropriate. For example, some documents need to be formal and conform to a formula or format, while others leave room for more creativity. Techniques you might use to reach one set of readers might be less effective when appealing to other audiences.

Bonus Tip

While you may still end up working with editing consultants, if you provide them with a higher calibre of rough draft, they will produce final drafts of more polish and sophistication.

Bonus Tip

This book is not English class in a nutshell. If you missed getting the school-based instruction, practice, and feedback you need, I recommend taking a course at your local community college or extension school. Another option is to work with a writing coach on specific weak spots.

I hope that you will begin to take your writing to a whole new level of power. The only risk you run is that of finding the writing process faster and more enjoyable.

GOT EXAMPLES?

This book features hundreds of examples from nonprofits, socially responsible businesses, government agencies, and more. Some come from my clients' work; others I excerpt from my previously published pieces; a number are the result of Internet research; and still others I invent, based on what I have seen in the field. I include websites for all of the genuine featured organizations; when I draw upon actual clients' work in my examples of suggested edits, I change names and details to ensure confidentiality.

I include a wide range of issues, especially those I care about or have been involved in over the years. You might notice that I have a soft spot for environmental, global poverty, gender, education, and diversity issues.

HOW IS THIS BOOK ORGANIZED?

This book covers a lot, from branding all the way to proofreading. I am not trying to go a mile wide and an inch deep here. Instead, I am aiming to provide you with the essentials of the various tools you need to wield as you go about ***writing to make a difference.*** You will find the following content:

> ***Top Frequently Asked Questions*** lists the top questions this book answers. It is a quick-start guide to finding what you need.
>
> ***Rate Your Skills Sheet*** helps you take stock of your writing skills before and after you read this book.
>
> ***Personal Cheat Sheet*** gives you a handy place to record the most relevant pointers you find as you read.
>
> ***Part I*** grounds you in the fundamentals: the three "what we're doing here" strategies you need to know as a writer in the public interest.
>
> ***Part II*** reveals the first six powerful techniques that will help you establish your organization's socially responsible context.
>
> ***Part III*** explores ten additional professional ways to write for results, from the beginning of your piece right through to the end.
>
> ***Part IV*** offers nine editing pointers to revisit, polish, and fine-tune your work.

Each chapter in Parts I-IV ends with a Writing Workout (i.e., exercise) that provides some hands-on experience with the writing technique just covered. In addition, each section ends with a "Section-at-a-Glance": a brief take-away summary that will help you remember key points.

The Appendices section includes additional lists and information that supplement the main body of the text, plus suggested answers to the Writing Workouts that need them.

The Recommended Resources section provides more than one hundred references for further reading.

HOW CAN YOU USE THIS BOOK?

You have probably already guessed that this is not a stuffy tome that yearns to collect dust on your bookshelf. Instead, I offer it as a feisty handbook: a reference that you will bookmark and use often.

This book will help you strengthen, sharpen, and tune up a whole slew of different documents you work on regularly. By cultivating these valuable skills, you will achieve a higher level of performance and boost your community impact.

You can get started right away. Here are eight ways to get the most out of this book:

1. *Consider it your personal (and portable) writing coach.*
   This book offers a smorgasbord of tasty bite-size nuggets, served up in chapters that are brief enough to enjoy in one sitting—perhaps during a lunch break or on a subway ride. Seek out the answers to specific questions, get advice if you are stuck on a writing problem, or get up to speed for your next assignment. Refer back to the book periodically to make sure you stay on track.

2. *Go step by step.*
   Maybe you like to absorb everything you can, using a methodical approach. Feel free to read this book from cover to cover and put my suggestions to the test as you go. You can join me as I follow the typical sequence of producing a document.

3. *Focus on the handy reminders.*
   Go ahead and adorn your bulletin board, file cabinet, or refrigerator with your favorite "Section-at-a-Glance" reminder sheets, cartoons, quotes, jokes, or whatever motivates you. A list of the chapter titles might even do the trick.

4. *Rate your skills and make your own Personal Cheat Sheet.*
   Use the "Rate Your Skills Sheet" (page 11) to help you evaluate your strengths and weaknesses. Then, as you read, keep track of the tips that mean the most to you and speak to your personal challenge areas on your Personal Cheat Sheet (see page 12). With these guides in hand, you can quickly remember things to work on and eventually master.

5. ***Read this book with others.***

   One of the best ways to learn is in community, where you can get lots of feedback. Try reading this book in a group and form your own writing circle (more on that in Appendix 10). Discuss the various skills you are learning, do the Writing Workouts together, and get input from other colleagues who are committed to improving their writing. You might also consider participating in a writing workshop. In addition, for ongoing conversations with me and your fellow public-benefit writers around the world, you can join the community of readers on the *Writing to Make a Difference* website (see page 364 for more info).

6. ***Train your colleagues.***

   This book can serve as an excellent group training tool. You can use it to cultivate a writing-positive culture in your organization, where you focus on improving writing practices and styles. Present the most relevant information at a board or staff meeting; hold a mini-seminar; or circulate copies of this book, selected "Section-at-a-Glance" summaries, or your favorite appendices. One idea is to ask everyone to read the same chapter and then take ten to fifteen minutes to work on the chapter's Writing Workout together. This is a great way to get the most bang for your learning buck.

7. ***Orient yourself.***

   Do what is best for your learning style. If you doubt you can learn to write better by simply reading a book and doing the exercises, you are probably right. You will fare far better if you use this book as an orientation to writing for the community-benefit sector, then enroll in a writing class or work with a writing coach.

8. ***Get creative (or silly).***

   Writing is not all serious stuff! Compete with your colleagues to see who can name all 25 techniques in this book. Jumble the letters in any chapter title to make a silly sentence, or take this book with you to ski country on a "working" weekend and use it as a sled. Well, you get my point.

AND OFF YOU GO!

Sharpen your pencils, check the ink in your pens, or get cozy with your keyboard. Just remember to be patient with yourself and to celebrate your successes. Happy writing!

Icons Explained

This book contains six illustrated icons that act as guideposts to keep you on track toward **writing to make a difference.** They include:

 Ask yourself: This question prompts you to have an internal dialogue, encouraging you to get involved in your own learning process.

 Caution: This alert helps you identify and avoid common trouble spots, pitfalls, or traps. Its warning should motivate you to pause and take a second look.

 Personally Speaking: I offer a glimpse into my own personal or professional experiences on the topic at hand, often reinforcing the point I just made in the main text. The icon is a caricature of me.

 Bonus Tip: This is a whisper in your ear, a little extra advice that is not "need to know." It tends to be more advanced or more technical than the main text.

 Joke: A humorous tidbit drives home my point or just tries to provoke a smile (or at least a tolerant snicker).

 Writing Workout: Get those writing muscles in shape by doing these fun exercises at the end of each chapter. They give you a chance to get your hands dirty as you absorb the material. I have designed each one to stimulate your creativity and to help you in your future pieces.

Note to Non-U.S. Readers

This book assumes at least a somewhat solid grasp of Standard American English. If English is not your native language, you should already have some good courses and practice under your belt. The book also freely uses U.S. idiomatic expressions (such as "under your belt"). But even if you are not familiar with a particular conversational phrase, the context should help.

Speakers of British, Canadian, Australian, South African, or other variations of the English language should also take note. There are quite a few grammatical, stylistic, and usage differences across the English-speaking world, but fortunately they are so minor that you should have little problem getting my drift (another one of those U.S. English idioms). For example, people in the U.S. refer to "nonprofit organizations," but others may call them charities, voluntary groups, or NGOs.

Finally, although I wrote this book with U.S. culture and politics in mind, it will definitely be useful to anyone, anywhere, who is **writing to make a difference.** Just be aware that documents tend to be less formal in the U.S. than in other countries.

Top Frequently Asked Questions—
& where to find the answers

I love it when clients ask me questions. Questions help me share exactly the information my listeners need to hear, and help me understand what is really on their minds. This in turn tells me more about how I can help them now and in the future.

Here are the top questions people have asked me (directly or indirectly) in my workshops, coaching sessions, and casual conversations. You will find answers throughout this book, and I have listed some spots to start looking.

Of course, as you dig into these matters, you may discover a host of other questions. I trust you will find answers in the following pages and in the books and websites I refer to in the Recommended Resources section.

QUESTION	WHERE TO LOOK
Where do I begin?	Part I
How can I turn our many features (services or products) into benefits and a compelling brand?	Part I
What can we do to establish our organization's credibility?	Parts I & II
How can I adapt my writing to create strong relationships with different readers?	Chapters B, 4, & 6
How can I spotlight my organization's role in the community?	Section IIa
How can I develop my writer's voice?	Chapters 4 & 15
How can I manage cultural and class differences?	Chapter 6
How can I overcome writer's block?	Chapter 7
How can I develop good writing habits?	Chapters 7, 8, & 17
How can I speed up my writing—or make more time for it?	Chapter 8
How can I capture my reader's attention quickly?	Chapter 9
How can I make sure my writing is clear?	Chapters 10-13 & Section IVb
How can I choose active verbs and avoid passive ones?	Chapter 11
Is there any special "lingo" I need to know (or unlearn)?	Chapter 13
How can I make my writing flow better?	Chapters 14 & 20
How can I come up with good closings?	Chapter 16
How can I get (and use) the feedback I need?	Chapter 17
How can I be concise and punchy, but still communicate nuance?	Chapter 18
How can I enhance the visual appeal of my document?	Chapter 20
How can I edit my own work?	Part IV
How can I brush up on my grammar and proofreading skills?	Section IVb
Have any rules of writing changed lately?	Section IVb

Rate Your Skills Sheet

This log will help you keep track of the skills you develop as you work through this book. Rate yourself on a scale of 1 to 10 (poor to great) on the following questions — both before and after reading Parts I through IV.

Of course, this sheet is for your eyes only. Even if you find that you are already happy with the majority of your skills, this rating sheet will come in handy as a reminder of effective writing techniques. If you see in yourself plenty of room for improvement, this sheet will help you track your progress.

SKILL	ASK YOURSELF: *Do you usually…*	BEFORE	AFTER
ABCs of Copywriting	• understand and advance your organization's brand?		
	• understand your intended readers and their needs?		
	• focus on benefits and not just features?		
Establishing Your Organizational Context			
Stressing Your Effectiveness	• emphasize your organization's mission and vision throughout your pieces?		
	• discuss important collaborations?		
	• tell your readers about the quantity, quality, and ripple effects of your organization's work?		
Focusing on Your Community	• emphasize the connections among your readers, the people you're writing about, your organization, and you?		
	• illustrate your organization with success stories?		
	• honestly address cultural and class differences?		
Pulling It All Together			
Keeping the Golden Words Coming	• know how to work through your writer's blocks?		
	• find ways to speed up your writing?		
Hammering Out a Draft	• hook your reader in at the very beginning?		
	• help your reader truly experience your words?		
	• maximize your verbs?		
	• make your points clearly?		
	• avoid unnecessary jargon and unexplained acronyms?		
	• guide your reader through your document?		
	• make sure your writing sounds right to your reader's ear?		
	• end on a high note?		
Editing Your Own Work			
Revising and Polishing: The Next Level	• step back from your draft and don an editor's perspective?		
	• write tight?		
	• use repetition to your advantage?		
	• appeal to your reader's eye?		
Fine-Tuning: Picky, Picky, Picky	• make sure your subjects, verbs, and pronouns all agree?		
	• use correct — and varied — sentence structure?		
	• have a handle on confusing word pairs?		
	• feel comfortable using a variety of punctuation marks?		
	• proofread well?		

Personal Cheat Sheet

If you examine my bookshelves, you will find volumes riddled with dog-eared or highlighted pages and handwritten reminders of key points. I often also make my own "cheat sheets" to summarize what I have learned. I can then easily refer to the most salient ideas when I need them in the course of my work. My students and clients have also liked this learning technique.

As you come across particularly helpful tips and ideas in this book, try jotting down some notes on this Personal Cheat Sheet. Use this chart for your own common trouble spots, to remind yourself of the suggestions that make the most sense to you.

Meanwhile, feel free to adorn your filing cabinet, bulletin board, or cubicle walls with handy notes about these items!

Some of my clients are a bit secretive about their efforts to clean up their writing. They keep their Cheat Sheets in a private drawer of their desk, hidden from coworkers and supervisors. While your learning process is clearly nothing to be embarrassed about — and, actually, speaks well of your self-motivation — you too may prefer not to be very up front about it. Just don't forget to pull out your Cheat Sheet and review it on a regular basis.

MY TROUBLE SPOT	HELPFUL SUGGESTION	PAGE # / MY NOTES

The ABCs of Copywriting

What do you think of when you first hear the word "marketing"?

A bunch of deceptive hyperbole with no substance? A sleazy game that shady characters play when they are trying to get you to buy something that you don't actually need or want? At some point, most of us have even said something like, "Oh, that's just a marketing ploy."

As a representative of a community-oriented effort, you definitely do not want your voice to be associated with empty promises. Fortunately, marketing does not have to be that way.

Your organization is not just about building a better mousetrap that serves the community. You also want people with rodent-control problems to be aware of you, easily access you, consider supporting you, and spread the word about your work.

People working in the public interest increasingly acknowledge that *we too* have to get out there and hustle to attract attention to ourselves. Terms such as "social marketing," "cause-related marketing," "green marketing," and even the old standby "outreach" come to mind. After all, if no one knows about your good work, you simply are not going to get very far.

So when I say "marketing" in the public-interest context, I am talking about:

Sharing information and enthusiasm about your work with interested people who may want to exchange their involvement or support for the value you add to them and their community.

That exchange is important. It is essentially an agreement, sometimes even a contract, between you and your reader. Remember: We are talking about dialogue that helps everyone win. That is what *writing to make a difference* is all about.

When you write on behalf of a community-benefit organization, you have to convey its work clearly, concisely, and persuasively. Your readers may include investors, clients, the press, activists, volunteers, colleagues, allies, and other stakeholders. You want to educate, inspire, and activate them. And to do that you have to write strategically to reach each specific type of reader.

This kind of writing is commonly known as "copywriting," and that is the term I use throughout this book.

When copywriting, you also want to cultivate relationships with your readers over the short and long term. You want to encourage them to see your work as credible, successful, and vital—a solid investment of their time and/or money. You are looking to strike a responsive chord, so that your relationship can grow from there.

To communicate to the right people, in a way that builds solid relationships, you have to treat *everything* you write as a potential marketing tool. The specific language you use will vary, of course, according to the type of document and the intended reader. (For example, you would not write a project or funding proposal in the style you use to write a brochure, flyer, or press release.) The tips I share in this book offer a wide range of concepts to consider, no matter what your writing task.

In Part I, we will take a sneak peek at three of the fundamental strategies found in all good copywriters' toolkits:

A ～Create and advance your brand.～
Concentrate on what your organization stands for and keep promoting it.

B ～Engage your specific readers.～
Get to know them and their worlds, and then join them there with your writing.

C ～Emphasize benefits more than features.～
It is not just what you do that counts, but also what it *means* to your clients and community.

You can use these three introductory chapters to help keep you on track, by coming back to them from time to time. The 25 tactical techniques in Parts II-IV will show you how to put these "ABCs" into practice in the context of your socially responsible organization. Turn the page and let's get started!

⌐Create and advance your brand.⌐

Every piece you write—whatever its own individual purpose—should have one overarching goal: to help promote your organization's brand.

What do I mean by "brand"? Your "brand" is your essence: your identity, your personality, your promise, your reputation. It is what your organization stands for.

Ask yourself: When someone hears about your organization, what set of images, attributes, feelings, and ideas do you want them to associate with it?

The answer is your brand.

Even if unintentionally, you are always building and reinforcing your brand. With time, if you are consistent enough, you can and should earn the familiarity and loyalty of your stakeholders. They will begin to relate to you, identify with you, and—yes—support you. As your brand becomes more known and liked, you will attract the people and organizations that can help your organization—and your community—succeed even more.

EXAMPLES

What do you imagine, think, or feel when you hear these organizations' names?

- National Parent Teacher Association
- Working Assets
- Amnesty International
- U.S. Environmental Protection Agency
- National Geographic Society
- Whole Foods Market
- Newman's Own
- Ben & Jerry's
- American Red Cross
- NAACP
- moveon.org
- Lions Club

Bonus Tip

If your organization has recently undergone a strategic planning process, you may have already articulated your brand. If so, this book will help you maximize that branding (or re-branding) in your written materials, with a focus on reaching your intended readers.

All have built their brands over time, and unless one of them has somehow escaped your notice, you probably have opinions or gut reactions to all their names. You may envision a logo or tagline, or remember being exposed to and relating to their messages.

Whatever your organization's brand, your documents have to uphold it. That is, as a marketing writer (copywriter) at your organization, your job is to advance your brand. Here is an overview of how to do that.

EMPHASIZE YOUR ORGANIZATION'S UNIQUENESS

You probably know more than most people do about the many outstanding public-benefit organizations improving your community. In this way, you are truly blessed and inspired. However, all of those organizations inevitably encounter competition for all kinds of resources. Everyone needs financial backing, people-power, public attention, market share, etc.

To make your organization stand out, you need to highlight what distinguishes it from similar groups. You must show how your organization is uniquely positioned to address a specific need that your community has expressed.

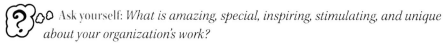 Ask yourself: *What is amazing, special, inspiring, stimulating, and unique about your organization's work?*

For instance: Does your organization deal with a particular aspect of an issue that no one else focuses on? Do you have a breakthrough approach or method? Do you work with a severely underserved community? Do you offer a product or service that solves a compelling social problem but is not readily available anywhere else? Do you have a history that has positioned you as the "go-to" organization in your community for years?

Those distinguishing characteristics are key parts of your brand and bear repeating (over and over again).

EXAMPLES

These bits of text ("copy") help define various organizations' unique qualities on their websites, in brochures, or in other marketing or fundraising materials:

1. When "Get Well Soon" seems a bit out of place, Kimo Kards™ are cancer recovery greeting cards that have just the right words to help a friend or loved one through the difficult journey of chemotherapy and other cancer treatments. Our messages are positive: designed to encourage and inspire men, women and children in different ways, including humor, scripture, and empowering words. Every card is "Created by Survivors for Survivors." *(www.kimokards.com)*

2. Our mission is to deliver now — and for future generations. With every step we take, we are committed to leaving a "green" footprint across the American landscape… The U.S. Postal Service is the only shipping company that has earned Cradle to Cradle^{SM} certification (administered by McDonough Braungart Design Chemistry, LLC) for the environmentally friendly design and manufacturing of its boxes and envelopes. In addition, the Postal Service has the largest civilian vehicle fleet in the nation, and over 43,000 of them are alternative fuel-capable. Since we primarily refuel at commercial retail fueling locations, our fleet generates demand for alternative fuels nationwide.

   (www.usps.com/green)

3. *International Development Exchange (IDEX) answers the Frequently Asked Question, "How is IDEX different from other international organizations?":*

   Since its inception in 1985, IDEX has made it a priority to support economic development initiatives in a way that is quite different from traditional large-scale philanthropy and prevailing models of global aid that are often top-down, paternalistic, and money-centered. IDEX's grantmaking model has evolved over the years, but remains focused on:

   - The value of community-based solutions and the wisdom of local leaders who are grounded in their communities.
   - Providing multi-year unrestricted grants so that local partner organizations can apply funds where most needed and can plan for the future.
   - Providing additional resources as opportunities arise. This may include participation in conferences in the U.S. or elsewhere or facilitating connections to fair trade organizations.   *(www.idex.org)*

If your organization is "too unique" (special in unfamiliar ways) you may generate initial resistance. Try to relate your work to things your intended readers already know and trust, as I discuss later in this chapter.

Your uniqueness must be so clear—and so relevant to your readers' individual or community lives—that it gets noticed and gets people talking about you. This defining quality of your organization makes you the best choice for your readers to support or work with.

 Ask yourself: *What is the* _____ *difference?*
[insert your organization's name here]

Some ways organizations have traditionally set themselves apart from the pack include:

- Outstanding credentials or experience
- Personal service and attention to detail
- High quality and value
- Superior effectiveness
- Speed or convenience
- Unusual ease of use
- Continuous innovation
- Widespread familiarity

And as a public-benefit organization, you can also talk about qualities such as:

- Community accountability
- Values-driven decisions
- Socially responsible sourcing and trading
- Environmental sensitivity and stewardship
- Community participation and collaboration
- A leading-edge point of view or approach

Your uniqueness is whatever your ideal readers want and are concerned about but cannot easily get elsewhere. Once you identify those unique selling points, you can begin to incorporate them into your copywriting.

You might even take this idea one step further by showing how your work in conjunction with others in your field sets your network of partners and allies apart from the rest. (For more on collaboration, see Chapter 2, "Maximize your collaborations.")

SHOW THAT YOU SHARE GOALS AND VALUES WITH YOUR READERS

People are reading your material because they feel that your organization's core beliefs and aims are aligned with theirs. Your job is to consistently show them that they are right. Connecting with your readers on this plane—appealing to both their hearts and their heads—gets the best results.

Ask yourself: *What is the very soul of your message?*

Your organization's mission embodies its passion, sincerity, and spirit. It energizes your brand and should shine through in every piece of writing you create. You are conveying not only literal subject matter, but also your organization's attitude and stance. By the words and methods you choose, you are saying a lot about who you are and why you do what you do.

EXAMPLE

Say you are writing a brochure that explains the importance of a specific aspect of your work. Your organization promotes child health and safety, and your brochure argues why lead paint should be removed from homes with young children. You and your colleagues understand the urgency, you are clear on what needs to be done, and you want to motivate parents to protect their children from the toxin.

Your brochure will advance your brand in that it will reflect your:

1. knowledge about the issue and how to handle it;

2. caring attitude about the pressing nature of the issue;

3. interest in making homes safer for youngsters;

4. unique ability to help parents in your community take positive action.

You will learn more in Chapter 1, "Spotlight your mission repeatedly," about focusing on your mission throughout your copy.

GIVE YOUR READERS GOOD REASONS TO TRUST YOU

As a copywriter, your intention is to create ongoing relationships with your readers. And all solid relationships begin with trust. One way to build trust is to demonstrate your familiarity with the problems your readers face. Show that you are in the know by citing what other experts in your field are saying. And back up your official, academic, or professional claims with on-the-ground testimonials from people who have used your service or product and are known by, or are at least similar to, your readers.

You can also reassure your readers with ways to lower their risk of working with you. For example, offer a satisfaction guarantee. Or tell them about an evaluation or feedback process (e.g., an online rating system) that will let them exchange their views about your effectiveness with other customers or clients.

Another idea is to describe your product or service by comparing it favorably with an easily recognized brand that your readers trust and value. Or, use a colorful analogy or metaphor that they can quickly grasp. The goal here is to reduce their unfamiliarity with your brand and encourage their interest in you and your work.

EXAMPLES

1. You may have seen this technique used in phrases such as, "If you liked X you will love Y" and the "Alternative Nobel Prize" (the popular name for the somewhat obscurely named "Right Livelihood Award"). Saying something is the Mercedes of solar heating systems (vs. the Ford or Honda) is another great example.

2. You may have bought a less expensive store-brand drug or food product that is marketed as equivalent to a well-known brand because it features the same active ingredients. Emerging musicians are often marketed by comparing their styles with those of more established stars.

3. Some marketers (and others) use the phrase "Disneyland for grownups" to describe Las Vegas, New Orleans, or Amsterdam. Such a comparison leaves no question as to its meaning.

Bonus Tip

Remember that you can never be 100% objective, no matter how hard you try. While your readers know you have a perspective, they also expect you to be clear and honest with your facts and opinions, and to explain your frame-of-reference.

In addition, your readers want to know that others they respect (often called "opinion-leaders") agree that your work is important and worthy of support. Highlight awards, great media coverage, and endorsements.

And, of course, when a few bad apples produce scandals, scrutiny of all public-interest organizations goes up. Of course, it behooves your organization to always be as transparent as possible—showing that your community can trust you to be open, honest, and accountable for what you do and say. Being a consistently visible and reliable presence is one important way to do this. And your documents can play a vital role in sending that message.

GO BEYOND PROMOTION FOR ITS OWN SAKE

When you are *writing to make a difference,* your two-fold goal is both to promote your organization as a part of a socially responsible solution *and* to educate your readers about key things they need to know in your issue area.

Constituent education is often the first step in marketing, especially if you are tackling a complex, often misunderstood problem that involves many variables, processes, or actors. Most of your readers are not specialists in your area, but their interests make them want to know more. You would be wise, then, to build an educational component into your organization's branding.

EXAMPLE

Let's imagine that, as a socially responsible business, you offer environmentally friendly laundry services to people in your neighborhood. While your customers surely know about their need for clean clothes, many of them may not be aware of the hazards of chemicals often used in the dry cleaning process. Your marketing, then, would need to include information about *why* you offer green services (as well as how you do so). Your branding should embody both of these aspects.

In this world of information overload, we all could use a guide to the most critical aspects of the issues important to us. We also want to hear about how we can personally get involved in solutions, presented in a way that we can relate to.

And that information is precisely what you and your organization excel at providing! Give it to your readers—repeatedly and consistently. The more value you can deliver, the more they will see your organization as worthy of their support, investment, or patronage.

Promoting your brand and appropriately educating your community work hand in hand.

PROJECT PROFESSIONALISM

Errors of fact or clumsiness of style can stop your readers in their tracks. You don't want to undermine the work you have invested in developing and promoting your brand, so make sure that you don't give your readers reasons to question your credibility. It pays to be mindful of the details—and to apologize for that rare mistake. It is often much easier to fix a slip of the tongue than a slip of the pen.

Double-check your facts and figures by consulting outside sources (preferably, more than one). Clean up any lingering problems in grammatical usage (Chapters 21-25 will be helpful). And review your work for its visual impact (see Chapter 20, "Make sure it *looks* right," for a brief discussion of layout and graphic design.)

WRITING WORKOUT

Take a few moments right now to think about your organization's unique brand and how you can improve your presentation of it through your materials.

STEP 1: Brainstorm five to ten key words and concepts that you would like your readers to easily associate with your organization. The words should describe your organization's essential identity. If you are so inclined, sketch out pictures representing each of your chosen words:

  A. The unique value you add to your community

  B. The attitudes or ideals you want to be known for

  C. The tone, style, and personality you bring to your work

  D. The reasons why your readers can trust you

STEP 2: Now consider the five to ten words that your organization currently uses to describe itself. Some places to look are your organization's name, tagline, and mission statement, as well as the organizational descriptions in your brochure, home page, newsletter, press releases, or funding proposals. Also think about your organization's logo, colors, and other visuals. Jot down some notes.

STEP 3: Next, compare the words and images you chose in Step 1 with the ones you found in your existing materials in Step 2. How are they similar? Or different?

STEP 4: If you found some discrepancies, choose three new "brand identity words" that you would like to begin incorporating in your copywriting. Discuss these changes with a supervisor or colleague. You may want to try experimenting with the changes to see how they resonate with your readers.

Engage your specific readers.

"FIRST IS OUR CORE CONSTITUENCY, NEXT COMES FRIENDS AND FINALLY PEOPLE SIX DEGREES OF SEPARATION FROM KEVIN BACON."

Writing to make a difference must be reader-centered and not writer-centered. You have to shift your attention, and your pre-occupations, from yourself to your readers. After all, they care about themselves, their communities, and their impact much more than they care about your organization.

To write is to engage in an intimate conversation with your readers. And for that you need to know whom you are addressing, and—most importantly—what they want to get out of conversing with you.

You might be unusally fortunate and already know exactly who will be reading your work, and why. But chances are good that you are at least a bit fuzzy.

For instance, if you are creating a flyer to post at specific locations or a funding proposal for specific investors, you may know exactly who will read it (or at least you have a good idea). But have you thought carefully about their specific interests and concerns, and their relevant informational, professional, or personal needs?

And what if you are writing a general-purpose brochure, newsletter article, or webpage? Then you are reaching a much broader group of potential readers, who all have particular needs. It can get complicated and more than a little confusing.

If there are any important cultural differences between you and your prospective readers, you will also need to navigate those waters. For instance, if you are not familiar with the ethnic or age group you are intending to reach, you must do some research and get solid guidance. (Chapter 6, "Write with reader diversity in mind," discusses this issue in detail.)

In this chapter, we will discuss the first step in engaging the readers you most want to reach: identifying them.

ASK THE RIGHT QUESTIONS ABOUT YOUR INTENDED READERS

Here are a few detailed questions to help guide your research.

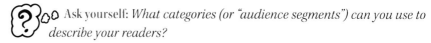 Ask yourself: *What categories (or "audience segments") can you use to describe your readers?*

They are not one monolithic group, but have important differences. For instance, are some of them healthcare providers and others patients? Under twenty or senior citizens? Urban or rural? Homeowners or renters? Businesspeople or policymakers? Staff or volunteers? New immigrants? Single parents? College graduates? Attorneys?

While you can categorize your readers in countless ways, try to identify the characteristics most relevant to your work. And don't be afraid to subdivide your audience segments, while you are at it. For instance, are you focusing on tax attorneys, public-interest attorneys, or workers' compensation attorneys?

As you start to pinpoint your audience segments, you will also want to consider how your readers categorize *themselves*. That is, which of their characteristics do they feel are most important, in terms of their relationship to your organization?

Personally Speaking

When I write in my personal journal, I know exactly who is going to be reading it: me, myself, and I. I can simply look in the mirror to get a good image of my reader. So I feel free to write with abandon, about anything, however I choose. I have no concerns about writer/reader differences or reader misinterpretations, or even reader interest. I highly recommend journaling, for these reasons. However, beware of confusing your own perspective with that of an outside reader. Navel gazing has a tendency to chase away everyone except your therapist and close friends. That goes for organizations, too!

EXAMPLES

1. Your readers might consider themselves leaders or followers, rich or poor, mainstream or alternative, outdoor enthusiasts or homebodies, very involved activists or bystanders, concerned citizens, environmentalists, artists, intellectuals, animal lovers, mothers, etc. They may also identify closely with any number of particular groups, based on politics, culture, ethnicity, religion, family, sexual orientation, and/or other factors.

    But within each of the above-mentioned groups we can think of several sub-groups, all quite different from each other.

2. Some people are early adopters of change and love all things innovative, cutting-edge, or experimental. Others are much more cautious and will want to wait until a new idea, product, or service has enough time to work out any initial bugs; they want to see a track record before coming on board. And then again, some people come down somewhere between these two extremes, preferring a blend of approaches.

    One of those people might jump at the chance to try a new techno-gadget. But she might not be the first to care how or where the gadget is made—or disposed of when it breaks down. Her neighbor might also love new technology but wonder from the outset about its origins and plan for repair, reuse, or recycling.

Just be sure to avoid stereotyping your readers. Simply because someone is a member of one audience segment does not automatically mean that he or she resembles everyone else in that group in other important ways. Everyone is unique—and no one likes to be treated like a faceless number or just a statistic. The more you can tailor your messages to the diverse needs of reader sub-groups, without patronizing or pandering, the better they will respond.

 Ask yourself: *What are your readers' hopes and fears?*

Think about what they value and practice. What motivates or concerns them most?

EXAMPLES

1. Your readers might be hoping to see a specific change in their community, such as improved public schools or better air quality. Or they may fear particular problems, such as local violent crime or compromised health from pesticides in their food supply.

2. Two well-known communications campaigns in recent years focused on the core concerns of their intended audiences and met with huge success. One, an anti-littering campaign sponsored by the Texas Department of Transportation, used the slogan "Don't Mess with Texas"® to acknowledge and celebrate Texans' state pride. In a national phone and Internet campaign, the HIV prevention and care nonprofit called Us Helping Us, People Into Living, Inc. used its "Down Low" messages to take into account the privacy concerns of its intended audience segment: African-American men who sometimes have sex with other men but do not talk about it.

Don't forget that your readers will likely be especially attracted to only one or two particular aspects of your organization's work. Emphasize the specific benefits you offer them—how you can help them realize their unique dreams—in those areas of special interest.

 Ask yourself: *What do your readers already know, believe, or do concerning your topic, and how can you build on that?*

Think about their levels of experience, background, and commitment, and write toward those. Start with the basics and move to the more advanced, using a glossary and footnotes if necessary and appropriate. Offer different information for as many of them as possible, in ways that they can easily access. You want to confirm what they already know or do, so you can usher them to the next phase.

EXAMPLES

1. Your readers may already know about the beauty of the natural environment in their state or region, but do they know how fragile it actually is, why it is threatened, and what could be done to protect it? Do they wish they knew more? And how will you convey that additional information to them?

2. A health organization's website may have different sections for heathcare practitioners, patients, and families. Or seniors, adults, teens, and children. Or even men and women. You can establish a baseline of knowledge or experience and then move on from there. Some constructions you might try include:

   - You may already know that _____ .
     But did you know that _____ ?

   - Because you have done _____ , you
     probably are dealing with _____ . Our
     organization can help you every step of the way.

   - Learn from the experiences of people like you who have used our services to go to the next level by _____ .

3. You will need to find out if your readers are newcomers, long-time supporters, friends of friends who endorsed you, or just casual onlookers. Maybe they are interested or involved in your issues, but have yet to discover your particular organization. Perhaps they have personal histories or experiences that connect to the stories you tell.

   Think about how important your work is to them. That is, is it something that they take an active interest in on a daily, weekly, monthly, or yearly basis? What would it take to increase that?

4. A reader who has invested $50 in your organization is quite different from one who has invested $5,000 or $50,000. Not only do these investors have different abilities to support you, but their knowledge, commitment, and interest in your organization might be different too. You need to bear these differences in mind when writing for these diverse groups.

   You may be working with an investor who is hands-off and just wants to know that his or her investment is going to the right place. Another may want to be intimately involved in decisions your organization makes. Each needs to know particular information to work with you in his or her preferred way.

Sometimes readers think they know about an issue or a community but actually are relying on misunderstandings. This can often result from a history of differences based on class, race, ethnicity, geography, gender, or culture. The root cause may also be just plain misinformation that folks have picked up along the way.

For instance, perhaps your readers are considering getting involved in your work because they think your beneficiaries are "poor victims," rather than people with great potential and strength who merely lack some crucial resources. Part of your organization's marketing work will be to introduce a clearer understanding of your issue, and the people it involves, in a way that reflects your brand.

Ask yourself: *Of course your readers want to "do the right thing," but what kinds of next steps are they open to?*

Many issues we deal with in the community-benefit sector are complex and confusing. In readers' fast-paced lives, they are often looking for clear explanations and easy ways to contribute to solutions. They are actively seeking out this information because it will benefit them. It is your job not only to know, but to advocate for, the most effective and appropriate ways for them to help their communities move forward.

> **EXAMPLE**
>
> Would your readers want to sign a petition? Write a letter to a politician or their local newspaper editor? Distribute flyers or make some phone calls to friends? Start using a product or service and then share their experiences with others?
>
> On the other hand, they may not be quite ready to take action. In that case, they may need concise, persuasive information that they can mull over and decide about later.

Ask yourself: *What are your readers' related interests?*

Strategic affiliations and collaborations often create win-win opportunities. If many of your readers demonstrate an interest in issues or activities that are closely related to your organization's work, think about ways you can connect on those other levels. That is, your product or service may add value to another product or service that they already find interesting. And if you can create a nice package that solves more than one problem or enhances your readers' lives in more than one way, tell them about it.

> **EXAMPLE**
>
> When a business and a nonprofit team up to promote each other through joint marketing and sales of a product or service, they create what is known as a "cause-related marketing campaign." The partners have researched related interests of their respective intended audiences and found points of overlap. The partnership can thus be fruitful for both of them. Some organizations that have done this include:
>
> - Tom's of Maine with River Network and American Rivers
> - Luna Bar with the Breast Cancer Fund
> - Whirlpool with Habitat for Humanity

BUILD ON THESE SAMPLE READER PROFILES

Now, let's begin to examine the interests of four broad categories of your likely readers. Below are some of their common characteristics; you will need to do your own research to find out more about your specific situation.

Journalists

Remember that each reporter (or editor) has different interests and comes to your piece with a particular mindset. In general, however, we can say that they:

- *are divided by "beat."* That is, they usually cover either an undifferentiated general interest in a geographical region, or they specialize by issue.

- *work for different types of media.* Examples include mainstream, progressive, alternative, ethnic, and neighborhood media.

- *are naturally skeptical or distrustful of community-benefit organizations.* They do not want to feel they are acting as mouthpieces for uncountered opinion. Many reporters have seen a lot and have become somewhat cynical (an editor once described himself to me as a "curmudgeon"). You need to make your news as factual as possible to appeal to their interest in getting the whole story.

- *are time-pressed and deadline-driven.* If you don't get back to them right away, your voice may get lost in the shuffle. Give them everything they need to cover you well—before they move on to the next story.

- *watch patterns.* They often assume that a person or organization that shows up everywhere has something valuable to offer. This means that the more familiar they become with you, the more likely they are to seek you out.

◉ *have a sense of civic duty—just like you.* They aim to cover their community in a way that serves the public. And they are always looking for highly relevant news and information.

Once you know which journalists are your intended audience—and the readers that *they* are writing for—you will understand the two main things they are looking for:

1. A newsworthy story that they can grasp quickly, about which they can get specific details relatively easily

2. Quotes from people involved in the action with whom their readers can identify

Investors

Members of this vital audience segment:

◉ have significant background and concern about your issue but may be unfamiliar with your organization's particular slant or niche;

◉ are often time-pressed and want direct and succinct answers to their questions;

◉ have the capacity to get financially involved, but may not have decided on an exact dollar figure;

◉ may be involved in supporting several organizations in your issue area, geographic region, or stage of development, and may be interested in leveraging any potential partnerships among these organizations;

◉ want to be inspired by your vision of success;

◉ have been around the block a few times and frequently talk to each other.

In addition, they are looking to invest in organizations or projects that:

◉ are likely to be successful in addressing an expressed community need by having a clear, direct, measurable impact in both the short and long term;

◉ have a realistic overall budget;

◉ involve the beneficiaries or clients in the planning and/or implementation of the proposed service;

◉ enjoy support and trust from many community stakeholders;

◉ play a unique role in collaborations with others in the field;

◉ will evaluate their strengths and weaknesses, act on suggested improvements, and serve as leaders in the industry.

A few questions or concerns on the mind of the typical investor include:

- ◈ How is the organization's work related to my needs or my community's needs?
- ◈ What has been the impact of my past investments?
- ◈ Who else is on board with this organization?
- ◈ Do I already have a relationship with the organization?

Brochure readers

Brochure readers are most likely in a hurry and will only give you a brief moment to grab their attention. Remember that you are competing with a limitless amount of information floating around out there.

They want to spend a few minutes on a document that cuts to the chase and gives them a compelling glimpse of how your world and theirs might connect. They are looking for a piece that can hit the highlights of your spiel. If you are lucky, your readers will be looking to gain a bit of exposure to a new idea or two. Even better, they may also pass along the brochure to interested friends.

Brochure readers may be people you encounter during presentations, conferences, trade shows, or meetings. They also may be passing through your office or worksite. Learn to listen to them whenever they talk to you, and take into account their ideas and reactions.

Brochures, meanwhile, can also be great for reaching highly specific types of readers. Think about policymakers, reporters, major donors, clients, and any other specialized group you often encounter.

Email readers

Your emails—such as e-newsletters—are probably aiming to reach a wide variety of readers, each with different interests and needs. However, those readers also have several things in common. In general, they are looking for a combination of these things:

- ◈ A reminder of who you are, what you are up to, and how they can work with you for the benefit of themselves and/or their community—*now*
- ◈ Inside information they do not have to dig up
- ◈ Expert advice or information
- ◈ A quick hit on whatever is new and up-to-date in your field
- ◈ Inspiration and hope about what is possible
- ◈ News about who else works with you

Most people are in a hurry-up-and-get-this-done frame of mind when they check their email. They are looking for specific things that will immediately help them enrich their lives or accomplish their tasks. And if they don't find those resources right away, they lose interest.

According to studies by leading web usability expert Dr. Jakob Nielsen, most people read up to 25% slower on a computer monitor than on paper. They dislike reading long emails, and will most often skim rather than read. Because they are impatient, they are likely to simply delete messages that seem vague, complicated, or trivial. And they usually will read only the first screen and/or the subheadings to decide if they should read further or ignore the message.

Remember that email readers are happy to forward your message on to others, if they find it useful. This is especially good to know when you are looking for people to help spread the word through online "viral" marketing (you will find more on email ripple effects in Chapter 3, "Reflect your true numbers").

GET OUT THERE AND GATHER MORE DATA

If you are having trouble putting together detailed reader profiles, have no fear. Check out these suggestions for doing market research:

- *Analyze event and service evaluation forms.* This is a gold mine of information you have at your fingertips. Most people have opinions about how they are treated or events they attend; all you have to do is listen. If you are not already compiling this data, start right away. Be sure to solicit frank responses by assuring anonymity and asking thoughtful questions.

- *Review purchase and investment records.* Not only will you find out who is investing in or buying from your organization (and how much), but you will also learn how and when. Sometimes a note on the person's record will give you a hint about her or his character.

- *Take online or print surveys.* Online surveys are increasingly simple, inexpensive, and fruitful. While dozens of companies out there offer this service, a quick poll on your website could also do the trick. Print surveys can be more difficult to deal with on your end, but they can be well worth the effort if they give you more of the information you are seeking and are more convenient for your readers. Just remember to offer an incentive for completing your questionnaire, such as the chance to win a special prize or a token of your appreciation.

- *Hold focus groups with different types of stakeholders.* This can be as simple as a casual chat during a community open house or envelope-stuffing party, or

Personally Speaking

I have used the free online survey services of **surveymonkey.com** and **zoomerang.com** and have gotten excellent results.

as formal as an agenda item at your next board meeting. You can also do this online with a chat room or blog. People love to be consulted for their expert opinions, and the synergy of people bouncing ideas around can help get the juices flowing.

- *Do individual interviews.* These work best for people who feel most comfortable speaking with one person at a time, or who have difficulty coordinating their schedules with others. Interviews also allow you to ask follow-up questions tailored to the individual respondents. Be forewarned, however, that this technique can be resource-intensive.

- *Attend gatherings where your readers naturally congregate.* This is otherwise known as "networking." If you watch and listen closely to your potential readers, you can learn a lot. Any time you strike up a conversation about your organization or project, listen for the signs of deepest interest or enthusiasm, as well as confusion or misunderstanding.

- *Review the media that reflect your readers' mindsets, attitudes, and concerns.* Make a habit of reading, watching, and listening to the media that your constituents consume—both the content (articles, programs, web posts) and the targeted advertising. Most likely, those advertisers have also studied their ideal audiences and how to reach them.

- *Study published opinion polls.* Research institutes of all kinds constantly find out what is on people's minds. Find the ones studying your constituents and track their findings.

- *Research what your constituents have previously supported, bought, or been involved in elsewhere.* You are looking for similarities to your service or product that do not compromise the uniqueness of your specific approach.

- *Finally, simply talk to others who also know about your readers.* Other staff members, volunteers, board members, outreach workers, salespeople, or clients might know more about your readers than you do. Strategic partners in your field or market can also be great sources of this type of information.

ONE LAST SUGGESTION: KEEP LEARNING

Your readers are always changing, as the world about them changes. Don't make the mistake of assuming that the people you wrote for a few years ago are the same today. They may surprise you. Be open to unexpected lessons, and know that understanding your readers is an ongoing process. On occasion, you may even find that you have a little re-branding to do.

WRITING WORKOUT

Engaging your readers is all about seeing things from their point of view. You have to know what they need to get out of your piece and then give it to them.

On the next page you will find a handy Reader Inventory chart that tracks some key reader information you will need for each type of reader. When you first start out, collecting all this data may seem like a huge task. But it will pay off later, as you use and re-use the information for different copywriting projects.

STEP 1: Try to fill out charts for at least two of your key audience segments. You might have to go on a treasure hunt around your organization to track this stuff down. Consider realistic ways of compiling any missing data. But don't worry if you have to leave some spaces blank for now. You may need to come back to them after you have read more of this book.

STEP 2: Do you see any overlaps among your types of readers? If so, you can write a single piece to appeal to more than one. Stark differences suggest that you are better off writing different types of documents for different readers, or at least segmenting your single existing document along those lines of difference.

STEP 3: Regularly revisit this Reader Inventory. You will need to revise it over time with new information you glean about your readers.

READER INVENTORY FORM

WRITING TO MAKE A DIFFERENCE: *25 Powerful Techniques to Boost Your Community Impact by Dalya F. Massachi*

READER INVENTORY FOR ‾‾‾‾‾‾‾‾‾‾‾‾‾‾‾‾‾‾‾‾
[name of the audience segment]

DATA	INFO I HAVE	HOW TO FIND OUT MORE
Demographics (age, race, gender, culture, sexuality, family status, occupation).		
Geographic location and size of community.		
Political or social affiliations that may relate to our issues.		
Their limitations (e.g., time, income, educational background, technology, disability, other responsibilities)		
Their values, hopes, and fears that we address—directly or indirectly.		
Why they care about our issues, organization, or program.		
What they already know or believe about our issues and/or our organization.		
What they want to know more about or understand better.		
Behavior concerning our organization or issues (commitment level, etc.).		
Their other personal interests or hobbies related to our issues.		
Any other attitudes they may have toward our issues or industry (e.g., conventional, enthusiastic, wary).		
Ways they get current information, or their reading preferences.		
Most appropriate information or tools they need to act or become informed.		

Emphasize benefits more than features

Do you know the big question on the mind of every reader of your organization's material? It is this: "What's in it for me?"

As far as your readers are concerned, it's all about the benefits you can offer them. You want to emphasize how your organization's product or service improves the lives of its constituents and their communities.

We tend to focus on all of the wonderful features of the services and products we offer. But if you try to see things from your readers' perspective, you will notice that they are most interested in buying or supporting benefits *that address their specific needs and values.*

For this reason, writing about benefits that matter to your readers is absolutely crucial in any kind of marketing or fundraising piece. I am talking about everything from a personal letter requesting financial support, to a general flyer about a service you offer, to a special report or white paper about your industry, to a website article.

Don't just concentrate on what specific things your organization does or makes, or how. Those are the various features of your work. While those are interesting and necessary to discuss, I suggest you emphasize *what difference your organization makes* — how your services benefit the users, your supporters, and/or the community at-large.

Ask yourself: *How will your service or product improve the lives of your readers and their community, in the short and the long term?*

Did you notice how I said *both* your readers *and* their community? That is because we work in the public-interest sector and not the conventional business world. Our stakeholders want to find ways to benefit both themselves and the world around them. So we might want to edit their big question to now read: "What's in it for *me and us*?"

Simply put, your job is to refine your copy so that it makes your readers feel good about the benefits you are offering. You want them to feel so good that they are willing to take a chance on you with their time, money, energy, or other resources.

Your writing has to persuade them that your product or service will help them achieve their goals, benefiting them and their community. And your pieces need to justify the space and time they occupy (e.g., room in email inboxes or reading time).

Eventually, you will compile especially effective phrases, paragraphs, and statements to recycle in your materials. But, of course, you will have to tweak and update everything to make sure it uses language that speaks most persuasively to your specific intended audience.

BUT FIRST, YOU HAVE TO CONVINCE YOUR READERS OF THE URGENCY

Before your readers will even think about getting involved with your organization's solutions, they have to be convinced that you are dealing with an urgent problem or important unmet need. Keep in mind that your readers are busy people and could easily be indifferent to — or unaware of — your issue or their own need for your product or service. Without an understanding of the problem — and its seriousness — they really have no reason to do anything about it.

If your organization has assessed the needs and realities of your community members with solid research (perhaps as part of a strategic planning process), you already know the types of problems you need to address. Your job as a public-interest organization is to advocate for and/or implement socially responsible solutions to those problems, delivering needed benefits to your constituents.

But what if you are trying to involve a segment of your community that is not that well-informed about the issue or its complexities? Then you will have to do some constituent education as part of your marketing work. For instance, you may need to explain the health benefits of organic produce, or how energy-efficient and reusable products save money (see Chapter A, "Create and advance your brand," for more information about educating your readers).

For now, though, we will assume that your readers know a lot about the needs or problems you are addressing. Their interest lies in how to solve those problems, and to reap the benefits of those solutions.

Personally speaking

This feel-good imperative reminds me of the old toothpaste commercials that implied that you would find love and romance if only you brushed with their minty fresh taste. Today's cell phone ads suggest that their products will win you lots of new friends and dates. While this is a blatant use of persuasive power, we can use that power in the public interest too.

LET'S START WITH YOUR FEATURES, BUT MOVE RIGHT TO BENEFITS

Consider the features of your work: the components or characteristics of the actual services or products your organization offers. The details of your features often include answers to questions your most interested readers might ask. Examples might be technical specifications or information on exactly how you carry out your programs.

Benefits, on the other hand, are the tangible and intangible outcomes you are striving for: the great results and powerful impact that your stakeholders will get from working with you.

EXAMPLE

Let's say that an organization runs a homeless shelter for families. It offers warm beds, restrooms, and other facilities. It also hires child care workers and counselors, uses volunteers, operates a soup kitchen, and offers services to help residents find more permanent housing or jobs. Those are all features of the organization's work.

The benefits are the positive effects that those things have on the shelter residents and the community at-large. Here we are talking about the difference the organization makes in addressing the problems associated with homelessness, both in the short and long term.

Some of those benefits may be:

- Increased stability and nutrition in the lives of homeless families
- Increased employment among homeless parents
- Fewer families living in cars or on the streets
- Less desperation, which often leads to crime, drug abuse, and other social ills
- The sense of being a community that cares for all of its citizens

Here are three related questions that can help you identify the benefits of your work:

Ask yourself: *What does your service or product mean to your reader and/ or community — personally, professionally, financially, physically, logistically, spiritually, and/or emotionally?*

EXAMPLES

1. *The Health Trust, which oversaw and partially supported the School Health Clinics of Santa Clara County, worked with me several years ago to document its benefits to the community. The language we developed then served the organization for years in many successful documents. Following is some of the text, which focuses on economic benefits:*

   - The School Health Clinics play a critical role in support of the educational process. They prepare children and families to be informed healthcare consumers and encourage self-responsible behaviors. The Clinics represent wise investments, as they lead to a healthy community and a healthy future workforce.
   - Each clinic visit will save the community from $160 to $2,000 in physician or emergency room costs.
   - School-based healthcare gives working parents a convenient healthcare alternative for their children, thus reducing costly disruption, distraction, and absence from their workplace.
   - Companies have better informed employees who are likely to make wise healthcare and lifestyle choices for themselves and their families. And healthy employees with fewer health risks give employers a negotiating advantage with health insurers. Thus, corporate financing of school-based healthcare can be part of a company's community development and philanthropic strategy. *(www.healthtrust.org)*

2. Four of the features of the services I offer through my socially responsible business, Writing for Community Success,* are:

   - Expert guidance from a published writer
   - Availability in person, by phone, and online
   - Customized advice
   - Specialization in socially responsible organizations

   Those four features in turn produce these four benefits:

   - You will quickly start to see improvements in your documents, with no more frustratingly long learning curves.
   - The work fits nicely with your busy lifestyle.
   - You will learn exactly what you need to know, exactly the way you need it, with no need to try to fit within standardized processes or timelines.
   - You will improve your writing with an eye toward improving your community.

---

* I know, I know. This is shameless self-promotion. But it also makes a great example.

Ask yourself: *What will happen as a result of the particular features you offer? And how does that satisfy the needs and desires of your readers?*

> **EXAMPLE**
>
> An organization that provides massage therapy to low-income cancer survivors might say:
>
> Your compassionate investment of $100 will buy a new clinic massage table *(feature)*, enabling our volunteer therapists to provide 50 additional revitalizing, healing massages per week to low-income cancer survivors like Jose *(client benefit)*. You will be helping your friends and neighbors enjoy happier, healthier, more productive, and (as suggested by recent medical studies) longer lives *(social benefit)*.

Ask yourself: *For each feature you offer, ask "So what?" How does that lead to something better for my reader and/or the community?*

> **EXAMPLE**
>
> Our company exterminates termites and other pests from your home or office with natural orange peel oil.
>
> | FEATURE | *BENEFIT* |
> |---|---|
> | Proven effective within 24 hours | *It will solve your termite problem quickly.* |
> | Nontoxic and natural | *It is safe, with no side effects for adults or children.* |
> | Fume-free | *You can use your home right afterward, with no waiting.* |
> | Plant-based | *It is not dependent on petroleum.* |
> | Guaranteed to keep your home or office pest-free for at least twelve months | *Saves you the expense and hassle of re-exterminating.* |
> | Consistent with an overall green lifestyle | *You will do your part for the planet.* |

LIST AND ORGANIZE ALL THE BENEFITS YOU OFFER

You probably have noticed that most people who get involved with community-benefit organizations like yours are not looking only for a practical benefit for themselves. Sure, they may be interested in the tangible things you can offer them. And they obviously value the work you do in your community. But they are also interested in the psychological and emotional benefits they can gain because of the nature of your work.

This fact defines socially responsible organizations, and you should take it seriously. It can help position your work in the forefront of your readers' minds.

Your organization's vision and mission will point you toward uncovering the many unique benefits you offer your clients and customers. I will go into how to use your mission in that way in Chapter 1, "Spotlight your mission repeatedly."

To start you down this path, I have listed some sample types of benefits, both practical and psychological/emotional, that your organization may offer to different constituencies. In the table below, I have divided constituents into two categories, but they may overlap at your organization. See how many apply to your work or to any particular aspect of it. Of course, your particular organization also will offer many others.

PRACTICAL BENEFITS *for...*	Investors, Volunteers, Other Supporters	Clients, Customers, Communities
A convenient opportunity, despite their hectic lives, to make a difference in their community	✳	
A chance to serve as a community resource — to share their good fortune or give something back in a way that matters to them	✳	
Small gifts or subscriptions	✳	
Special recognition for their involvement	✳	
Tax deduction or rebate	✳	
Access to unique expertise that addresses a key problem in a socially responsible manner	✳	✳
Environmental sustainability	✳	✳
Interactions with other people with whom they share values, beliefs, concerns, and struggles	✳	✳
New skills and/or understanding	✳	✳
Preparation for the future	✳	✳
Improved health and well-being		✳
Reduced cost or risk		✳
Safety for family, friends, or community		✳
Time savings		✳

PSYCHOLOGICAL/EMOTIONAL BENEFITS *for...*	Investors, Volunteers, Other Supporters	Clients, Customers, Communities
A sense that they are part of a winning team that is making the world a better place	✳	✳
Feelings of being kind, generous, trustworthy, helpful, important, conscious, and contributing citizens	✳	✳
Improved morale, excitement, or inspiration	✳	✳
The knowledge that they are doing their part to solve a problem that directly or indirectly affects them	✳	✳
The knowledge that they are empowering themselves and others to make their own decisions	✳	
Increased confidence		✳
Feelings of personal dignity		✳

Keep these factors in mind when you are trying to understand your readers (that is, get inside their heads). If your written pieces acknowledge and support these needs in your readers, you will be on your way to instilling a sense that your organization is an important part of their lives. You can do that by naming these benefits whenever they come up, or at least implying their presence.

EXAMPLES

1. A wealthy donor is interested in contributing financially to his community on a global level, but is unclear about how to go about it. Let's say that your organization is involved in international work focusing on women and girls, and you want to reach out to this reader. How would you do it?

   In a letter to him, you would touch on the benefits — both practical and psychological or emotional — that he would receive from investing in you and your partners overseas. Depending on what you know about the person, you may mention things like:

   ☙ Your organization hopes to offer him the opportunity to make a difference in the lives of women and girls around the world by partnering with the experts on your team;

   ☙ Your organization has a great track record of success stories;

Sometimes your readers will be interested in the specific features of your service or product, and somewhat suspicious if you only focus on benefits. If that is the case, respect their need to know and give them the data they need to make up their own minds. Explain how and why the features of your organization's service or product can lead directly to the benefits your readers might seek. This situation exemplifies the importance of knowing your readers.

> ◉ His generosity is a way for him to give something back and do his part by empowering others and helping prepare them to join our global community;
>
> ◉ By joining your circle of donors, he will be able to meet regularly with others who share his commitment;
>
> ◉ Your organization is a registered nonprofit and all gifts without an exchange of goods or services are tax-deductible.
>
> 2. Your organization's products — t-shirts made of organic cotton and sewn in factories certified to be sweatshop-free — display award-winning local artwork that is silk-screened by a union shop using soy-based inks. Your prices are competitive with other high-quality t-shirts that sport none of these special features.
>
>   I am sure you can name several of this product's many benefits for the individual consumer, the community, and the environment!

 Ask yourself: *How can you find out more about your constituents' motivations for getting involved with your organization and the benefits they seek?*

Bonus Tip

What if you know your reader is comparing two or more similar products or services with similar benefits? In that case you may want to talk about individual features that set you apart from others. Chances are good, though, that if you can identify a particular set of benefits that you alone can offer, the relevant features will simply help back you up.

Chapter B, "Engage your specific readers," offers a full slate of ways to gather this information, including simple focus groups, surveys, and observation. By using these techniques, you may discover benefits of your service or product that you have been overlooking. For instance, constituents may be using your work in ways that you have been unaware of. You can then integrate your new knowledge into your growing reader databank.

Once you have some clarity about their relevant needs and interests, you can tailor your messages to emphasize the benefits that are most meaningful to them. One way to do that is with quotes and personal stories. Chapters 4, "Connect on a person-to-person level," and 5, "Share stories," show you how.

Identifying and promoting the benefits of your product or service also help to further establish your organization's brand. That is, the benefits you offer should align well with your intended image in your readers' minds.

CONSIDER BENEFITS YOU OFFER TO OTHER ORGANIZATIONS, TOO

Not all your readers will come to your work as individuals. Some of them will represent other organizations, and may have slightly different concerns.

Ask yourself: *What benefits would they need to be aware of to make a case for engaging with you? And what would hold them back?*

All of these concerns should be on your mind as you write for these intended readers.

EXAMPLE ~~~~~~

Let's say that your reader works at a funding institution or an organization that works in a field closely related to yours, and she is concerned about the issue or challenge your organization addresses. Then she stumbles upon your document.

She would be interested in learning about your work in terms of benefits to her and her organization, such as how it will:

- ⊚ fit with her overall mission and strategic direction;

- ⊚ work in conjunction with other things she already has or does;

- ⊚ help her fulfill her responsibilities to her community;

- ⊚ help her avoid a negative outcome;

- ⊚ make her look good in the eyes of her supervisor, colleagues, and/or stakeholders.

Bonus Tip

Interestingly, many marketers have found that people will reward you if you slightly understate, but then over-deliver on, your promise of features or benefits. If your readers are pleasantly surprised, they will come back for more.

WRITING WORKOUT

This exercise will help you identify key benefits of your organization that you will want to mention in many types of marketing materials.

STEP 1: Draw a line down the center of a piece of paper. On the left-hand side, write down three features of an important product or service that you offer. Make sure there are a few blank lines between them.

STEP 2: On the right-hand side of the line, write down at least two benefits to your readers, the community, and/or the environment that go along with each feature. That is, consider your readers' point of view and see what difference those features will make in their lives — as if they were asking you: "So what?"

STEP 3: Now dig a bit deeper and think about why each benefit is so important to your readers (the next level of "so what?" questions). Does the benefit touch on a core value, belief, need, or desire? Will it mean that greater things will be possible for them in the future? Jot down these second-order benefits as well.

STEP 4: Consider how the benefits (from both Step 2 and Step 3) match up with your organization's brand. They should align well.

Bonus Tip

You may want to put together what is often known as a "positioning statement." This sentence (or two) summarizes your organization, product, or service in terms of its unique benefits and who would appreciate them. The information you summarize here about the brand you are building will be useful as an internal document for any kind of copywriting that you do.

For best results, do this exercise with all of your organization's products and services. By doing so, you will begin to develop a list of benefits that you can repeatedly refer to and draw from.

~Section-at-a-Glance: The ABCs of Copywriting~

CHAPTER A: CREATE AND ADVANCE YOUR BRAND

Every piece you write—whatever its own individual purpose—should have one overarching goal: to help promote your organization's brand.

What do I mean by "brand"?

Your "brand" is your essence: your identity, your personality, your promise, your reputation. It is what your organization stands for.

 Ask yourself: *When someone hears about your organization, what set of images, attributes, feelings, and ideas do you want them to associate with it?*

The answer is your brand.

- Emphasize your organization's uniqueness.
- Show that you share goals and values with your readers.
- Give your readers good reasons to trust you.
- Go beyond promotion for its own sake.
- Project professionalism.

CHAPTER B: ENGAGE YOUR SPECIFIC READERS

Writing to make a difference must be reader-centered and not writer-centered. You have to shift your attention, and your pre-occupations, from yourself to your readers. After all, they care about themselves, their communities, and their impact much more than they care about your organization.

To write is to engage in an intimate conversation with your readers. And for that you need to know whom you are addressing, and—most importantly—what they want to get out of conversing with you.

- Ask the right questions about your intended readers.
- Build on sample reader profiles.
- Get out there and gather more data.
- One last suggestion: keep learning.

Section-at-a-Glance: The ABCs of Copywriting

CHAPTER C: EMPHASIZE BENEFITS MORE THAN FEATURES

Do you know the big question on the mind of every reader of your organization's material? It's this: "What's in it for me?"

As far as your readers are concerned, it's all about the benefits you can offer them. You want to emphasize how your organization's product or service improves the lives of your constituents and their communities.

 Ask yourself: *How will your service or product improve the lives of your readers and their community, in the short and the long term?*

Did you notice how I said *both* your readers *and* their community? That is because we work in the public interest sector and not the conventional business world. Our stakeholders want to find ways to benefit both themselves and the world around them. So we might want to edit their big question to now read: "What's in it for *me and us?*"

- But first, you have to convince your readers of the urgency.
- Let's start with your features, but move right to benefits.
- List and organize all the benefits you offer.
- Consider benefits you offer to other organizations, too.

Part II

Establishing Your Organizational Context

You now understand the big picture of how you can use *writing to make a difference* to help your organization market and fundraise. Next, let's discuss specific techniques to advance those goals.

We begin by focusing on your specific organizational context. Because you write for a community-oriented organization, you need to be clear about the special niche your organization fills in your community. What unique contribution do you make? Why and how?

Any strategic planning you have done will serve you very well here. After all, if you have spent the time on that work, it would be a shame to never quite use it in your marketing.

In Section II a, "Stressing Your Effectiveness," we explore some tips for turning your good planning and management practices into outstanding documents:

- ◉ How you can transform your mission and vision into marketing messages

- ◉ The value of highlighting how you work in collaboration with others

- ◉ How to write about the impact of your work, using both quantitative and qualitative measures

Section II b, "Focusing on Your Community," then offers lots of details about how to focus our writing on the most important people to us: our various readers and their communities. You will learn ways to relate to these groups by both bringing your own personality into your writing and seeing your organization through the eyes of your constituents. This section also emphasizes how to ensure that your perspective is as inclusive as possible.

"You write in order to change the world, knowing perfectly well that you probably can't, but also knowing that literature is indispensable to the world… The world changes according to the way people see it, and if you alter, even by a millimeter, the way… people look at reality, then you can change it."

— James Baldwin

Section 11a   *Stressing Your Effectiveness*

I n this section you will learn how to:

- ◈ Keep the spotlight on your organization's mission and vision as you market yourself

- ◈ Write about your organization's contributions to community collaborations

- ◈ Go beyond traditional ways of 'doing the numbers' as you measure your organization's impact

Spotlight your mission repeatedly 1

H ave you advanced your organization's mission today? Your readers are eager to know about it!

Every marketing or fundraising piece you write needs to speak to your organization's reason for existing in the first place. That is, each page should remind your readers that you never forget what you set out to do in your community.

Every values-driven organization has a specific mission to make a positive difference in the world. My guess is that you already know what yours is. You may not have memorized your official mission statement, but you are clear on the essence of your organization. Your mission, after all, is a key part of your organization's brand (as discussed in Chapter A, "Create and advance your brand").

LITZLER

"I'VE NEVER SEEN OUR MISSION AD LIBBED SO WELL BY A VOLUNTEER."

Personally speaking

I have often found it interesting and useful to write up a personal mission statement, and then check if my activities align with it. The New Year, birthdays, anniversaries, and other milestones make fine times for this kind of taking stock. Politicians' publicists do this all the time because they must continuously re-brand their clients. Check out your favorite public figure's website to find her or his personal mission statement.

To each of your readers, your mission, or perhaps some particular aspect of it, is the heart of the matter. They want to hear that it is central to everything you do. They want to know that your work continues to be relevant to their lives and the life of their community, even as times and circumstances change.

There is no shame in reminding yourself of your organization's mission statement once in a while. Some people I know even plaster it on the wall or make it their screensaver to keep it at the top of the mind and on the tip of the tongue.

Your mission should inspire and motivate support and commitment from those who share your concerns. Your organization's name alone should cause your mission to spring to mind.

However, if you — and your colleagues — do not revisit your mission statement regularly, and ideally fine-tune or update it on occasion, you can get stuck in out-of-date patterns of branding. This is true for both start-up organizations (whose missions are usually still evolving) and more established groups. For instance, a client organization of mine had focused for decades on the needs of all low-income families, but recent demographic changes in their county compelled them to focus on new immigrants, with the associated cultural and linguistic challenges.

Even more dangerously, if you are not careful to monitor your work in light of your mission, your organization could easily lose its sense of direction. The Cheshire Cat in *Alice in Wonderland* summarized why you need a strong, relevant mission: "If you don't know where you're going, it doesn't matter which way you go."

Of course, your readers might not come out and ask, "What is your mission?" Instead, they might want to know what you do (how you benefit your customers and the community), how you do it (products and services featured in your work), and why you exist at all (why you are needed).

Help them out by frequently reminding them of your goals and how you are consistently making progress toward them. You cannot assume that your readers will instantly recall who you are or exactly what you do — and that includes both die-hard supporters/patrons and casual online surfers who may have stumbled across your website. But repetition will certainly help!

Here are some tips for maintaining a focus on mission in your copy.

HIGHLIGHT THE OUTSTANDING STRENGTHS OF YOUR MISSION

Continually remind your readers of what is innovative about your mission. No one likes to reinvent the wheel or be part of something garden-variety. Show that you play a special and essential role in your field: a role that cries out for involvement from your readers. Identifying the uniqueness in your organization's mission and style is a crucial aspect of furthering your brand.

Ask yourself: How is your mission unique within your field, and how does that give you a special niche?

Your mission may be to implement an entirely new solution to an age-old problem that has been haunting your community. Or maybe you are striving to improve or expand what already has begun to work. Either way, identify what about your mission makes it extraordinary.

EXAMPLES

1. *Por Fin Nuestra Casa ("finally, a home of our own") has the mission:*
   To raise the standard of living for families who currently reside in dangerous or substandard conditions.
   Not so unique, you might think. But the organization then fleshes it out with an innovative model:
   We advance this cause by creating shelters from low-cost recycled materials. PFNC utilizes surplus shipping containers resulting from the United States' consistent trade deficit. These containers serve as the building block of PFNC housing, but go through an extensive conversion process to make them a home. PFNC offers an affordable housing solution that is scalable and fully portable. Each PFNC unit includes First World amenities for a price of less than $10,000 (US).
   (www.pfnc.net)

2. *Seventh Generation is a pioneer in its industry, and that makes it stand out:*
   Established in 1988, Seventh Generation is the nation's most widely recognized brand of natural household and personal care products. For 20 years, the closely held Burlington, Vermont-based company has been at the forefront of a cultural change in consumer behavior and business ethics.
   One of the country's first self-declared "socially responsible" companies, Seventh Generation is a business that operates according to a new and different set of principles and values that in many ways are a marked departure from those long considered "traditional." Its business practice is focused on offering people avenues to express their idealism, passion, and commitment to causes larger than themselves at every point along its supply chain — from suppliers and partners to shareholders, customers and its own staff.
   (www.seventhgeneration.com)

Another way to point out your organization's unique value to your community is to ask your readers to imagine a world *without* anyone working to advance your mission. What void would that leave? And how troubling would that picture be?

> **EXAMPLE**
>
> Imagine our urban neighborhood if the Westside Teen Center suddenly disappeared…
>
> Very few places would remain for our young people to continue to develop their hearts and minds after the school day ends. Without supportive adult mentors and role models, our children would lose critical opportunities to get tutoring help, build new leadership and social skills, discover their unique talents, interests, and strengths, and prepare for their futures. They also would no longer have a safe place to mingle and relax with their peers.
>
> Our teens must deal daily with grinding poverty and all of the risks and problems that come with it. Without a positive, empowering "home away from home," they would be left with few alternatives to unhealthy or illegal activities on the streets. Drug trafficking, a proliferation of gangs, and increased violent crime would likely soon follow.

DESCRIBE HOW YOUR WORK EMBODIES YOUR GUIDING PRINCIPLES

Back away from the practical specifics and take a bit of a philosophical approach.

Ask yourself: *What fundamental values or concerns lead your readers to your organization and its mission?*

For instance, you and your readers might particularly value the physical and emotional health of young women; the dignity of refugees; the artistic expression of senior citizens; the conservation of wildlife in your region; the science education of middle school students; or waterways free of pollution.

Because of your shared values, you can make some basic assumptions about what your readers understand and agree on. In your written pieces, build on those assumptions about what works, what does not work, and what important beliefs should be upheld. You will naturally hit on the core thoughts and feelings your readers harbor, as they pertain to your mission and activities. (For more about shared essential concerns, check out Chapters 4, "Connect on a person-to-person level," and 6, "Write with reader diversity in mind.")

Ask yourself: *How would your organization complete this sentence to clarify shared assumptions about the world, how it works, and what is important?*

"Our organization focuses on _____ and we value _____ .
We believe our work is important in the world because _____ ."

EXAMPLE

Our organization focuses on girls' education around the world, and we value equal opportunity, economic and social development, and self-actualization for all. We believe our work is important in the world because an educated girl is more likely to grow up to create a healthier life for herself, her family, and her community than she otherwise might have. Decades of studies have shown us that girls' education is the key to the economic development of communities and entire nations.

Many socially responsible organizations explicitly talk about their values and guiding principles in their marketing materials. So can you.

EXAMPLES

1. *Presidio School of Management believes that:*
   Traditional business skills won't take students far enough. Our courses are designed to cross disciplines, teach through experience both in and outside of the classroom, and provide a new framework for talking about both business and sustainability.

   Our educational philosophy provides students not just with a skill set, but also with a unique perspective on solving the world's most pressing problems — leading to action driven by their vision and values.

   (www.presidiomba.org/vision)

2. All of ShoreBank's leaders and employees are expected to demonstrate the following values in their daily activities and decision-making:

   - Integrity and Excellence
   - Respect and Inclusion
   - Collaboration and Local focus
   - Triple Bottom Line: building wealth for all in economically integrated communities, promoting environmental health and operating profitably
   - Innovation   *(adapted from www.shorebankcorp.com)*

Once you have identified what is most meaningful to your organization, those values and beliefs will inform the rest of your copywriting, illuminating your message.

EVOKE A VISION OF WHAT YOUR COMMUNITY WILL BE LIKE ONCE YOUR ORGANIZATION HAS FULFILLED ITS MISSION

Your mission is not only about short-term results. It is also about your long-term vision. Your readers want to be inspired by the world you would like to see. Your organization, of course, will play a role in realizing that vision — so help your readers visualize it right now.

Ask yourself: *If your organization were to meet with great success and fully accomplish its mission, what would that look like?*

You may want to ask this simple question of your colleagues as well. Perhaps your organization even has a formal "vision statement."

EXAMPLES

Here are a few vision statements of values-based organizations:

1. *Foundation Center:* We envision a world enriched by the effective allocation of philanthropic resources, informed public discourse about philanthropy, and broad understanding of the contributions of nonprofit activity to civil society.　　　*(www.foundationcenter.org)*

2. *Brown Paper Tickets:* We are here to change the ticketing industry. Years of unfair pricing and mediocre service have resulted in these practices becoming the norm. No longer. Leading by example, Brown Paper Tickets will guide the industry into a new era of affordable ticketing and quality service. Others in the industry will be forced to change their ways or lose the markets they currently dominate.　　　*(www.brownpapertickets.com)*

3. *Global Exchange:* We envision a people-centered globalization that values the rights of workers and the health of the planet; that prioritizes international collaboration as central to ensuring peace; and that aims to create a local, green economy designed to embrace the diversity of our communities.　　　*(www.globalexchange.org)*

You might also develop a more informal image of what you are working toward. For instance, some organizations have held community gatherings or stakeholder retreats to paint murals or assemble collages representing the world they want to create.

Generally speaking, community-benefit organizations like yours are working to:

◈ Advance	◈ Facilitate	◈ Protect
◈ Broaden	◈ Help	◈ Provide
◈ Build	◈ Improve	◈ Restore
◈ Connect	◈ Increase	◈ Reverse
◈ Create	◈ Initiate	◈ Save
◈ Cure	◈ Inspire	◈ Serve
◈ Decrease	◈ Integrate	◈ Stop
◈ Develop	◈ Preserve	◈ Strengthen
◈ Discover	◈ Prevent	◈ Support
◈ Eliminate	◈ Promote	◈ Transform

or in another way change something vital in our world. Think about the specific ways you envision changes happening, and bring those images into your documents.

For more help with making your mission and vision vivid for your readers, see Chapter 10, "Show, don't just tell." And for help maximizing the power of your action words, check out Chapter 11, "Focus on the verbs."

CONNECT THE DOTS FOR YOUR READERS OVER TIME

When writing about your current or past activities, show how they create an ongoing story of accomplishing your mission. You want to convince your reader that you have your eye on the ultimate goal — every move gets you closer to it.

As you spotlight the advancement of your mission, explain the specific changes you are helping to bring about. Changes can be small, such as an "aha" expression spreading across a child's face, or the sight of a few hundred freshly planted trees in an otherwise barren urban landscape. They can also be large, such as a change in voting patterns in a national election, or a growing widespread preference for renewable fuels. But all successes are steps in the right direction. Help your reader see the progression over the long haul — and how the whole is actually far more than the sum of the parts.

Ask yourself: *How would you complete this paragraph?*

"Our mission is to _____ . Over the past _____ years we have done this by _____ . Currently we are taking our mission into the future by doing _____ ."

EXAMPLE

Suppose your organization is about to launch a new product, service, or policy, or expand something you already are offering. It is your job to write about this change in a way that engages your intended readers. You will want to explain why your organization is introducing this change: how it will help advance your mission both now and in the long run. You may also have internal reasons for introducing it (generating a new revenue stream, increasing your visibility, staying competitive in your industry, etc.). But your readers are specifically interested in how it will benefit *them and their community,* and that ties right back to your mission.

The change you are initiating will help solve the community problem at the core of your organization's issues of concern — so emphasize that. In conventional business, the rationale for service or product changes is something like, "to serve you better." But in socially responsible organizations, we have the goal of also serving our community and environment better. By emphasizing how your organization's new actions tie closely to your mission, you advance your brand — on the cutting edge of your issue.

USE YOUR MISSION AND VISION AS OVERARCHING THEMES

Over time, organizations often develop programs, products, and services that can be quite diverse. If this describes your organization, help your readers keep track of how your mission and vision provide the unifying theme for your various projects. Your readers can then quickly see the connections between whatever program you are writing about and their continuing support for your brand.

EXAMPLES

1. *From the 2005 Annual Report of the Lawyers' Committee for Civil Rights of the San Francisco Bay Area:*

   For nearly 40 years, we have provided legal representation in three broad program areas: race, poverty and immigration. Our ability to employ a range of advocacy strategies in addressing these expansive program areas has become a crucial part of our organizational identity.

   Ask a cross-section of Lawyers' Committee clients to describe us, and you would likely receive a wide range of responses. For students in California's under-funded and increasingly re-segregated public schools, we are passionate advocates of equal access to education. For refugees, we are a path to asylum and a life free of persecution. For victims of large-scale retail discrimination, we are defenders of every customer's right to non-discriminatory service. For disenfranchised voters, we are the challengers of unfair voting districts and the enforcers of equal representation laws. For Muslim, South Asian and Middle Eastern communities enduring post-9/11 backlash, we are the courage to defend their legal rights despite a hostile political climate.   *(www.lccr.com)*

2. *The Ella Baker Center's website describes its broad vision:*

   The safest neighborhoods aren't the ones with the most prisons and the most police. They're the ones with the best schools, the cleanest environment, and the most opportunities for young people and working people. That's what we want for urban America: justice in the system; opportunity in our cities; and peace on our streets.

   Those three ideas — justice, peace and opportunity — guide all of our work at Ella Baker Center. They are the foundation of our four campaigns and initiatives.   *(www.ellabakercenter.org)*

While writing for a multi-issue organization, point out the various ways it carries out its mission. But beware of being too general, vague, or all-purpose. You want to be sure to depict the organization's niche in a way that does not also describe many other organizations. For example, you would want to steer clear of nondescript language such as: "We aim to help communities address environmental challenges and build a better future shaped by all."

WRITING WORKOUT

This exercise will get you thinking about how to integrate your organization's mission and vision into your marketing and fundraising copy. You will find that it is an extension of the Writing Workout in Chapter A, "Create and advance your brand."

STEP 1: Review your organization's mission statement and vision statement, as they provide good starting points. Even if the precise wordings are not particularly helpful to you, they should embody a sense of what your organization believes about the world and what needs to get done. A written articulation of your organization's core values or principles and a recent strategic plan are also great documents to read through. If you have a copy of the minutes to a recent board or staff meeting or retreat, find and consider the comments that address what your organization is about and what it stands for. Run a highlighter pen over some of the most important words or phrases.

If you have not already filled in the blanks contained in the two "Ask Yourself" questions on pages 53 and 56, please do so now.

STEP 2: Now look at some of your organization's published marketing and fundraising materials. Are your activities discussed in terms of the values and goals you identified in Step 1? That is, does the writing reflect shared values, assumptions about the world, and your organization's mission and vision? Notice what the materials say about both short-term and long-term goals and achievements. Jot down some notes that come to mind.

STEP 3: If you found that your materials do not quite accurately portray your organization from a mission or vision perspective, spend some time thinking about how to change that. What can you do right now to reinforce your organization's unique, mission-driven brand, through the words, concepts, and style you use? Try making these changes over the next one or two weeks, and see how it strengthens your copywriting. (You may eventually want to update your organization's mission statement, but that process will likely take more time.)

Maximize your collaborations 2

Given the astronomical proliferation of values-driven organizations in the last few decades, many of our readers are wondering: "How come you all don't just combine forces?" Good question.

No one — investors, customers, clients, etc. — likes to see duplication of effort among barely distinguishable parties. It certainly makes marketing and branding a tougher job as well!

But we are so passionate and concerned about our own sub-issues, services, and products that we can neglect the potential allies out there. In fact, instead of finding ways to cooperate, we often adopt a competitive attitude.

Please don't get me wrong. I am the first to agree that healthy competition keeps organizations on their toes. What I bemoan is the frequent tendency to allow narrow organizational interests (such as maintaining the status quo or protecting fragile egos) to take precedence over larger community interests.

If you can show that you are not only aware of your potential collaborators, but also working with them to make an even bigger difference than you could make alone, you will be ahead of the game. Your readers will respond.

Emphasizing how you work collaboratively shows your readers that you are strategically maximizing your precious resources. It also demonstrates that your organization is in the know about your field as a whole. Seize every opportunity to showcase that cooperative work!

After all, successful businesses have long known that strategic partnerships are the way to go. An example from the conventional business world is the growing number of marketing partnerships of airline frequent flyer programs. These partnerships mean that customers can earn miles or get discounts with a host of credit cards, hotels, car rental companies, restaurants, and even retail stores. In turn, the businesses involved reap the benefits of expanding their market share.

Finding a way to connect to another organization just to be able to say you are "collaborating" will not work. It will fool no one. Be strategic about your choice of partners and work in a genuine way that benefits all parties involved — especially your clients. If you focus on everyone's strengths in a way that truly improves each organization's work, your effort will succeed. If not, go back to the drawing board.

As I mentioned in Chapter B, "Engage your specific readers," many nonprofits have teamed up with corporate sponsors through "cause-related marketing campaigns." This chapter offers several other ways to use your collaborative work to improve your marketing and fundraising pieces.

DESCRIBE YOUR ORGANIZATION'S UNIQUE ROLE IN COLLABORATIVE EFFORTS

Your work to advance your organization's unique brand involves illustrating how you contribute essential threads to your community's interwoven fabric. You serve as a crucial resource and contributor to social and/or environmental responsibility.

Collaboration combines your organization's power with that of other organizations that share your values, in a strategic effort to benefit a larger number of people than you could alone.

Ask yourself: *How does your work fit into the larger picture of your community's well-being?*

For instance:

- Are you picking up where other organizations leave off (geographically, economically, demographically, or otherwise)?

- Are you breaking new ground or starting a trend that will create forward-looking possibilities for your field or industry?

- Do you serve a crucial intermediary function that other important systems need in order to work well?

- Are you providing needed support for other community organizations to progress (facilitation, information exchange, equipment, research, etc.)?

Your organization offers unique perspectives, expertise, and resources to groups in your community that work on related issues. Together, your efforts take your collective work to a higher level.

Personally speaking

I strongly advocate collaboration and networking. I believe that when two or more organizations are working on the same or similar issues they can find ways to enhance each other's work. I often feel frustrated when several community-benefit organizations try to do extremely similar work — in isolation. Clearly, if they worked together they could summon a whole new level of power. But fruitful collaboration requires particular attention and effort. Unfortunately, these elements are not always in the plans.

EXAMPLES

1. The Henry Street Settlement's employment program and Recycle-a-Bicycle, Inc. co-sponsor a youth development project that blends environmental education with job training. New York City youth and young adults from low-income neighborhoods repair donated bicycles and reintroduce them into the community through retail sales or donations. Participants also learn about the environmental benefits of bicycling and conservation. The project's other collaborators include local public schools and after-school programs. Since opening its doors in 1995, the initiative has recovered or spared 109 tons from the city's waste stream. *(www.henrystreet.org)*

2. The AMBER (America's Missing: Broadcast Emergency Response) Alert network, headed by the U.S. Department of Justice, broadcasts emergency messages when a law enforcement agency determines that a child has been abducted and is in immediate danger. The broadcasts include information about the child and abductor, such as physical description and information about the abductor's vehicle. Other partners include broadcasters, transportation agencies, and the wireless industry — all contributing to the joint effort to spur the community to help in the search for and safe recovery of the child. *(www.amberalert.gov)*

3. Needful Provision, Inc. is a nonprofit in Oklahoma whose for-profit arm, Preparedness Systems Intl., LLC, employs low-income people in its area to produce odorless, community composting toilet "kits" and related items. An affiliated business in Kenya, Quick Lift, Ltd., will then sell the kits via a unique global barter trade program that helps African villagers buy the items without paying cash. *(www.needfulprovision.org)*

Whenever you find a strong connection between your organization and another, in terms of work and target audience, you will also find a stellar opportunity to mutually benefit. By working together, you:

- build on each other's strengths and complement each other's weaknesses;
- avoid duplicating services by coordinating and streamlining your work;
- learn from each other's experiences;
- begin to see relationships among the issues and approaches that you focus on;
- share information and resources instead of having to find them individually;
- begin to reap the benefits of economy of scale.

All of these benefits of collaboration should feature prominently in your written pieces.

EXAMPLE

One effective appeal letter from the Union of Concerned Scientists began by posing a question on the minds of many of its readers: "There are too many environmental groups. Why don't you folks work together?"

The letter then went on to show how collaboration is a "guiding principle" for this organization of scientists and citizens:

We share our findings with other environmental groups, decision-makers in government, and local citizens' groups to achieve our common goal: a cleaner,

Bonus Tip

Many international, national, and regional networks facilitate collaborations among socially responsible organizations. National and International examples include: the Social Venture Network, B Corporation, America Forward, Business for Social Responsibility, the Institute of Green Professionals, Business Ethics Network, and Future 500. Regional initiatives include the Sustainable Business Alliance in the San Francisco area's East Bay, Maine Businesses for Social Responsibility, the Sustainable Business Network in New York City, the Green Exchange in Chicago, and the Jean Vollum Natural Capital Center in Portland, Oregon.

By participating in a collaborative network, your organization can carve out a unique role while reaping the rewards of collaboration, in both your marketing to different constituencies and your internal organizational development.

> healthier environment and a safer world…You probably know many of the organizations we collaborate with — the Sierra Club, Natural Resources Defense Council, World Wildlife Fund. There are scores of others, and UCS stands ready to work with them — combining our expertise and political muscle with the millions of concerned citizens who are collectively our members…
>
> By joining the Union of Concerned Scientists, and connecting with our online Action Network, you won't just be giving your moral and financial support to UCS's efforts. You'll be strengthening the entire Environmental Movement. *(www.ucsusa.org)*

EXCHANGE ONLINE CONTENT WITH YOUR PARTNERS AND AFFILIATES

The organizations that you work with have their own websites, blogs, social networking profiles, podcasts, and/or e-newsletters. So you can easily share your content. This can mean less work for each of you, as well as new and valuable information for your separate constituencies.

Consider interviewing each other, posting guest articles, linking your websites, and endorsing each other's new ideas, products, or services. Well-established ethical online marketers are notorious for these practices — and you can join them.

CONSTRUCT JOINT DOCUMENTS

Collaboration in copywriting gets out your shared messages in a powerful and consistent voice. With less competition for public attention on similar issues, your readers can focus on the collective credibility and clout of the contributing organizations. Looked at another way, repetition of the same copy reinforces the message.

For instance, the reports of the United Nations Intergovernmental Panel on Climate Change are the world's most authoritative on the topic. Their assessments carry much more weight than that of any individual scientist. Joint statements that draw from a large pool of public opinion operate in a similar way.

Also, shared authorship can facilitate a robust exchange of ideas and insights. You can learn and borrow from each other, mutually feeding off of your energy, encouragement, and confidence. Perspectives and skills will spread beyond your organizational silos. Collaboration also encourages and models debate and discussion of best practices and current thinking.

What types of documents can organizations create together? Here is a short list of ideas:

- A joint website that becomes the gateway for information on the partners
- Joint press releases about events you are participating in
- Cooperative opinion pieces that carry the voices of multiple organizations
- Collaborative special reports

⊘ Joint newsletters, either online or print

⊘ Collaborative event announcements

⊘ Joint grant proposals for projects that require several partners

If you are serious about working collaboratively, all partners need to be involved in the initial planning. Of course, the diverse partners bring a wide variety of perspectives to the table. And your documents need to reflect your common ground as well as your significant areas of difference.

To accomplish this, you must establish an inclusive process that balances the needs of all partners. Name a single coordinator or editor to assign, collect, and unify the various pieces that each party submits. With that person's leadership, the group needs to do a few structural things:

1. agree on the document's scope and purposes as a marketing tool, geared to your intended readers;

2. discuss the main messages you are aiming to convey, given your shared vision;

3. decide how similar the pieces need to be, or if they can diverge (each appearing in a different voice, under a different byline);

4. divide up the writing and editing tasks.

You also have to agree on how you will share suggested edits. These will range from general comments on the document's content, structure, and tone to nitty-gritty wordsmithing. To directly encourage input, provide fill-in-the-blank lines to be completed with additional information, and devise a way to alert each other to places that need additional feedback.

Several word processing and online collaborative writing systems include features that keep track of changes and comments made by several people. Examples include the "track changes" feature in Microsoft Word®, blogs, wikis (changeable online archives), email discussion groups, and chat rooms. If you use an online document storage system, you will be able to access joint documents from any computer, and receive an online message when a collaborator makes a change. Tag services enable you to earmark websites to share with your collaborators.

In addition, I suggest reviewing Chapter 17, "Edit the big picture," and Appendix 8, "Editing Checklist," for further guidance about helping improve others' drafts.

Sometimes we may think that relative lack of experience or knowledge on the topic at hand renders our opinions marginal. Avoid this tendency! Anyone can contribute valuable perspectives, even if it is only expressing confusion about what a writer means to say. A less well-versed reader can also help writers gauge a document's fit with the background of intended readers.

Bonus Tip

Collaborative writing can immensely benefit your organization. If you have existing relationships with some or all of the other partners, a collaborative writing project can strengthen these ties — and it can also spark new ones. In addition, collaborative pieces offer excellent opportunities to mentor the less experienced writers in your group.

Personally speaking

In my writing workshops, participants love exchanging ideas with each other about their pieces. Frequently the synergy is exactly what they need to move to the next level of effectiveness. Writers throughout the ages have known this secret, and now you do too.

EXAMPLES

1. CONCUR, Inc., an environmental policy analysis and dispute mediation firm, facilitated what it calls "joint factfinding" with the New York Bight Initiative. Under the auspices of the New York Academy of Sciences, this collaborative decision-making process focused on the management of pollutants in an extremely stressed ocean region (the Bight) next to the New York Harbor. The process involved 22 different groups representing a wide spectrum of backgrounds, ranging from Clean Ocean Action to the Chemical Manufacturers Association. The process had to elevate the discussion beyond the long history of disputes among the interest groups.

   How did they ultimately reach consensus and produce an 80-page report, with five chapters of findings and one chapter of management strategies?

   First, they negotiated and agreed on a draft outline for the report. They then underwent months of closely facilitated meetings, with the facilitators acting as the group's secretariat — producing five successive drafts.

   The group focused on making technical findings and terms accessible to all involved—scientists and non-scientists alike. They also identified facts that they agreed on and reached consensus on 26 recommendations. When necessary, they agreed to disagree. *(www.concurinc.com)*

2. As part of a two-year collaborative project sponsored by the W.K. Kellogg Foundation, entitled Transforming Philanthropy in Communities of Color, eight organizations worked together to produce one joint marketing piece. The National Community Development Institute and the University of North Carolina-Chapel Hill teamed up with six local community organizations. They each had specific roles to play in the writing, editing, and production of the booklet, which features case studies from each of the partners. The collective format highlights the collaboration among them. *(www.ncdinet.org)*

3. Citizens for Sensible Transportation worked together on three related ballot measures for the November 2008 election in Santa Clara County, California. The core group included a business-oriented conservative Democrat, a Libertarian, an anti-tax Republican, a moderate Democrat, and three progressive Democrats. The representatives ranged from people who thought global warming was a hoax to people who felt that curbing global warming required drastic, immediate action.

   The group succeeded by focusing on the specific phrases and concepts they agreed on in various working drafts and refrained from attacking items they did not favor. They also paid close attention to their writing's clarity and appeal to the largest possible number of voters. *(www.novtatax.org)*

Of course, collaborative writing projects are about more than words on paper. Many interpersonal communication issues may also arise, and you need to recognize them when they do. A healthy dose of diplomacy and understanding will come in handy as you pay special attention to issues of:

- ◉ Mutual trust and respect

- ◉ Competition or intellectual ownership

- ◉ Power differences

- ◉ Everyone doing a fair share of the work

- ◉ Jealousy

- ◉ Differences in background or culture

- ◉ Individual egos

Some people are highly independent. If you truly enjoy working alone and need total control over your document, you probably would do well not to try to write in a collaborative manner.

I suggest that you first decide on some ground rules on topics such as:

- ◉ What is each person's role in the process and responsibility to the group?

- ◉ How available will each person be at critical points in the process?

- ◉ How open is everyone to constructive criticism: Are you encouraging or even expecting it from each other?

- ◉ How can you integrate individual strengths, skills, knowledge, work styles, rhythms, and approaches to complement one another?

- ◉ How will you handle areas of disagreement or different interpretations of the same thing?

- ◉ What are your budget and timetable, and how swiftly will you need to swap ideas and drafts?

- ◉ Which technologies and methods will you use, so as to accommodate everyone's comfort level?

ADDRESS CONCERNS ABOUT COLLABORATING TOO MUCH

If you collaborate too much, will your organization get lost in the crowd? While this can be a risk, you can agree that each partner will carve out a specialty or niche around which to lead any collaborative efforts. Your organization will then become the "lead author" on jointly published documents or document segments that focus on this area.

In this way, you add to your credibility by becoming known as the expert on a particular piece of an issue, while not detracting from your partners' time in the limelight. You will also establish a position as both a team player and a leader.

 WRITING WORKOUT

Get a bit of practice articulating the collaborations your organization engages in.

STEP 1: Think about at least two other partner organizations you regularly work with on a particular project. What unique capabilities and experiences does each of you bring to the mix? Write a bit about each contribution.

STEP 2: Now consider how the parts work together to enhance your collaborative work. Create a metaphor or analogy to describe it. Examples may include a well-oiled machine, a healthy body, a delicious salad, an ecosystem, a functional family, the two wings of a bird, an efficient three-legged stool, or a beautiful multi-colored mosaic. Write a brief piece invoking your metaphor to explain how your collaboration operates.

STEP 3: Share the piece you have just written with your collaborating partners. Solicit their feedback and maybe even turn this piece into a collaborative writing project. You may want to consider posting it on your website or including it in the "About Us" section of your next collaborative document. Your partners may also want to use it in their own marketing material.

Reflect your true numbers 3

"AT THE HEART OF OUR RESEARCH AND DEVELOPMENT IS A RIGOROUS EENIE, MEENIE, MINIE, MOE MATRIX."

We in the U.S. love our numbers! If you can tell us how much, how fast, how tall, how far, how old, how big, or how small, we are happy campers. We like to measure and count things. We are drawn to definition, lines, and edges. For centuries, we have cherished an appreciation for the elegance of proportions and the predicting power of statistics.

Your readers relate to numbers because numbers reflect visible, tangible outcomes in communities. People have come to expect to hear about your organization's results in this way.

At the same time, as a socially responsible organization, you are aware of how accountable you are to your many stakeholders: your clients, customers, members, investors, staff, volunteers, board, the natural environment, and the larger community. You address a vital need and create valuable benefits, without running roughshod over anyone involved.

Focusing on the numbers is a powerful way to demonstrate accountability. You might want to simply count the number of individuals, families, communities, animals, or natural resources that your organization directly serves or works with. Such a tabulation may seem pretty straightforward. *Not so fast!*

Your impact on the community is actually much greater than that. Think about other ways you can measure and illustrate the difference your organization is making. Although collecting this new data may initially take a while, it will pay off later.

Let's look at a few ways to toot your organization's own numeric horn.

Bonus Tip

Administrative and technical staff members often know best exactly how to collect this sort of data. They can help you figure out what fits easily into existing tracking systems and will require the least amount of hassle.

DOCUMENT YOUR RIPPLE EFFECTS

These days it is almost impossible not to have an effect on people who see, hear, or read about your work, or who know someone connected to you. That is, you touch the lives of all those who come in contact with your efforts, and not only those with whom you interact directly.

For instance, your organization may serve a modest absolute number of clients each month, but your actual audience is much wider—particularly if what you are doing could be easily replicated. Also, some efforts—such as legal cases, public policy advocacy, or train the trainers initiatives—are designed to have much broader implications than their immediate outcomes. Chances are good that if you are involved in groundbreaking work, you are doing lots of public presentations too — and you should keep track of the number of people you are speaking to.

Consider also the phenomena of website linking and email forwarding, often called "word of mouse" or "Internet viral marketing." When readers love what they see in your online materials, sending it on to their friends takes only a click or two. They might also post it on a personal blog or online social networking page.

EXAMPLES

1. *Better World Books is a global online bookstore that brings literacy and opportunity to people around the world. It documents not only the number of books it sells, but also the social, environmental, and economic ripple effects it is after. That is, the number of:*

   - books collected through book drives
   - books directly sent to literacy organizations worldwide
   - pounds of metal shelving reclaimed from U.S. libraries
   - tons of carbon offset in shipping their books
   - full-time jobs (with full benefits) created
   - tons of books saved from landfills   *(www.betterworld.com)*

2. *A great way to show your organization's numbers and use word of mouse is with an email signature line. Here is one from VIA (Volunteers in Asia):*

   - 45 years
   - 15 countries
   - 1,600 American volunteers
   - 4,000+ Asian undergraduates
   - Countless lives changed   *(www.viaprograms.org)*

Printed materials can make the rounds too—both those you create and those you contribute to with articles, columns, and the like.

As ripple effects take time to accumulate, you need to keep your organization visible by continually making "impressions." This marketing term means, essentially, the individual exposures of your target audience members to your messages. Most marketers agree that you need to make at least five (some say seven, or up to nine) impressions before the average reader will take notice.

Another way you can create a tidal wave beyond your initial splash: Work with strategic partners. Do you collaborate with one or more allied organizations? If so, you can cross-promote to reach larger circles of interested folks. By including each other in your written materials, you show your readers that your organizations are leveraging and maximizing your resources, financial and otherwise. (See Chapter 2, "Maximize your collaborations," for more information.)

Finally, many socially responsible organizations are contributing to wholesale social changes over years or decades. For instance, manufacturers of environmentally sound products no longer occupy the fringe of their industries, but now influence what consumers can easily find at stores and shops nationwide. Of course, if you have a way to measure how your organization has helped create a more socially responsible marketplace of products, services, or ideas—on a local, regional, national or global level—bring those results to the foreground!

HOME IN ON THE COLORFUL DETAILS OF YOUR ORGANIZATION

Ask yourself: *What interesting numbers at your organization can you point to that show the day-to-day hard work you do—and also demonstrate the widespread effects you have?*

If you look beyond the standard numbers about your organization's direct or indirect impacts, you can find many other compelling statistics. Some organizations have even found that they can turn such numbers into a fun board game that they then offer to their communities.

Another way to look at the numbers at your organization is to think about what size holes your organization would leave if it suddenly disappeared from your community. Help your reader see what is actually at stake here.

For instance:

- How many thousands of families would lose their healthcare?

- How many endangered species would probably go extinct?

- How many more cubic feet of waste would end up in your town's landfill each year?

Bonus Tip

How can you begin to track the impressions you make?

You can start by estimating the foot traffic, circulation, or broadcast market of the locations you target with your messages. You also can note any spikes in traffic on your website or blog—and additional links to your site from other sites—after each email announcement. Some email software actually registers how many people click on your embedded links. Always ask people who contact your organization how they heard about your work. And investigate other indicators you can track to learn about your long-term direct and indirect impacts on your community.

Bonus Tip

If your organization leverages the power of pro bono expertise and other resources, you probably make much more of a community impact than you otherwise could. Your supporters want to know about that! Calculate the dollar value of donated services or products ("in-kind donations"), and show how those resources multiply the effectiveness of each actual dollar invested in your organization. Make sure to talk about any another financial incentives—such as funds from institutions or individuals that will only come to your organization if "matched" by other money.

Investors are keen on getting a large bang for their buck or return on their investment.

EXAMPLE

Harper's Magazine does a great job with its "Index." This simple monthly feature shows how numbers can make a statement and tell a story. Just a few statistics or dates can shine a light on important—or at least funny—trends in our world.

You can do a similar thing. What creative data can you put in your organization's index? How about:

- Number of solar panels used when outfitting your new green building

- Ages of the youngest and oldest patients at your community health clinic

- Number of additional volunteers at your organization, as compared to last year

- Number of hours they put in

- Amount of money your clients (and the larger community) saved

- Number of thank-you notes you received

- Client satisfaction rating you received in your most recent evaluation

- Number of other organizations or communities that consulted you last year for advice or guidance

- Total percentage of your organization's budget that comes from generous individual supporters

- Average number of organic apples that students in your environmental education class picked on a recent field trip

- Number of out-of-state hits your website received last month

- Number of additional people you can reach this year through new organizational partnerships

- Number of students and young people who spoke at your annual conference this year

- The year a recycling program began at your organization; percentage increase in recycled matter between then and now

- Percentage decrease in net carbon emissions from your new fleet of electric delivery vans

EVALUATE THE QUALITY OF THE DIFFERENCE YOU ARE MAKING— NOT JUST THE QUANTITY

Beyond bean-counting (quantitative measurement) is the rich and varied world of quality assessment. No doubt you would like to find out how much people value your organization. You want to hear their voices and their experiences, right? You could even learn a thing or two about how to make your work more effective and helpful in the future. You might also find out about related services or products that may be of interest to your readers; this information may suggest potential organizations you can partner with.

In Chapter B, "Engage your specific readers," I suggested several ways to use market research methods to learn more about your readers' opinions. Examples include surveys, focus groups, and one-on-one interviews. But what questions should you ask?

Ask yourself: *What are some ways to tell that your work is benefiting your community? What milestones or benchmarks can you use?*

Some common indicators include:

- A growing interest in or rate of use of your product or service
- A higher average score in a post-test than in a pre-test
- Stated or observed relevant behavior changes (over time)
- Interest in recommending the product or service to others

You might also ask folks to rate, rank, or compare the benefits or outcomes of your services. This technique is especially prevalent online. Provide a scale for your readers to use: one to ten, useless to very helpful, terrible to great, irrelevant to extremely important, one star to five stars, etc.

You may want to ask them to what extent they perceive your service or product to be important, valuable, cost-effective, inspirational, practical, beneficial, timely, efficient, professional, or environmentally and socially responsible.

EXAMPLE

Several years ago, I worked with Legal Services for Entrepreneurs (LSE), a project of the Lawyers' Committee for Civil Rights of the San Francisco Bay Area. LSE matches new entrepreneurs with pro bono business attorneys. The project did a major study of its effectiveness in 2003, and was then able to use the data in grant proposals, brochures, reports, newsletters, etc. We used quotes from study respondents to further illustrate our findings (a technique I discuss in Chapter 5, "Share stories").

Bonus Tip

People often will want to participate in a survey if they know that the results will be reported back to them, and ultimately will be used to help them and their communities.

But in this hyper-busy world, they may need an extra push to spend a few moments evaluating your work. It is a wise idea to offer an incentive for turning in a completed survey, answering a few questions on the phone, or attending a focus group session. A group meal, entry into a prize drawing, a small gift, or a link from your website to theirs might do the trick. If you can afford a small cash token of your appreciation, so much the better.

> ✍ 87% of respondents reported that they could not have gone else-where to receive legal help for their businesses.
>
> "LSE gives people an opportunity to compete when they would otherwise be unable to do so."
>
> "Legal issues [are] a barrier to entry into the market. Having a way in, the resources, is invaluable."
>
> ✍ Approximately 75% of client respondents said they felt more confident in running their businesses because of receiving LSE services.
>
> "[LSE] brought [my business] to a professional, real level, and made my company real to clients, so they would have the confidence to do business with me. In turn, I had more confidence."
>
> "[LSE assistance] made me feel more official, like I really was in business. It made me feel important and that my business was important, and that people cared about it and wanted to help me make it successful." *(www.lccr.com)*

If at all possible, evaluate your impacts over time. Right after attending an event, receiving a service, or buying a product, a person's initial response may not be entirely accurate. People often need time to process new information and integrate it into their personal or professional lives. That is, a product or service may continue to increase in value to users months or years down the line. On the other hand, looks can be deceiving; implementation problems may not emerge for a while.

TAKE CONTROL OF YOUR USE OF RAW NUMBERS

They say that numbers don't lie—but don't be so sure. How you report, manipulate, and interpret numbers matters a great deal. The emphasis you place on some numbers rather than others—or how you slice and dice them—can translate into vastly different reader understandings. Do not let yourself get carried away and cross the line between accurate and questionable presentation. Double-check that your comparisons do not misrepresent your data.

If you are not careful, numbers can confuse, mislead, or overwhelm your readers, most of whom would not claim to be statisticians, mathematicians, or engineers. Although we generally like the concreteness of numbers, many people have math anxiety and shrink from too many calculations or statistical manipulations. Mathematician John Allen Paulos' best-selling 1988 book *Innumeracy* tells of how many Americans are not confident, competent, or comfortable dealing with any math beyond balancing a checkbook. Few of us even have to do that these days.

So, a good rule of thumb is to limit your raw numbers to only one or two per sentence. Instead of listing an array of numerals, you can use simple comparative phrases such as "were cut in half," "tripled in the last decade," or "only a tiny fraction remained."

EXPRESS NUMERICAL DATA IN CONTEXT

If you provide context and a sense of perspective, your readers are likely to understand what your numbers represent. They are also likely to want to know more of what you have to say, rather than zone out. And knowledgeable readers are confident readers, standing ready to engage on the tough issues.

EXAMPLES

1. Evo.com, an online marketplace, screens and rates consumer products for their green attributes. The company uses a one- to five-leaf scale of environmental soundness.

   Evo's software and human editors take into account a host of criteria, such as where each product is made, materials used, transportation involved, production process, and other environmental impacts. Lots of complexity there! All that data becomes a simple number of green leaves that the website then relates to readers to help them comparison shop within a common framework. The company plans to develop a user community to help rate products and flag "greenwashing" violations, where a product is not quite as green as it seems.   *(www.evo.com)*

2. *Timberland, a manufacturer of outdoor footwear, has developed its own way to measure the environmental impact of its products: their "Green Index." This rating system summarizes details about the product's climate impact, chemicals used, and resource consumption. The three individual scores are added together and divided by three, to produce a final rating between zero and ten. The company describes its efforts this way:*

   Timberland considers the Green Index a starting point on the path to increased sustainability and transparency. Our hope is that other like-minded companies will join us in developing an industry-wide index for comparing the environmental impacts of our design choices. We also hope to inspire consumers to ask questions, and make informed decisions about their purchases.   *(www.timberland.com)*

The Advocacy Institute and Berkeley Media Studies Group use the term "social math" to describe an especially effective technique. Here, you express numbers in terms of a social context familiar to your readers. That is, you make comparisons to easily understood items or ideas by using vivid word pictures.

EXAMPLES

1. *The Frameworks Institute evaluated all the statistical results from the U.S. Department of Education's 2005 study, "Calories In, Calories Out: Food and Exercise in Public Elementary Schools," and crafted this message:*

   Exercise is something that children need every day. But half of all students attend schools that have reduced their phys ed class to just one or two days per week. Part-time fitness is no more effective than part-time reading or math instruction.   *(www.frameworksinstitute.org)*

2. *In the early 2000s, Dr. Jo Marie Griesgraber of Oxfam America made an oft-quoted comment that provoked quite a bit of discussion about the global proliferation of small arms:*

   Two years ago in Nigeria, an AK-47 could be had in exchange for two cows. Now the price is down to one cow. And in the Sudan, you can get an AK-47 for a chicken.   *(www.oxfamamerica.org)*

You can also use social math to turn huge or unfathomable numbers into smaller, tangible units. For instance, the Nature Conservancy wrote that: "Every second of every day, a slice of rainforest the size of a football field is mowed down. That's 86,400 football fields of rainforest per day, or over 31 million football fields of rainforest lost each year."

And no doubt you are familiar with the convention of describing a large number of something by asking your reader to imagine the objects all laid end-to-end to circle the globe or extend to the moon a certain number of times.

Finally, another common strategy is to contrast current spending on something your organization opposes or does not value (e.g., advertising cigarettes to young people) with what that same amount of money could buy if it were spent on things that your organization endorses (e.g., health education). Or, compare the cost of addressing your organization's issue with the cost of ignoring it.

EXAMPLE ∼∼∼∼∼∼∼∼∼∼∼∼∼∼∼∼∼∼∼∼∼∼∼∼∼∼∼∼∼∼∼∼∼∼∼∼∼∼∼

The organization Business Leaders for Sensible Priorities shows how the federal budget breaks down, and argues that a whopping $60 billion per year could be redirected from funding the Pentagon to funding other programs—without harming U.S. national security. The bipartisan organization suggests how that same money could otherwise be spent. They say that we could do all of the following things:

⊚ Provide health insurance to nine million American children

⊚ Rebuild or modernize all our public schools over twelve years

⊚ Retrain a quarter of a million workers

⊚ Cut our reliance on foreign oil in half over ten years

⊚ Restore recent cuts in lifesaving medical research

⊚ Invest wisely in Homeland Security by inspecting cargo containers entering our ports

⊚ Save six million children who die of hunger-related diseases in impoverished countries annually

⊚ Begin to reduce the national budget deficit

(www.sensiblepriorities.org)

A few other highly effective ways of expressing numbers in context include:

1. Using graphics: Show numeric comparisons and relationships with pie charts, line charts, and even simple cartoons. Help your readers process raw numbers by offering visual cues. (To learn more, turn to Chapter 20, "Make sure it *looks* right.")

2. Using historical sequencing: Arrange trends or events at your organization on a historical timeline and relate what was happening in the wider world during those same years.

3. Citing outside verification: If any recent independent studies measure or compare the benefits of organizations similar to or including yours, feature them. Back up your own findings with published numeric results and quotes from external experts.

Note that the Frameworks Institute also showed how this method can backfire if you choose the wrong things to compare. They tested the following sentence in focus groups:

"Most people in Africa support their entire families on the equivalent of what Americans spend on pet food."

They found that the audience heard:

"You want me to choose between my pets, whom I love and care for, and people in other countries."

This social math comparison inadvertently attacked people's nurturing values and forced them to make a false choice. So, the researchers concluded,

"Paying attention to the values inherent in your social math equation is an important consideration in determining its effectiveness."

WRITING WORKOUT

Here you will collect some new numerical data and begin to use it in your copy.

STEP 1: Check your database and ask around the office for the data your organization currently monitors. Review old annual reports. Make a list of what you find. Also note interesting numbers that you would like to track further.

STEP 2: Now dig a little deeper for other numbers. You have had a direct impact on a certain number of people (or animals)—in both the short and long term. What about the indirect impacts (ripple effects) you have had on others? Jot down at least two new ways you can find out about those impacts, in terms of both quantity and quality.

STEP 3: Make a plan to integrate these thoughts in the next evaluation document you write. This might be anything from a brief feature in your next newsletter or on your website, to a formal research study that takes several months.

STEP 4: Consider some accessible ways you could express the data you collect, using at least one of the techniques you read about in this chapter. For instance, how might you fill in these blanks (feel free to modify the sentences to fit your organization)?

A. In the time it takes to _____ (something your readers are familiar with and/or is related to strong values they hold), _____ (problem related to your issue) is also happening.

B. Every day in the United States, a total of _____ (event related to your issue) occur.

C. _____ (your product or service) is one of the best investments you can make. Every $1 you invest translates into a savings of $_____ per year because _____.

D. Studies have shown that people who use _____ (products or services that your organization provides) see results in terms of _____% more _____ (benefits you offer) over _____ (weeks, months, or years).

⌐Section-at-a-Glance: Stressing Your Effectiveness⌐

CHAPTER 1: SPOTLIGHT YOUR MISSION REPEATEDLY

Have you advanced your organization's mission today? Your readers are eager to know about it!

Every marketing or fundraising piece you write needs to speak to the advancement of your organization's reason for existing in the first place. That is, each page should remind your readers that you never forget what you set out to do in your community.

- Highlight the outstanding strengths of your mission.

- Describe how your work embodies your guiding principles.

- Evoke a vision of what your community will be like once your organization has fulfilled its mission.

- Connect the dots for your readers over time.

- Use your mission and vision as overarching themes.

CHAPTER 2: MAXIMIZE YOUR COLLABORATIONS

Given the astronomical proliferation of values-driven organizations in the last few decades, many of our readers are wondering: "How come you all don't just combine forces?" Good question.

No one — investors, customers, clients, etc. — likes to see duplication of effort among barely distinguishable parties. It certainly makes marketing and branding a tougher job as well!

If you can show that you are not only aware of your potential collaborators, but are also working with them to make an even bigger difference than you could make alone, you will be ahead of the game. Your readers will respond.

- Describe your organization's unique role in collaborative efforts.

- Exchange online content with your partners and affiliates.

- Construct joint documents.

- Address concerns about collaborating too much.

Section-at-a-Glance: Stressing Your Effectiveness

CHAPTER 3: REFLECT YOUR TRUE NUMBERS

We in the U.S. love our numbers! If you can tell us how much, how fast, how tall, how far, how old, how big, or how small, we are happy campers. We like to measure and count things. We are drawn to definition, lines, and edges. For centuries we have cherished an appreciation for the elegance of proportions and the predicting power of statistics.

Your readers relate to numbers because numbers reflect visible, tangible outcomes in their communities. People have come to expect to hear about your organization's results in this way.

- Document your ripple effects.

- Home in on the colorful details of your organization.

- Evaluate the quality of the difference you are making — not just the quantity.

- Take control of your use of raw numbers.

- Express numerical data in context.

⁓Section⁓ *1b* *Focusing on Your Community*

These chapters discuss the essential skill of focusing your attention on your community. In this section, you will learn how to:

- ✺ Connect with your readers' humanity

- ✺ Improve your storytelling skills

- ✺ Write for an increasingly diverse readership

Note: If you have not already tried the Writing Workout in Chapter B, "Engage your specific readers," do so now. It will be especially helpful to you in this section.

⁓Connect on a person-to-person level⁓ 4

You and I — and others in values-driven organizations — share the bottom-line goal of making the world a better place. Even if your focus is animals, or natural resources, or art, or media, or food, or technology, or any number of other subjects, at the root of it all is *people* and how we treat each other and our environment.

After all, humans are social animals. We live and breathe in community and will wither away without it.

As a writer, you need to take this knowledge to heart. People want to read about people. They also give to other people in many ways (money, time, contacts, and other resources). For your readers to want to listen to you, or for them to be moved by your piece, they need to relate to you — and those you are writing about — as people. They have to know, like, and trust you.

That is, your readers want to see how you, your organization, and your clients share their human-centered values.

Your job is to invite your readers to see how your material relates to their own experiences. The more your readers personally identify with your presentation, the more they will feel connected to your words and ideas. They will feel understood and plugged-in.

Personally speaking

I chose to write this book in a conversational style because I wanted to cultivate a personal connection with you, my reader, on a topic that you may normally consider a bit…shall we say…dry. I wanted to engage your interest, inspire and support your writing process, and invite you to join me on a journey of community outreach through self-expression. I use many idioms, anecdotes, popular culture references, analogies, and other devices to make myself good company along the way.

That person-to-person connection, that rapport, is what you are striving to create — as consistently as possible. To do that, you need to be a good conversationalist on paper. Use as intimate and dynamic a voice as you can get away with, given whatever parameters you have to work within. And always keep in mind your reader's expectations!

This chapter offers you some ways to establish and maintain connection.

MEET YOUR READERS WHEREVER THEY ARE

If you have read Part I, especially Chapter B, "Engage your specific readers," you probably already have a good sense of your readers and their contexts. And since they are reading your documents, they have already demonstrated some interest related to your work or your issues.

Your readers have taken the first step by being open to hearing from you. It is now your turn to reach out to greet them. By making it easy to engage with you, you make it more likely that they will come closer, stay a while, come back again, and want to be involved with you over the long term.

Like the family doctor of yesteryear who made house calls, go to where the customers are. Only use your words and not a stethoscope.

Ask yourself: *How can you use your knowledge about your readers to improve your pieces?*

The short answer: Tie your work to their specific needs, interests, and concerns.

FOCUS ON ONE READER AT A TIME

The good news is that your document will, most likely, be read by one person at a time. In a sense, you and your reader will create a private world together. That means that you can write toward only that one person.

So, try to visualize a typical reader (or maybe two or three). You might even want to post a picture of that person in your writing space to serve as a constant reminder of whom you are talking to. You want to make sure that what you have to say is going to be understood. While each reader will interpret your words differently, you can do your best to make it easy for her or him to integrate what you are saying.

A simple way to start adopting the mindset and voice of a copywriter is to think and write in terms of "you" (the reader) more than "we" (the organization you are representing). Remember that your job is to make your piece beneficial to your readers, even as they are reading it. You are not writing it to hear yourself talk.

Most organizations have an "About Us" section on their websites, in their brochures, etc. But why not add a bit that is about your *readers*?

EXAMPLES

1. *With an environmental educator in mind, you may write something like:*
   As a middle-school science teacher, you are always looking for fresh, up-to-date material on today's pressing issues. With diminishing resources in our public schools, you may find it increasingly difficult to keep up with the times. On the Ecokids website, you will discover a wealth of high-quality classroom resources updated every semester to reflect changing frontiers in the environmental sciences. Get teaching materials that will inspire your students with dozens of lively class discussion starters, coupled with engaging and educational indoor, outdoor, online, and offline activities.

2. *With a vacationer in mind, you could write:*
   When you go on vacation you want to be free of concerns and worries. You want to enjoy yourself in whatever way feels best. But let's face it: There simply is no escape from this interdependent and globalized world. Your actions—wherever and whenever they may occur—do indeed affect other people and the planet.
   Now our socially responsible eco-tourism company makes it easy to let your concerns take a hike while your feet do too! We worry about the ecological footprint you're making so you don't have to.

3. *1% for the Planet has socially responsible businesspeople in mind as it presents this piece in its website's "About Us" section:*
   To be perfectly honest, it's not about us. It's about businesses recognizing that industry and ecology are inherently connected. It's about realizing the positive effects of connecting businesses, consumers and nonprofits through philanthropy. And it's about understanding that the true cost of doing business can be mitigated by a simple pledge to the planet.
   Since 2002, 1% For The Planet has inspired members of the business community to contribute 1% of sales to environmental groups around the world. In return, this growing alliance of companies is given the opportunity not only to see their self-worth rise, but their net worth climb as well. *(www.onepercentfortheplanet.org)*

RELATE TO YOUR READERS' EMOTIONS

I cannot emphasize enough that your reader will remember how you make her or him *feel* — the emotions you elicit — more than anything else you say or do.

Let's try a little thought experiment.

Think back to the last time you read the materials of another community-benefit organization. It might have been a website, a brochure, a newsletter, a fundraising letter, a thank-you note, an opinion piece, whatever.

Ask yourself: *What were you feeling?*

On an emotional level, you probably wanted or needed the writer to conjure up some of these:

◈ Appreciation	◈ Empowerment	◈ Joy
◈ Belonging	◈ Encouragement	◈ Love
◈ Compassion	◈ Excitement	◈ Safety
◈ Dignity	◈ Inspiration	◈ Well-being

If you felt some of that good stuff, you probably stuck around to continue reading. It made you feel hopeful about yourself, your community, and your world (i.e., it offered you emotional benefits). Those positive strokes fed your soul and gave you the motivation to read on, maybe even act on what you read. Without those positive strokes, there would not have been much to spur you on.

Now, as a writer, remember that your readers are seeking these very same things. Your task is to reflect your personal understanding and experiences of these common human feelings, and then relate them to your organization.

> *Find a subject you care about and which you in your heart feel others should care about. It is this genuine caring, not your games with language, which will be the most compelling and seductive element in your style.*
> — Kurt Vonnegut

> **EXAMPLE**
>
> You want your young children to be safe and healthy. You drench their bare skin with sunscreen and they never leave home without warm clothes on. You always use seat belts. You avoid lead paint.
>
> But have you ever thought about the pesticides that contaminate the school playground your children use every day? Parents for Playgrounds has! Let us tell you about what we have found in our community...

BUT BALANCE OUT EMOTIONS WITH AN INTELLECTUAL TOUCH

You are not only trying to appeal to your readers' hearts. You are also interested in reaching their minds.

We all know people who like to wrap their heads around hard facts. They are reading your piece to learn more about your issues, including the historical context and current trends, political controversies, how your work fits into today's world, and other verifiable information. They may want to know about the academic or philosophical theories behind your perspectives.

Even those people, however, need an emotional component to their understanding.

It is up to you — the writer — to strike a balance by providing a blend of facts and feelings. Most of the press strive to do this by including a variety of news, features, human-interest stories, editorials, personal columns, and analysis. Some media outlets, such as *The Daily Show*, serve up a healthy dose of entertainment along with up-to-date information. Each person can then choose the mix that feels right.

ASK QUESTIONS

Have you every noticed how much public-interest writing these days appears in the form of a question? That is because asking written questions is our equivalent of the dialogue that can be so irresistible in great fiction or in person.

As psychologists know, human beings are hard-wired to solve problems and will automatically try to answer whatever questions are asked of us. We will either answer silently to ourselves or listen or read on to see if the answer is provided for us — or both.

Questions to your readers simulate person-to-person interaction.

"TURNS OUT THE PHILANTHROPY GENE IS IN BETWEEN THE RISK-TAKING AND THE HAPPINESS GENES."

LITZLER

EXAMPLES

1. *Original:* The recent squabble over whether the Transportation Authority can afford a people-mover to the airport is only the latest in the local transit debate.

   Suggested revision: Can the Transportation Authority afford a people-mover to the airport? That question is only the latest in the local transit debate.

2. *Original:* Our organization, Climate Crisis, is collecting the community's comments on climate change, and will soon share the feedback with our legislators. If you would like to have your voice heard, please fill out this form.

   Suggested revision: Want to have your say about climate change? Climate Crisis and your legislators are all ears! Just fill out this form.

> " *Writing, when properly managed, is but a different name for conversation.* "
> — British writer
>   Laurence Sterne

This is the idea behind the ubiquitous Frequently Asked Questions (FAQ) documents on the web and elsewhere. In fact, writers have been asking and answering questions for eons. Question-and-Answer interviews and advice columns are examples. Why has this technique stuck around so long? Because it works.

Ask yourself: *What questions keep coming up in phone conversations, in face-to-face meetings, at events, and at other times you interact with clients, members, volunteers, and other stakeholders?*

Also consider what questions you *wish* your stakeholders would ask. If you stay away from the simple yes or no answer, you will elicit more thinking. Try to ask questions that begin with words such as: how, why, how much, which, where, when, what, and who (avoid do, can, will, and should).

Your questions should sound realistic — as if someone could or did actually ask them at that moment. You might want to keep a file of these questions as they pop up, and ask others in your organization to do the same.

> **EXAMPLES**
>
> - "How can young people be part of your planning process?"
> - "When was the last time you needed a helping hand?"
> - "Which candidate would you choose?"
> - "What do you mean by that?"
> - "Hey — who's in charge here?"
> - "What can one person do?"
> - "How does this work?"
> - "Where do we go from here?"
> - "Why is this so important?"
> - "What if you still are not clear?"

After asking a question or two, you are not obligated to answer right away. It is fine (at times, a good idea) to continue the suspense, encouraging your reader to stay with you. You can use phrases such as "Before I tell you the answer..." to fill in some background information. But always make sure to deliver on your promises before you wrap it up.

By the way, questions often make great headlines (see Chapter 9, "Start with a punchy opening") and can also contribute to the flow of your document (see Chapter 14, "Keep your piece flowing smoothly").

While I recommend including questions and answers to enhance your piece's conversational tone, pay attention to how you use this technique. Ask questions and provide answers in a simple and straightforward manner. That is, avoid questions or answers that lump together more than one concept at a time. Phrasing questions in the negative can also lead to confusion. For instance, take a look at these questions and their answers:

1. Let's say you asked your readers this question:

   "*If you knew a product on your bathroom shelf may cause cancer or damage your reproductive system, you probably wouldn't use it, right?*"

   You assume that your reader will answer that question with a resounding "NO." Your follow-up might then be:

   "*Of course not! But that, unfortunately, is exactly what millions of Americans do every day.*"

   But wait a minute: that answer is quite confusing! While you mean that millions of Americans are using harmful personal care products without knowing about their potential danger, you are actually saying that they are using harmful products even though they know about the risks they are taking. Re-read it and you will see what I mean.

   Instead, separate the two concepts in the answer to arrive at some clarity:

   "*Of course not! And neither would millions of other Americans. But, unfortunately, they aren't aware of the potential dangers lurking in their bathroom cabinets.*"

2. In the 1985 film *Clue*, Colonel Mustard asks the butler:

   "*Am I right in thinking there is nobody else in this house?*"

   That question starts an avalanche of confusing back-and-forth questions and answers. Notice how he asks about two things at once: the correctness of his thinking and if there is nobody else in the house. On top of that, he does not ask if *anybody* is in the house, but he chooses the negative pronoun instead.

   He eventually gets around to the simplified version of his question:

   "*Is there anybody else in the house?!*"

   And he gets a straight answer: "No!"

RELAY YOUR PERSONAL EXPERIENCES

Because you and I work in community-benefit organizations, we have a special opportunity — if you like, an obligation — to express great enthusiasm for our work. Yes, we need to be able to rattle off statistics, citations, and relevant facts and figures about why our efforts are important. But we also can infuse our writing with personal passion for the great work we do.

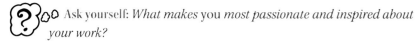 Ask yourself: *What makes you most passionate and inspired about your work?*

Have you ever stood in awe of the tremendous things your organization can and does accomplish — and the fact that you are a part of it? Have you ever found yourself aglow as you share a profound moment with a successful client whose heartfelt smile is contagious? What about those times when you finally win a battle that you and your colleagues have been fighting for years or decades? Sometimes a personal reason for being involved in your organization is what keeps you going.

Let that excitement, exhilaration, energy, and commitment shine through. It is one of the special gifts you can share with your readers. They will tune in to the feelings in your voice and be drawn to listen.

In fact, all your personal experiences can provide fuel to feed your writing fire. And your readers are likely to share some of those experiences — or at least relate to them on a personal level. Highlight that common ground, and you will be on your way to establishing a genuine relationship.

> **EXAMPLE**
>
> *Eva Paterson, Founder and Executive Director of the Equal Justice Society, loves jazz. She pens a blog entitled "Eva Paterson Riffs on Civil Rights." In an entry in support of the legalization of same-sex marriages, she wrote of her personal experience:*
>
> "This epic battle has personal relevance for me. In 1970, I fell in love with Gary Paterson, who is white, at the height of the Black Power movement. Our love antagonized both black and white people … When we decided to marry, Gary's parents were so appalled that first we eloped to Hawaii and then settled in Oakland. Gary did not speak to his parents for almost seven years. We had epithets yelled at us in public. What gay men and lesbians are experiencing now as they seek to marry feels very familiar to me.   *(www.evapaterson.com)*

Even if you have not personally experienced a particular event or circumstance that you know your readers have, you can still use this technique. How? Simply become the ghostwriter or editor for someone else in your organization (staff, volunteer, client, investor, customer) with a story to tell.

TALK ABOUT YOUR SHARED SOCIAL CONTEXT

You and your readers no doubt share some of the same social context. Identify these components and underline that similarity. "We're all in this together," as the saying goes.

For instance, your context could include a shared locality or event, a culture or history in common, or a socio-economic hardship you all are living through. You can also empathize with the realities of your readers' everyday lives. Examples might be the chronic rushed feeling of never having enough time to get everything done, or frustration with traffic jams, or disappointment with politicians or other high-profile figures.

EXAMPLES

1. *Let's say your organization promotes dental checkups as part of essential healthcare. But everyone hates going to the dentist. You might want to take a hint from Bill Cosby, who found a way to talk about this common experience in his routine,* The Dentist:

   Dentists tell you not to pick your teeth with any sharp metal object. And then you sit in their chair and the first thing they grab is an iron hook! Now the dentist pulls out a needle. This is to deaden the pain. So you open up…"

2. *I began a newspaper opinion piece about my complex ethnic heritage by recalling an experience whose outlines are common to most adults who went to school in the U.S. (that is, my likely readers):*

   It was an early autumn morning when my seventh-grade homeroom teacher passed out the forms. "Race/Ethnicity — check only one." I was confused.

   Maybe the choices were the four that the U.S. Census Bureau has traditionally used: White, Black, Asian/Pacific Islander, and American Indian/Alaskan Native. I'm sure that Hispanic was included in some way. But there was definitely *not* a place to check "other" or even "mixed."

   I still have trouble with such categories. So do many other people I know.

   My mother was born in the U.S. and is Jewish, and her parents were immigrants from Eastern Europe. So what would I consider to be her ethnicity?

   Then there's Dad. He's from Iran and has rather dark skin and hair. His complexion isn't black, but it isn't white either. And his home country is in Asia, last time I checked.

   "Just write down *white*, Dalya," my parents told me that night many years ago…

Because of the cultural and socio-economic diversity of your readers, finding experiences that resonate may seem difficult. You can find common denominators if you stick to images that appeal to the senses or to widely held core values and beliefs. (For more on these strategies, see Chapter 6, "Write with reader diversity in mind," and Chapter 10, "Show, don't just tell.")

Check out the *Dilbert* comic strip, *New Yorker* cartoons, any good stand-up comedy routine, *This American Life* on National Public Radio, or "Life in These United States" in *Reader's Digest* to see this technique in action.

ADMIT THAT YOU ARE HUMAN TOO — AND WE ALL MAKE MISTAKES

While you want to accentuate the positive aspects of your work, it is okay to occasionally share struggles or weaknesses too. By writing about both your successes and challenges, you can encourage your readers to see your organization as one made up of genuine, down-to-earth people like them.

The key here is to show how those lessons are always leading you to a better tomorrow.

For instance, perhaps your board or staff lacked a specific skillset or important understanding a year ago — but you are now working to get up to speed. Or maybe your office recently experienced a break-in and you lost the data you needed to efficiently communicate with your readers — but you have implemented an improved security system to prevent the problem in the future.

Admit your mistakes, share your lessons learned, and explain how you are moving forward. Your readers will recognize and appreciate your integrity.

EXAMPLES

Most people find true confessions utterly irresistible. How many times have you stopped to hear about the misdeeds of someone you admire, and what she or he learned from the experience?

Popular books along these lines include John Perkins' *Confessions of an Economic Hitman* and Richard Bitner's *Confessions of a Subprime Lender: An Insider's Tale of Greed, Fraud, and Ignorance.*

In an article I excerpt in Chapter 6, "Write with reader diversity in mind," I confess to my personal gaffe concerning racial stereotypes and snap judgements about others.

WRITING WORKOUT

Use this exercise to start thinking about the types of people you would like to connect to and how you will do so.

STEP 1:   Choose someone you know personally (an acquaintance or friend) who is not yet involved in your organization, but who is part of your intended audience. You may want to refer to your Reader Inventory from Chapter B, "Engage your specific readers," for some suggestions about whom you might focus on.

STEP 2:   Notice the particularly compelling characteristics of that person. Take your time — preferably over the course of a couple of days. Observe and keep notes. Do your best to pretend you are a fly on the wall. You are looking for evidence of the person's talents, unique style, personal history, sense of humor, doubts or unresolved internal conflicts, likes and dislikes, habits, eccentricities, communication style, facial expressions, preferred tone of voice, fashion sense (or lack thereof), etc. Look especially for indicators of her or his values, motivations, and emotions.

STEP 3:   Now picture that person in a relationship with your organization (as a client, donor, customer, volunteer, etc.). What challenging issues in your chosen character's personal or professional life could your organization be part of resolving? And how can you — as an individual — relate on a human level to him or her? Jot down your thoughts, implementing at least two of the techniques from this chapter.

STEP 4:   Repeat the above process as often as you can. The more practice the better, as your intended audience will grow and change over time.

Note: *This Writing Workout fits well with the one at the end of Chapter 5, "Share stories."*

" Once in East Africa, on the shores of an ancient lake, I sat alone and suddenly it struck me what community is. It is gathering around a fire and listening to someone tell us a story. "

— Bill Moyers

⁀Share stories⁀ 5

As children, we always loved it when someone said, "Let me tell you a story," or "Once upon a time." Even though we are now adults, that part of us has not disappeared. We are still more likely to remember anecdotes, examples, jokes, rhymes, and juicy tales than dry facts. Stories make the world go 'round! Use them.

In fact, in the previous chapter, "Connect on a person-to-person level," I featured quite a few stories. Stories form bonds from one person to the next. Without a mutual sense of story, we cannot truly understand each other.

By sharing stories with your readers, you will render your messages personalized, catchy, and relevant. Feature your various constituents: clients, customers, volunteers, members, donors, staff, board, and strategic partners. Slice-of-life word snapshots will help put a face and voice to your work in a way that goes far beyond mind-numbing statistics. Telling a brief account of someone's story can crystallize your message for your readers.

(Statistics, studies, or opinion polls can complement your stories with nitty-gritty facts and figures that illustrate the big picture. For more information about using numbers in that way, check out Chapter 3, "Reflect your true numbers.")

Keep in mind that your readers want to know how your organization addresses issues that concern them in *their own* communities. They may define those communities according to geography, demographics, occupation, educational background, attitude, political affiliation, life experiences, etc. Whatever the case, they are looking for improvements you are making in what they see all around them. It is your job to point out those changes as vividly as you can.

Ask yourself: *How can you show that are you playing an important role in your readers' communities?*

"With storytelling we enter the trance of the sacred. Telling stories reminds us of our humanity in this beautiful broken world."
— Terry Tempest Williams

Think about some stories that might illustrate your answers. Every day, values-based organizations improve people's lives. And every time that happens, a potential story is born.

Stories of people who have used your service or product should be core to your copy. Often called "case studies," these before-and-after stories illustrate how people similar to your intended readers have found the benefits or results they were seeking by working with you. Your readers may well want to work with you too.

BUILD ON THE FEATURES OF ANY GREAT STORY

Think back to English class, and recall the five basic components:

1. *Memorable characters:* These are people your readers can recognize and identify with. They are people whom your readers truly care about, and usually include heroes, antagonists, and/or an outside narrator.

2. *A clear sequence:* Here we are talking about three phases: (1) a well-defined beginning with something to hook the reader in; (2) a middle, with a dramatic plot and theme; and (3) an end or resolution that ideally involves your organization or reader, maybe even with a twist.

3. *Conflict, controversy, or conspiracy:* A problem logically or ethically troubles the main character(s), and thus troubles your reader.

4. *Interesting setting:* This includes a time and place that convey the atmosphere or social climate you want to depict.

5. *Point of view:* The perspective can be that of your main character, the narrator, or someone else who is telling his or her side of the story.

Our culture is full of classic storylines and themes that pop up over and over again. These easy-to-understand templates surround us every day. I am sure you recognize these examples:

Using a frame that emphasizes isolated individuals – and neglects their social context – can mislead by providing only partial information. Remember that many characters in your pieces live within societal systems that are often stacked against them. For example, they may be dealing with environmental racism or a lack of economic opportunity. You can encourage your readers to adopt a larger perspective of the issue at hand if you include information about the relevant socio-economic environment your characters find themselves in.

EXAMPLES

- Good vs. Evil, Us vs. Them, Good guys vs. Bad guys

- Underdog solves a big problem, finds justice, or wins a competition (David vs. Goliath, Little Engine that Could, Tortoise and the Hare)

- Neighbors help each other in time of need or tragedy (barn raising, the good Samaritan, the Golden Rule)

- Doing one's part as a good global citizen

◈ Rags to riches or from down-and-out to happy and productive

◈ Hero turns personal tragedy into community force

◈ Migration trek from old country to new country

◈ Triumph of hard work, education, determination (the American Dream, the self-made person, or "pull yourself up by your bootstraps")

◈ Success from seeing beyond stereotypes

◈ The 100th monkey that brings about critical mass

◈ Struggle for personal identity and meaning

◈ Consumerism vs. the simple life

◈ What goes around comes around

You can plug into these pre-existing stories with details from your organization. All you have to do is add a bit of background to some recent letters or comments you have received from enthusiastic folks in your community.

EXAMPLES

1. Jacob Levitt is a student with a mission — to prevent child labor, and to ensure fair labor practices for everyone, young and old. Jacob, now 13, first learned about child labor when he was in sixth grade and his class began a lesson on it. He was horrified to learn that children around the world were sold into slavery and forced to work long hours, and he also wanted to find out more about the issue in the hopes that maybe he would be able to do something about it.

   Like a lot of kids, Jacob loves sports, and so he decided to combine his love of sports with his growing interest and sense of injustice over child labor issues. Jacob has since become one of the youngest and most dynamic supporters of our Fair Trade Sports soccer balls. He organized a meeting with the Northampton Soccer Club, where he explained unfair labor practices and convinced the group to begin using our Fair Trade balls. He's now trying to encourage Northampton High School to team up with the Northampton Soccer Club on a bulk order. He's also hoping to get the city of Northampton Recreation Department to consider using Fair Trade Sports soccer balls in their leagues.
   (storyline: good global citizen)   *(www.FairTradeSports.com)*

2. When he finished his ten-year prison term for bank robbery, William Green was determined to turn his life around. At the JVS Technology Access Center, he explored career options, learned to write a resume and cover letter, and practiced how to answer difficult interview questions about his past. In his new job as a prep cook for a catering company, William has become a model employee! "JVS accepted me. They were warm and friendly and took the time to help," he said.
(storylines: triumph of hard work; from down-and-out to happy and productive)   *(www.jvs.org)*

Another simple and effective story pattern that helps your readers interpret facts and large issues is the Problem X causes Problem Y and Problem Y causes Problem Z type of story.

EXAMPLE

Eating meals full of trans-fat, cholesterol, and sugar will eventually lead to health problems such as diabetes, cardiovascular disease, and cancer. And those health problems often kill.

Bonus Tip

Staff meetings are great places to dig up stories. Conversations with coworkers around the water cooler, at lunch, or after work can also be goldmines for raw material. Always keep an eye and ear out for stories (or even jokes) that others in your organization are telling. Build a stockpile of little gems that you can then polish when the time comes. Better yet, ask your colleagues to include client or customer vignettes in any regular program reports they have to submit.

Or you can show how one benefit can lead to others.

EXAMPLE

Head Start benefits children from low-income families by preparing them to enter elementary school ready to succeed. Studies show that these children then repeat fewer grades, graduate from high school more often, earn higher wages, depend less on welfare, and are charged with fewer crimes than their counterparts who did not participate in the program.

(www.nhsa.org)

Remember: Your stories need not be long to convey your point. Just a few paragraphs, even a few lines, might do. However, if you have the space — perhaps across several editions of your newsletter, updates to your website, or other regular pieces you publish — there is no need to confine them to isolated incidents. You can tell stories in installments, focusing on a slowly unfolding adventure or ongoing trend you are following. You may even want to set up each installment to lead to the next stage of your organization's continuing thread or plotline, like episodes in a television series.

EXAMPLE

The International Male Contraception Coalition publishes an e-newsletter that follows the ongoing saga of research and development in the field. The publication marks milestones, examines setbacks, and tracks press coverage. A few of the headlines from 2008 explore continuing threads in its story:

- "FDA approves new home sperm count test" (important for monitoring male contraceptive effectiveness)

- "RISUG Update" (promising contraceptive they have been tracking)

- "New Gates Foundation strategy includes contraceptive development"

- "Start-up companies working on male contraceptives"

- "From folk remedy to contraceptive product formulation: papaya seed extract" (the beginning of a series of articles on male contraceptive ideas beyond the U.S. borders) *(www.imccoalition.org/newsletter.php)*

GIVE YOUR CAST OF CHARACTERS TOP BILLING

Your organization's issue is full of information: facts, figures, ideas, processes, and controversies. As a storyteller, you should have the opportunity to temper this often bewildering blizzard of data with personal perspectives of the people you write about. If you do that, your readers will be able to see the real-life context in which your issue is playing out, involving people whose lives are similar (or very different) from their own.

The last great novel you read or movie or television show you watched most likely centered around its characters. Your organization also centers around its "characters" (clients or customers).

Ask yourself: *How can you help your readers feel the urgency, exhilaration, relief, inspiration, surprise, humor, poignancy, suspense, or other aspects of your characters' experiences?*

Show how your characters' lives improve as they work with you. Perhaps they learn some new information or a skill that they then use to rise out of despair. Or they could uncover a new resource (internal or external) that becomes crucial to their lives. Maybe they adopt a new attitude or forge a new relationship that allows them to find what they have long been seeking. Or they find a more effective way to make their values or beliefs a prominent part of their lives.

Whatever major change occurs in your characters, tell your readers about how your organization played a part.

> "*Your reader will only be interested in the problem as long as he's interested in the character [or person] who has it.*"
> — Scott Meredith

Sometimes you will find it helpful to create a composite character to represent several people at once. That's entirely legitimate — as long as you clarify somewhere that you are using that technique and not trying to misrepresent the facts.

If you have to convey technical material, try relaying it through the story of an individual you know your readers will find compelling. For instance, show how students in your math education program apply formulas and equations in their everyday personal lives; how a complex disease affects a child's afternoon on the playground; or how a new law will directly impact the families who ask for your advice every day. Use a story to follow your characters through an important time in their lives, step by step.

EXAMPLE

This story from one of my clients centers on a great character, but it easily could have been a dull human resources piece. Notice how both the narrator and his subject make great characters.

When I was the Human Resources Director at a religious institution, the grande dame of the reception staff was named Joan, and she had been one of the organization's first employees back in 1962. She chain-smoked and had the voice to prove it.

She would routinely answer the phone with the name of the organization, followed by a blunt "What do you want?" One day she left me a message that read: "Someone with an Italian last name called, and there was a seven and a two in his phone number." Once, when a visiting official walked past her desk to meet with our director, she barked: "Where the hell do you think you are going?"

I thought to myself: I teach a course on performance problem solving. I know what I am doing. This should be easy!

I was wrong.

I sat down with Joan to have "the talk." I spoke with her about the importance of her role and explained that we needed her to project a sense of hospitality and service that would make people feel welcome and important to us.

Joan sat there quietly and listened. Finally I asked her, "So tell me, Joan. What are my concerns, as you understand them?" She thought for a minute and said, "You are concerned that I work here and you want to fire me."

That is not what I intended to convey…

How did this end? The organization soon hit a budgetary crisis, and Joan took a severance package.

In truth, I try to think of ways I could have managed her differently, and it still eludes me. I did learn a valuable lesson though. The message you send is not the same as the one received. Never take for granted the clarity of your own communication.   *(Source: Bill Coy, Nonprofit Consultant)*

Joan's story reminds us that community-oriented organizations themselves often include compelling characters. Remember to look within for great stories. For instance, you might write about how your small but amazing staff and dedicated volunteers have overcome hardships of their own and are driven to make an impact well beyond the expected. You can also tell the story of how an investor initially got interested in your organization and has supported it ever since. On a significant anniversary of your organization, you might want to write about the trials and tribulations your founders went through.

USE PLENTY OF INTERESTING QUOTES

Break out your tape recorder (imaginary or real) and listen to the voices of your characters. They want to be heard and taken seriously, and your readers want to hear what they have to say. Using people's actual words will infuse your piece with a real-world genuineness. We all like to listen in on other people's conversations, and using plenty of quotes can approximate that. Quotation marks are also pretty darned eye-catching!

Using quotes will add texture to your writing by introducing a variety of personal styles, tones, rhythms, etc. That variety will help keep your readers interested and engaged. You want to have more than one sound dominate your virtual airwaves, so your readers stay tuned in. (Chapter 15, "Make sure it *sounds* right," goes into further depth on this.)

Include both short and long quotes that illustrate how people felt or what they experienced before, while, and after working with you. Most of the quotes you gather should somehow endorse your organization's work (these are usually called "testimonials"). Be sure to ask your interviewees: "How did you benefit from the experience? And what do those benefits mean to you?"

EXAMPLES

These two examples include quotes from both the organizations' direct clients and other beneficiaries of their work.

1. Adriana Razo came to ALAS, a program of Women's Initiative for Self-Employment, with years of distinguished child development experience, both as a teacher and a program director. "For many years, owning a business of my own did not seem possible to me," she said. After conducting market research and developing a solid business plan with ALAS, she knew it *was* possible.

   Adriana now runs a high-quality bilingual program that focuses on arts and academics for children ages two to five. "I offer a bilingual program that provides children of diverse backgrounds a cultural connection, she explained. "It's an opportunity to appreciate cultural and social differences amongst each other in a safe and caring classroom environment."

Sandra, a mother of one of Adriana's students, expressed her gratitude: "I am so happy about the cultural exposure, bilingual education, and love that David gets here. I can sleep well and focus at work. My son is in good hands."   *(www.womensinitiative.org)*

2. *Ashbury Images is a nonprofit business that offers custom-printed specialty items, while providing jobs, training, and support services for young adults recovering from substance abuse and homelessness. In their brochure's "rebuilding lives" section, they feature quotes from several of their employees, including this one:*

"I have a long history of substance abuse in my family, and at 18 I became addicted to heroin. I moved around a lot as a kid…and never really understood the power of community until I came to Ashbury Images. For the first time in my life I feel like I belong and that I am wanted and appreciated. I know this sounds a little goofy, but I can finally see the light at the end of the tunnel and feel like everything is going to be okay." — Karen

The brochure goes on to feature quotes from satisfied customers, such as this one:

"I have utilized Ashbury Images since 1993 and I absolutely love them! I tell all of my friends and colleagues about Ashbury Images because not only are they a company with a great mission, but their work is excellent. Their product knowledge, honesty, customer service, product quality, and ability to meet deadlines are unparalleled." — Alison Richardson, Director of Student Activities, University of San Francisco

(www.ashburyimages.org)

A quote is most powerful when you mention the name, title, and/or brief description of the person who said it. If you can, provide the person's photo along with the quote.

So where do you come across powerful testimonials? Of course you will want to conduct personal interviews with your characters. But remember that people often feel more comfortable saying what they honestly think in anonymous settings, so written evaluations can yield great quotes too. You may not be able to cite the speaker's detailed identity, but an outstanding testimonial is worth its relative anonymity. Overheard comments can work the same way.

In addition, in seeking testimonials you may want to offer sample quotes from others. Sometimes folks are willing or even eager to share their experiences, in their own words, but first want to hear what others have said.

Once you have finished listening, make sure to edit your quotes. At first, you may be tempted to just use everything. Instead, the quotes you choose should be tasty morsels of specific personal experience, opinion, or outstanding fact that leap out of the speaker's mouth, into your story, and off the page. Vague generalities (e.g., Mario said, "The museum was great!") do nothing for you. In general, only include quotes that add to your story, saying more than you could as an observant narrator.

Get to the point quickly and with pizzazz — especially if the person used any interesting or colorful language. You can rearrange quotes to flow more logically or to bring out important points sooner than the speaker did. Feel free to quote people using ellipses (…) when you want to fast-forward to the best sound bites. If you need to, clarify the statements by cleaning up the grammar.

EXAMPLES

1. *Original:* "Low-income teens from the industrial core of the tri-city area came to the Richmond Marsh to help restore its native plants, which had evolved to coexist with local wildlife. They spent all day and transplanted seedlings, pulled out bucketfuls of weeds, and picked up litter. It was a great opportunity for them to learn about the natural environment. A lot of these kids have never before been beyond the city streets," said Gary Pollock, the Natural Science curriculum director.

   Suggested revision: Low-income teens from the industrial core of the tri-city area helped restore the native plant habitat in the Richmond Marsh. They spent a full day transplanting seedlings, pulling out bucketfuls of weeds, and picking up litter. "A lot of these kids had never before been beyond the city streets," said Gary Pollock, the Natural Science curriculum director. "This was a great opportunity for them to learn about the natural environment."

2. *Original:* "Your non-violent communication and conflict resolution classes were so helpful to my students! Their behavior changed dramatically over the course of the year. You taught them to sit down and listen to each other. They used to settle disputes with fistfights and screaming matches. And tried to bring weapons with them to school. But with the new peaceful mediation skills they learned, they have begun to realize that violence helps no one," explained a seventh-grade math teacher at Carter Middle School.

Suggested revision: A seventh-grade math teacher at Carter Middle School explained what happened before her eyes:

"Your non-violent communication and conflict resolution classes…taught [my students] to sit down and listen to each other. They used to settle disputes with fistfights and screaming matches, and tried to bring weapons to school. But with the new mediation skills they learned, they have begun to realize that violence helps no one!"

Bonus Tip

If you receive some less-than-flattering comments, don't discount them. If they are constructive criticisms that you are working to address, they may come in handy when you are ready to tell your readers about improvements you have made.

When using quotes, you want to make sure to convey not just the words the person said, but also the intent, context, and feeling behind them. Be true to the speaker's key points and do not focus on tangents that go unexplored.

In addition, you don't want to quote someone saying something false or misleading. Try to stick to quotes based on people's firsthand experiences, and check up on any questionable facts.

Finally, don't detract from a solid quote with a cutesy verb. Old standbys such as "said," "explained," "added," and "asked" are fine. Another popular way to present quotes is in a straightforward question-and-answer interview format, where you can just label the quotes as questions or answers and omit the quotation marks.

CHOOSE YOUR SPEAKERS WISELY

Ask yourself: *Whose opinions matter the most to your readers?*

No one can keep up with all the news of interest. Instead, we rely on what respected people think and the recommendations and arguments they make. These opinion-leaders help us navigate through a maze of information and chatter. Their authority derives from experience, education, official status, celebrity, publications, or all of the above.

Bring their voices into your piece. They will help validate your claims, enhance your credibility, and build trust in your brand. Your judgment will demonstrate your familiarity with your field — and with how it relates to your reader's situation.

WORK AROUND ANY DIFFICULTIES YOU HAVE OBTAINING QUOTES

What if you cannot get an exact quote, or the ones you have don't sound so great? No problem. Just paraphrase the source and clarify that you are not directly quoting, but you are maintaining the spirit of the spoken words.

If you have time, try rephrasing the quote to more clearly portray what the person meant to say, and run it by him or her for approval. Most often, the speaker will appreciate your efforts to make the quote sound better. Once approved, you can use the doctored quote as if it were the original (i.e., with quotation marks and all).

Another way to get around a shortage of attractive quotes is to pull out a spectacular phrase or shocking statistic from your piece and make it a "pull-quote." That is, blow it up in size to provide a tantalizing tidbit to draw in your reader — even though it might not be an actual quote from anyone other than you, the writer. (For more info on other ways to make your pieces visually appealing to your readers, read Chapter 20, "Make sure it *looks* right.")

Personally speaking

My work producing programs with community radio stations has taught me to seek out good quotes and then maximize them in my pieces. My ears have become fine-tuned to the words my characters use. Another thing that works for me is listening to well-crafted radio documentaries, dramas, and audiobooks to learn their creative techniques. I have included some more information about this in Appendix 3, "Writing for Audio."

WRITING WORKOUT

In this exercise, you will practice crafting an imaginary case study with fictional quotes. Of course, if you have a real case study that you would like to punch up, please do so.

STEP 1: Jot down some notes about a typical problem in the life of an imaginary client that relates (directly or indirectly) to the work of your organization. Feel free to model that person after a real client or two. (If you wrote about a particular person in the Writing Workout in Chapter 4, you can use that character.)

Focus on the specifics of your character's situation, her/his concerns, and options. What choices does your hero or heroine make? And why?

STEP 2: Now imagine yourself and the character engaging in a dialogue about that experience — before, during, and after his or her contact with your organization. Write out (or record) a few paragraphs of your conversation, including the questions you ask of each other. If you are able to have a real conversation with a friend playing the role of the "character," that is better than imagining.

STEP 3: Choose some juicy quotes that truly stand out and help tell the client's story. If you really liked the question-and-answer conversation you had with your character, pick out the liveliest exchanges that illustrated the gist of the interview. You can slice, dice, or paraphrase them if you prefer. Just keep them true to what was actually said or intended.

STEP 4: Use your knowledge of your character's experience and the quotes you chose to construct a brief story to share with your readers. Make sure you include a clear beginning, middle, and end. Convey the atmosphere or social climate in which the action is taking place. Your story can be from the point of view of your character (using the first-person "I") or from an outside observer's perspective (using the third-person "she" or "he"). See if you can evoke at least one of the basic human emotions listed in Chapter 4, "Connect on a person-to-person level."

Write with reader diversity in mind 6

LITZLER

I am sure you have noticed that socially responsible organizations are diversifying. While there are more kinds of them than ever before, I focus here on how they are becoming more inclusive of all people across lines of race, class, ethnicity, culture, gender, age, ability, sexual orientation, education level, life experience, geography, etc. You can see this both in the people who make up your organization and in those you serve.

"OH, I'D HAVE TO SAY MY CLIMB TO THE TOP STARTED WHEN MY GRANDFATHER FORMED THE COMPANY."

I say: "Finally!" It has been a long time in coming.

This long-awaited broadening demands additional levels of respect, understanding, sensitivity, and cultural competency. I am talking about not only organizations that focus on diversity as core to their activities, but *all* values-based organizations.

Unfortunately, that next level of awareness does not just spontaneously appear. We all need to discover and challenge our biases as we try to write pieces that engage all of our constituents throughout our changing communities.

Often the different groups of people working with or for your organization — clients, staff, investors, board members, partners, and others — are different from each other, sometimes in a variety of ways. They might know little about each other, or have misunderstandings, or harbor resentments resulting from historical differences of power and privilege. Some entrenched systems of discrimination got started long ago, and we might not realize how much they still affect our current attitudes and behavior.

Even those of us with the best of intentions cannot escape the cultural waters we swim in. So if we want to use our writing to effectively market our organizations or ideas in a more diverse climate, we have to learn to navigate those waters in new ways.

Ask yourself: *Exactly whose perspectives and priorities are you promoting with the stories you tell?*

Those of your staff? Your funders? Clients? Board members? Potential clients? A particular sub-group or individual? Are you excluding any important voices?

Personally speaking

I generally avoid the phrase "politically correct," because I question its legitimacy in describing the evolution of the English language as it grapples with inclusion. U.S. culture is changing and so must our language, regardless of politics. Still, I recognize that some people would describe this chapter as "PC." To them I say, "To each her or his own."

Be prepared to spend extra time getting this right. While it is true that we often have extremely tight deadlines, that is no excuse for letting our prejudices or assumptions go unexamined or unchallenged.

Although this chapter certainly does not aim to be a comprehensive guide to cross-cultural communication or sensitivity, I can give you some pointers about what to watch out for in your writing. After all, language is at the root of any culture. As writers, we need to be aware of the power we hold in our pens and keyboards.

EMPHASIZE THE SIMILARITIES IN PEOPLE'S LIVES

Look beyond obvious or immediate differences. The fact is, we all share similar concerns for well-being, happiness, and dignity. Chief among them might be:

- Health
- Safety
- A sense of belonging
- Loving relationships
- Education and opportunity
- Self-esteem
- Spiritual connection
- Creativity
- Striving to be our personal best

Bonus Tip

If you are versed in psychological theory, you may notice that this list is remarkably similar to Abraham Maslow's hierarchy of needs. That is, these are key aspects of our lives as well-rounded human beings.

But — and this is important — while people may use the same words for these general goals and values, the terms themselves may hold different meanings in different contexts, communities, and cultures. And, of course, the ways to attain these goals can also vary.

EXAMPLES

1. "Loving relationships" could include all loving unions. But must those partnerships be comprised of two people of the opposite sex in a lifelong, exclusive commitment? Or might they also encompass other arrangements: same-sex unions, deep platonic friendships, short-term relationships, non-monogamous connections, etc.?

2. Let's look at "education." Does it imply a high school diploma or a PhD, practical street smarts or academic theory, factual knowledge or abstract thinking, formal instruction or informal training, spiritual or experiential learning, mental, emotional, or physical education?

3. "Health" could focus on your body, mind, and/or spirit. It could refer to either long-term or short-term well-being. And does having a disability make someone "unhealthy"?

Culturally appropriate writing requires that you dig beneath the surface to unearth common human themes that transcend superficial differences. To do this you must re-examine your word choices and ensure that they are as inclusive as possible.

WATCH YOUR ASSUMPTIONS AND PRECONCEIVED NOTIONS

Everyone has prejudices and biases, and many of these have become entrenched in the English language. The question is whether we proceed as if we were oblivious to them, or become aware of and actively critical of them.

EXAMPLES

Consider the assumptions inherent in these statements:

- Our organic cotton tights come in black, suntan, and flesh color.

- Mothers can leave their children at our beautiful daycare center during the workday.

- Everyone is welcome at the event—and bring the grandparents with you!

- Over 300 doctors attended the convention, along with their wives.

- Our founding fathers carved this great state out of the wilderness.

- Mrs. Imoto is remarkably spunky for her age!

- Confined to a wheelchair, Jorge still manages to live an active, productive life.

Creatively debunking stereotypes can address misconceptions or misunderstandings in a nonthreatening way. Make sure your sentences show your awareness that a wide range of people can occupy any role.

EXAMPLES

I have revised some of the sentences that appear above:

- Our organic cotton tights come in a variety of colors that look great with all skin tones.

- Parents can leave their children at our beautiful daycare center during the workday.

- This event has something for everyone, from ages two to 102.

- Over 300 doctors attended the convention, many joined by their families.

How might you revise (improve) the others?

Assumptions can also get us in trouble when we try to interpret the actions of people or cultures unfamiliar to us. The meaning of an activity might be completely different to an outside observer than to its participants. Anyone who has been surrounded by a new culture will tell you that.

The following pairs of words interpret the same scene or person, but they carry very different connotations:

- Demonstration vs. riot
- Made a scene vs. stood her ground
- Hysterical vs. adamant
- Enthusiastic vs. fanatic
- Rampaged vs. marched
- Assertive vs. abrasive
- Salvage vs. loot
- Zealot vs. patriot

Don't let your writing assume that everybody *should* think or behave according to the rules of the dominant or mainstream culture. Not everyone understands or uses words the same way you do. Even what may seem like innocuous words — such as "success," "action," "evidence," "logical," "good parenting," and "family" — may carry different meanings for different communities.

Therefore, it behooves us writers to put every story into its appropriate social or cultural context. For many marginalized groups, history is crucial to that context. But remember that official histories are written by the victors. You may need to look beyond a conventional explanation to a second opinion.

To be sure, we tend to be leery of the unknown. We often assuage those fears by making assumptions, pigeonholing people in our thoughts. I am suggesting, instead, that you honestly question your own level of personal discomfort. When we admit and examine our ignorance, we have the opportunity to approach the unfamiliar with genuine curiosity, sensitivity, and respect.

EXAMPLE

I share my own personal mishap and realization in this story, writing for a mainstream newspaper whose readers are mostly white:

As I rushed through the unfamiliar airport to find my departure gate, I saw out of the corner of my eye a well-dressed, dark-skinned middle-aged man pushing a cart full of luggage.

Without thinking, I automatically assumed he was a skycap and began asking for directions.

A few seconds later I turned my full attention to this man and realized he was an executive on a business trip. I sheepishly smiled. "Oh. I'm sorry. I thought that was someone else's luggage." I quickly turned away.

I wonder: Would I have made the same knee-jerk assumption if the man had been lighter skinned? Probably not.

I should have known better. Despite my conscious attempts to avoid stereotyping people of color, I need to always stay on my toes. It is just too easy to find that my racial prejudice is showing.

When I turned away from the "skycap" I was embarrassed. There I was, so concerned about diversity and cross-cultural understanding, yet catching myself in prejudiced thinking. It was not the first time, nor would I assume it to be the last.

I also wonder how he felt about the interaction. How often do things like this happen to him? I mistook him for a skycap, but what have others assumed about him? Has he endured racial profiling as a shoplifter, under-qualified job applicant, or worse? What other daily insults does he encounter? Assaults on his intelligence, professionalism, motivations, or dignity? I can only guess.

REVISIT YOUR CHOICES IN HOW YOU REFER TO SPECIFIC GROUPS

On a regular basis, check in with the words and phrases you use to describe people who are not members of your own culture — especially if you are a member of a dominant group. As a writer in your community, it is your job to ask questions, listen to the many answers, and adapt.

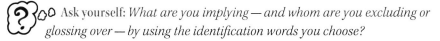 Ask yourself: *What are you implying — and whom are you excluding or glossing over — by using the identification words you choose?*

Some common cases are:

- Minorities vs. non-whites vs. people of color
- Native Americans vs. indigenous peoples vs. American Indians
- America vs. the United States
- The handicapped vs. the disabled vs. people with disabilities
- Latino vs. Latino/a vs. Hispanic
- Kids vs. young adults
- Homosexual vs. LGBT vs. queer
- The homeless vs. homeless individuals and families
- Victim vs. survivor
- Community vs. population
- Gypsies vs. Roma people

Make sure that if you replace the person or group in your sentences with yourself or your own group, it does not sound odd or offensive (e.g., "the _____ population living in our neighborhood really lowers the property value"). If it does, you can be sure that it is also going to sound that way to the people you are writing about, and to those attuned to their perspective.

You may find that you need to discuss your word choices with others in your organization. One client of mine had a lengthy discussion with her staff and board chair about what to call the people who use their services: clients? beneficiaries? consumers? They eventually had to take the matter to the full board.

In addition, the English language is chock full of words that are not quite gender-neutral (including personal pronouns, as discussed in Chapter 21, "Reach agreement on your subjects, verbs, and pronouns"). One common way to make nouns gender-free is to substitute the male or female suffix with "person" (e.g., spokesman becomes spokesperson). An alternative to that solution is to change the root noun into an appropriate, related verb and add the suffix "-er," "-or," or "-ist" — or eliminate the suffix altogether. Notice how changing a word's structure directly changes its connotation.

EXAMPLES

NOUN + GENDER-SPECIFIC SUFFIX	VERB + GENDER-NEUTRAL (OR NO) SUFFIX
Anchorman	*Anchor*
Cameraman	*Camera operator*
Chairman	*Chair*
Congressman	*Legislator*
Craftsman	*Artisan*
Deliveryman	*Delivery clerk*
Fireman	*Firefighter*
Housewife	*Stay-at-home parent*
Middleman	*Go-between or intermediary*
Policeman	*Police officer*
Salesman	*Sales associate or representative*
Statesman	*Diplomat*
Stewardess	*Flight attendant*
Weatherman	*Weather forecaster*
Workmen	*Workers, laborers*

LOOK OUT FOR EUPHEMISMS OR CODE WORDS

We often consciously or unconsciously try to cover up our biases or stereotyped worldviews by sugar-coating our words. We may hint at what we mean (maybe with a wink and a nudge), but don't come out and say it. Using these covert phrases is *not* the best way to cultivate a trust-based, transparent relationship with our readers!

EXAMPLES

What do these euphemisms really mean?

1. Our community thrives on good neighborhoods.

2. We sell the finest in ethnic products.

3. Don't you miss the good old days, when men were men and women were women?

4. The Siletz Indians were relocated to reservations.

Sentences like the one above about "relocation" often use the passive voice to avoid real discussion of oppression or discrimination. I examine the use of the passive voice to gloss over difficult topics in Chapter 11, "Focus on the verbs."

AVOID THE MELTING POT SYNDROME

Few people still talk about the U.S. as a "melting pot" where we all simply blend into one big (bland?) American soup. Today we prefer more of a tossed salad, with distinct ingredients that flavor each other, or at least a very chunky and savory stew.

Especially if race, ethnicity, class, subculture, or other differences among people are important to your organization, don't disregard them in your writing. Even though these topics can be hot-button issues, explain what is really going on and why. You will better serve the people you feature in your stories when you acknowledge their realities. In addition, you will reflect well upon your organization's integrity.

GET ADVICE BEFORE YOU GO PUBLIC

Of course, we writers need to be familiar with our communities. But we may have to write about cultural systems that we have limited personal experience with. Be honest with yourself and ask for help; check in with several people from that culture.

It would be great if you had some of these experts on staff, but what do you do if your staff lacks enough diversity? Make sure you have a few people (volunteer or paid) who are well-connected to the culture in question and are willing to review your important documents for bias, stereotypes, and misunderstandings.

Obviously, the best people to offer advice would be the actual people you are writing about. What bothers them about the ways their communities are portrayed concerning the issue at hand? How can your organization do better? (For more guidance on getting feedback, go to Chapter 17, "Edit the big picture.")

Bonus Tip

Although this book focuses on the English language, I don't mean to suggest tuning out non-English words you come across. Clearly, you must reach out to your readers of all cultures, on their own terms (literally and figuratively). Newly introduced words and sounds convey the echoes of not-so-foreign countries, and our language further evolves.

As you become clearer about your organization's use of updated and culturally appropriate language, look out for non-English terms that may be emerging — or are already widely circulating — in your community.

Even if you have significant diversity within your organization, don't automatically assume that those people will act as representatives of "their" cultures. Most people do not want to (and cannot) speak for an entire community.

WRITING WORKOUT

STEP 1: Do a diversity audit of your organization's documents by reviewing four or five of the most recent pieces written for readers inside or outside of your organization. Look at both the text and the graphics.

As a reader, what messages about different people are you getting? Are you picking up on any assumptions about people of different races, ethnicities, genders, ages, abilities, sexual orientations, classes, education levels, life experiences, and/or geographic areas?

Think about the voices represented — as well as those that you don't hear.

STEP 2: Chances are good that you could work on some aspect of cross-cultural communication and human diversity in your organization's documents. Jot down two or three things you can do in the next one to three months to take steps in the right direction. How can you be sure to take those steps? For example, can you bring up such issues at staff meetings? Distribute this chapter to your colleagues and share with them the results of your "diversity audit"? Create a standard test for unintended bias on each document before it goes public?

Note: Some of the examples and exercises in this chapter are adaptations of those in *Writing for Change: Raising Awareness of Difference, Power, and Discrimination,* by Janet Lockhart and Susan M. Shaw (www.tolerance.org/kit/writing-change).

⟶Section-at-a-Glance: Focusing on Your Community⟵

CHAPTER 4: CONNECT ON A PERSON-TO-PERSON LEVEL

You and I—and others in values-driven organizations—share the bottom-line goal of making the world a better place. Even if your focus is animals, or natural resources, or art, or media, or food, or any number of other subjects, at the root of it all is *people* and how we treat each other and our environment.

After all, humans are social animals. We live and breathe in community and will wither away without it.

- ✒ Meet your readers wherever they are.

- ✒ Focus on one reader at a time.

- ✒ Relate to your reader's emotions.

- ✒ But balance out emotions with an intellectual touch.

- ✒ Ask questions.

- ✒ Relay your personal experiences.

- ✒ Talk about your shared social context.

- ✒ Admit that you are human too—and we all make mistakes.

CHAPTER 5: SHARE STORIES

As children, we always loved it when someone said, "Let me tell you a story," or "Once upon a time." Even though we are now adults, that part of us has not disappeared. We are still more likely to remember anecdotes, examples, jokes, rhymes, and juicy tales than dry facts. Stories make the world go 'round! Use them.

- ✒ Build on the features of any great story.

- ✒ Give your cast of characters top billing.

- ✒ Use plenty of interesting quotes.

- ✒ Choose your speakers wisely.

- ✒ Work around any difficulties you have obtaining quotes.

⁀Section-at-a-Glance: Focusing on Your Community⁀

CHAPTER 6: WRITE WITH READER DIVERSITY IN MIND

I am sure you have noticed that socially responsible organizations are diversifying. While there are more kinds of them than ever before, I focus here on how they are becoming more inclusive of all people across lines of race, class, ethnicity, culture, gender, age, ability, sexual orientation, education level, life experience, geography, etc. You can see this both in the people who make up your organization and in those you serve.

I say: "Finally!" It has been a long time in coming.

This long-awaited broadening demands additional levels of respect, understanding, sensitivity, and cultural competency. I am talking about not only organizations that focus on diversity as core to their activities, but *all* values-based organizations.

- Emphasize the similarities in people's lives.

- Watch your assumptions and preconceived notions.

- Revisit your choices in how you refer to specific groups.

- Look out for euphemisms or code words.

- Avoid the melting pot syndrome.

- Get advice before you go public.

~Part~ III

Pulling It All Together

Now that you have examined your organizational context from your perspective as a copywriter, and you are clear on how to connect to your readers and their communities, let's move on to using that knowledge to assemble your piece.

At this point, you may need a little nudge (and pronto!) to get and keep your writing juices flowing. Section IIIa, "Keeping the Golden Words Coming," offers a slew of strategies to overcome writer's block and to prep yourself for faster writing. You may find yourself turning back to these tips again and again as you progress through your pieces.

Section IIIb, "Hammering Out a Draft," then takes you on a journey from the beginning of your piece right through to the end. You will find lots of creative ideas to make your pieces stand out from the dry materials we often see coming out of socially responsible organizations. I have borrowed techniques from the worlds of journalism and creative writing, plus a tad from classic literature.

You will probably recognize some of these techniques from English classes, and you will benefit from pointers on how to apply them to your ***writing to make a difference***.

"Today marketing depends on writing more than it ever has in the past...[great writing] gives you a serious competitive advantage, because you will be able to break through the clutter of bad writing."

— Jay Conrad Levinson,
author of *Guerrilla Marketing*

⁓Section⁓ III *Keeping the Golden Words Coming*

This section offers you several ways to keep your writing moving forward. You will learn how to:

- ✑ Take control of the Writer's Block Demon
- ✑ Use time-saving devices
- ✑ Find a writing system that works for you

Feel free to come back to these two pivotal chapters as you proceed through this book. You may find them more helpful once you are in the thick of on-the-job drafting and editing.

⁓Power through your writer's blocks⁓ 7

Along your journey of *writing to make a difference* you will have to deal with the Writer's Block Demon. Why do I say that? Well, my friend, it happens to all of us.

The dreaded attack may come at any time, in any place, and you need to be prepared. If you harbor memories of painful English classes or believe that you "can't write," the Writer's Block Demon can be especially ferocious.

A typical scenario might be: You get a writing assignment and you just cannot seem to get started. You can't think of an interesting word to say about your topic. It has all been said before—and oh, so much better. Besides, you suddenly see all of the absolutely pressing housecleaning or emailing or other distracting work all around you, crying out for your attention. And then, hours or days later, you realize that you have barely enough time left to finish your piece before the deadline.

LITZLER

"I MISS YANKING THE PAGE OUT OF THE TYPEWRITER, CRUMPLING IT INTO A BALL AND THROWING IT AT THE TRASHCAN."

Bonus Tip

According to the Myers-Briggs Personality Indicators, everyone has a different way of approaching writing projects. A few examples:

✳ If you are mostly extroverted (motivated and energized by other people and outside influences), you might appreciate how well you work under the pressure of an external deadline. The introverts among us will probably want to carve out some inner-directed quiet time and space especially for our writing.

✳ If you like to get your information from the concrete, detailed facts around you, you are probably great at methodical research. If you are the intuitive type, on the other hand, you may prefer to think big, letting your ideas flow freely without regard to ordering them.

✳ If you make decisions mostly as a thinker, an outline might help you a lot. If you are more the type who makes decisions based on feelings, you would probably do well to follow your instincts as you write.
(http://facstaff.buffalostate.edu/smithrd/PRWrite/mbti.htm)

Sound familiar?

Here are some specific suggestions that have worked for me. Try out one or two that strike your fancy the next time you need to overcome the Writer's Block Demon. If those don't work, try another. The big secret to victory is plain and simple: practice, practice, practice.

Trust that in time you will find which methods work best with your personality and work style. Have faith that the world is waiting to hear from you. You would not want to disappoint.

FIRST, STEP BACK A BIT AND FIND OUT MORE ABOUT YOUR READERS

Sometimes you have to know more about your readers to feel confident about engaging them. Make sure you are familiar with Part I of this book (especially Chapter B, "Engage your specific readers"), and consider getting more informed about your readers' interests, hopes, and fears.

That might include reviewing client and customer testimonials to uncover how they have used your services or products and how they benefited. What did they like most—and least? And what attracted them in the first place? You can also do some web surfing to find out what people are saying about trends in your field, related problems they encounter, etc.

If you are not in daily contact with your intended readers, you probably will need to speak regularly with people who are: your organization's clerks, salespeople, receptionists, direct service providers, and any other front-line people. Ask them what your clients and constituents think are the key benefits and features of your work. Have your colleagues discovered any unexpected connections or interests among your target audience? What is the most popular way for your readers to interact with your messages (e.g., through your website, flyers, email, or postal mail)?

You can also ask these front-line people their opinions of some of your copywriting ideas. Do they think the ideas will resonate with your intended readers? Why or why not?

CONSIDER YOUR APPROACHES

Let's assume that you have a great handle on who your readers are and where they are coming from, but you still cannot shake that Writer's Block Demon.

Some people, especially if they are non-linear thinkers, write in bits as thoughts randomly pop into their heads. If you are a stream-of-consciousness person, don't worry about the format for now; simply write down all that you want to say, and categorize later.

Others folks, more the traditionally organized types, set up folders (real or virtual) where they can drop in segments as they write them. Of course, the more linear among us follow an established path and write a beginning, middle, and end, in that order.

Still others combine methods they have heard work for other writers. For example, you may find a few Writing Workouts in this book that you really click with, and reuse them several times. Or perhaps you want to integrate some great technique you have learned about from a poet, novelist, or screenwriter.

PREPARE YOUR WRITING AREA

Clear your workspace so that it is comfortable, inviting, and not mixed up with your other work or personal things. If you can, try carving out a specific "writing area" in your home or office—either in a private space where nothing else happens, or in the middle of hustle and bustle if you prefer that environment. You might find that retreating to that place at the same time every day helps you focus on the task at hand. And when you are ready, you can get up and walk away, knowing that you have completed your writing duty for the day.

Ask yourself: *Do you like background music, television, or quiet? Natural, subdued, or super-bright light?*

Do whatever it takes to make the space your own. For instance, some people prefer writing while standing up or lying down. If that works for you, try to find a way to make that happen at least some of the time. You may also want to decorate the space with inspirational images or quotes. If you are creating a Personal Cheat Sheet (**see page** 12), post it on the wall to keep you on track.

By the way, your writing area does not actually have to be only one place. With laptops and wireless Internet access, you can try out different locations to give yourself some variety and test the impact of new surroundings on your writing. Cafes, libraries, parks, and gardens are some of my favorite writing areas. One friend of mine claims that she is most productive in a hot tub.

FIGHT OFF THE URGE TO PROCRASTINATE

Most of us have spent a night or two (or more) cramming to meet a deadline. To cut down on those incidents, I suggest that as soon as you get a writing assignment, you start keeping track of your ideas about it. Those ideas can be specific things you want to include, more general thoughts about the topic, or words and phrases you come across in everyday life that might relate to your piece. If your piece is going to have sections, separate your notes accordingly.

By starting the writing wheels in motion, you will subconsciously clear the way for relevant ideas and experiences to enter your world. Suddenly you will realize how many things that come into your life actually connect to your writing project.

Personally speaking

I carry a small notebook around with me wherever I go. But I could just as easily take notes in a PDA or record my voice on a portable device. I both capture my inspirations and keep track of interesting tidbits I pick up along my way. I jot down notes for my current writing project as well as ideas for future pieces. Going back through these notes later is a great way to relive my recent "aha" moments and maybe even add an additional thought that has been brewing in my mind. A journal is an expanded version of this little notebook, and I also recommend keeping one. It has helped me more times than I can count.

After all, most writing is done away from the typewriter, away from the desk. I'd say it occurs in the quiet, silent moments, while you're walking or shaving or playing a game, or whatever, or even talking to someone you're not vitally interested in. You're working, your mind is working, on this problem in the back of your head.

— Henry Miller

You may find, after making a list of all that needs to happen, that your original scope of work is actually a bit too broad — especially given your time constraints. If so, see if you can scale it down or subdivide and save some of it for a later project.

In fact, you have probably already experienced a similar phenomenon. How many times have you learned a new word one day and then noticed it everywhere for the next week?

This happens because you have focused your attention on that specific topic, even if you are not actively pursuing it at every moment. The same thing holds true for your writing intention. Once you commit to working on a piece—even if only in your head—you begin "writing" it in a larger sense.

If you have been entertaining thoughts about your piece, when you sit down to commit words to paper you will already have some starter material. Nothing can torpedo your creativity faster than a blank page staring you in the face. Trust me: If you wait until the last minute to get started, you will increase your probability of getting an ulcer *and* decrease the quality of your end product.

CUT YOUR TASK DOWN TO SIZE

Sometimes you may feel that your writing assignment is so overwhelming that you freeze up. It seems like a big, tangled mess that you simply cannot bring yourself to tackle. Well, it may sound like a cliché, but if you zero in on smaller parts of the piece you are writing, you can break it down into manageable chunks. And if you list them all and cross off each one as you accomplish it, you can track your progress.

Set up milestones for yourself and celebrate when you reach them. Your reward for a job well done may be a favorite snack or a special outing. For example, you may set your goal at a certain number of pages per day, or a few paragraphs on a sub-topic or two. As you begin to reach more milestones, your small bits and pieces will fit together into larger components that increasingly resemble your envisioned final product.

LISTEN TO YOURSELF

Sometimes people shut down when it comes to writing, yet are very free and easy with their speech. That can be a real strength! Since your writing should sound as conversational as possible, if you have a gift for sounding good in person, you are already halfway there.

My clients often know exactly how to say something orally, but their knowledge gets lost somehow in the writing process. I ask them to tell me what they are trying to say, and we jot down their exact words. Give it a try yourself:

Pretend you are chatting with a friend (your intended reader). Imagine talking about your own personal experience using your organization's products or services—or watching someone else use them—and how your organization made a real difference. Then try to persuade an unsuspecting colleague to be your sounding board as you practice aloud. Take notes; you may even want to record your conversation. Finally, review your piece with the eye of an editor. Pull out the juiciest and most important pieces of information, images, stories, stylistic turns, and the like.

You can also hear your voice, in a more figurative sense, if you use an instant messenger on your computer. Find a friend who happens to be online and ask if you can chat for a few minutes about "work stuff." The act of expressing yourself in writing—while interacting with a friend—may help grease your writing wheels and get them turning a bit. The great thing about carrying on a written conversation is that you automatically produce a wonderful archive that you can borrow from and build upon.

USE WORD ASSOCIATION

Brainstorm a few central words about your topic. Then write down whatever comes to mind when you think of those words, one by one. Let your mind go wherever the words take it. Give yourself permission to think without boundaries, requirements, or stipulations. If you want, add arrows to show how each word relates to the next word or phrase. Got an artistic bent? Include some drawings to represent your ideas.

If you have ever played a party game where you give your partner clues to guess a word then you have some experience in this technique. Here you are trying to branch out from a single keyword or concept by following your train of thought.

You will probably end up with a long list of places you might go with your piece. Try to map out or group similar ideas, and you will eventually have a solid outline. Mapping and word association work especially well if you are a visual thinker and like to work with pictures and spatial relationships. (You can find more about this technique in Chapter 12, "Get crystal clear.")

KNOW THAT YOUR FIRST DRAFT SHOULD *NOT* BE PERFECT

In fact, if your first draft is perfect, you are probably doing something extremely *wrong*. Yes, you read that correctly! If you think the first stab at your document is the best it will ever be and should be framed in gold, think again.

A common reason for writer's block is the fear that you will not get it right the first time. I am here to tell you that professional writers *never* produce fine-tuned, flowing pieces the first time around. This is exactly why your word processor's editing functions were invented.

On your first pass, it is a good idea to write more than you need and cut it down later. For now, ignore your "internal editor"—that nagging voice inside your head that questions everything you write. He or she will have plenty of time after the initial creation stages to run wild. (Remember that Part IV of this book offers an array of editing tips.)

JUST START WRITING—ABOUT ANYTHING!

Make it easy for yourself by not having astronomical expectations your first time out of the gate. That is, whatever you write is entirely acceptable: whether it is about what

> "*The beautiful part of writing is that you don't have to get it right the first time, unlike, say, a brain surgeon.*"
>
> — Robert Cormier

Personally speaking

Even though I have been writing for publication since childhood, most of my pieces still go through at least three drafts.

you did or did not have for breakfast this morning, or the cosmic origins of the universe, or your uncensored opinion of how your organization's marketing or fundraising efforts are going. Encourage yourself to write whatever flows from your fingers.

Simply warm up your keyboard by writing about something you personally know, feel, or think—whatever is on your mind. At first this may seem like a waste of precious time. But you will soon see that it helps set in motion the process of creating something new. One idea is to set an alarm clock to go off five or ten minutes after you start. You have to keep writing that entire time, no matter what. Don't worry about errors of any kind.

Then, when you are ready, that momentum can carry you all the way through the writing task at hand. You may even find that some of what you have written in those first freewriting moments is actually quite good and ultimately usable.

If you write every day, whether or not you have writer's block, the whole process will become familiar to you. It will take the form of an old friend anxiously waiting to hear the next episode of your drama. Start out with a brief routine—similar to stretching when you are just beginning to exercise—and gradually work your way through. It is especially important to stretch your writing muscles between deadline projects so you stay in shape and give yourself a bit of freedom to move and play.

Entire books have been written about beating back the intimidation that comes from a bad case of writer's block. Check out a few of them in the Recommended Resources section of this book. There you will find scores of warm-up exercises to get your pen or keyboard moving after a stall.

Here are a few of my favorites:

1. Pretend you are an inanimate object that comes to life. Write a short story or scene from its perspective, using the first person.

> **EXAMPLE**
>
> I love the sound that my teeth make when I bite down on fresh, strong, clean paper as it comes out of the printer. My teeth marks are always straight and I almost never fail to produce a perfect metal curl on the other side. My home is right near the office window, so I get a great view of the office park and my polished chrome accents have a special way of gleaming in the sunshine. My caretaker always seems to know exactly when I'm hungry, and she always fills me up. I am, of course, an everyday stapler—but I feel like so much more!

2. Find a magazine or newspaper article with a great headline, first line, or last line. Then take that snippet and write a short article around it—even if you have to make up some facts.

3. Pretend you have just landed in the future or the past. Write a letter to an older or younger version of yourself to explain your organization as it exists today. (What would you choose to talk about?)

4. Turn off your computer monitor and start typing. You will not be able to see what you write, which prevents your internal editor from sabotaging you. When you are satisfied, turn your monitor back on and behold the unfettered creativity before your eyes.

MEET UP WITH A WRITING BUDDY

Writing can be a lonely business, but it doesn't have to be that way. It is much more fun and often more productive to be accountable to someone else who is also in the writing game. That could be a coworker, a friend, a partner—anyone. Even if that person is not writing something that is anything like what you are writing, or is on a different schedule, having that mutual connection and focus will help. If you are the competitive type, you may find that you and a buddy can spur each other on to see who can write more in a single session. Or, simply seeing another writer work on her/his craft beside you might be all the motivation you need.

To get the writerly camaraderie going, meet with laptops or notebooks in hand to write together and bat around ideas. Read each other a few particularly exciting or troublesome passages, and swap suggestions. If you have different schedules, or if you prefer to write alone, you can opt to meet regularly to discuss your projects. If you are not geographically close, email and phone calls can also work.

Agree that you will both trade off giving each other feedback. But even a quick check-in ("I got a few more pages done today!") can help. You also may want to form a writing circle or join an online community of writers (see Appendix 10, "How to Form and Sustain a Writing Circle," for more info on that).

IF ALL ELSE FAILS, TAKE A BREAK

Don't waste time trying to come up with brilliant ideas if they are just not flowing. Get a healthy snack, exercise, read a book (unrelated to your work), or play with a stress ball. You might also want to do some meditation or stretching.

Take a brief nap, or sleep on it and return the next day. Take a moment to think about your topic right before bedtime. You will be amazed at the things you can fix after your subconscious mind has had time to undergo the creative process. You will be fresher when you wake up and may also have a new perspective or insight.

You might even feel like you are ready for a lengthy break —perhaps a week or more. If you have that luxury, this may be the time to ask for outside opinions. Flip to Chapter 17, "Edit the big picture," for more info on how to do that most effectively.

Personally speaking

I love taking breaks. Physical exercise really works for me, and I make sure that it plays a role in my life—even at my busiest times. Plenty of hearty snacks and beverages also keep me going. A break might only be five minutes—enough to eat an energy bar or refill my glass with fresh water.

I also invite my creative muse to visit me at night, with note taking gear by my bedside. I swear by the miracle of inspiration that happens just before I sleep and just after I awake in the morning, or even in the middle of the night. Sometimes the stream of ideas will flow so freely that the notes I take at those special times are the most productive of my whole day.

WRITING WORKOUT

STEP 1: On your Personal Cheat Sheet, note a few un-blocking techniques that have worked for you in the past. Then write down at least two new ideas from this chapter, to try out the next time your written words get stuck before they see the light of day.

STEP 2: Choose one new idea to try right now, even if you have not been visited recently by the Writer's Block Demon. Give it a whirl. Then write a paragraph or two about your experience: Did it help you? Did it prevent a full-blown case of writer's block? Or did it simply tell you that you need to look for a stronger cure?

STEP 3: The evil cousin of the Writer's Block Demon might also be afflicting you: The Time-sucking Vampire. If so, check out the next chapter.

Set up for efficiency 8

LITZLER

"WE'LL BE ON TIME EVEN IF IT MEANS WORKING STRAIGHT THROUGH TWO EXTENSIONS TO THE DEADLINE."

T ime. Everyone wants more of it, but it seems to slip away faster every year.

In community-benefit organizations, time is the one commodity that may be even scarcer than money. And even if you are rolling in dough, I am sure you want to be as efficient as you can be.

Writing is a craft like any other: You need to take the time to develop your skills and hone your work into masterpieces. However, in our line of work, other pressing priorities—such as caring for clients, meeting new investors, leading departmental meetings, or organizing the community around timely issues—may seem much more urgent. Interestingly, though, all of those other tasks involve some kind of writing. So working on your writing efficiency can actually help you do *all* of your work faster.

Think of how much more you would be able to accomplish if you could speed up your writing. That goes for both the increased number of pieces you could write **and** all the great things they would bring your way.

The good news is that there are several things you can do to help move that process along.

DEVELOP YOUR WRITING RHYTHM

Ask yourself: *What time of day are you at your peak?*

Are you a morning person or a night owl? Do you get the most done before breakfast or lunch, right after dinner, or when all is quiet after the lights go out? Armed with that information about your internal clock, make sure your writing time comes during those hours of maximum efficiency.

Now, you may think that the only way to write well is to have the luxury of huge blocks of uninterrupted time. Not necessarily! While this may be true at some points in your writing process, it is not always the case—especially if you are just

> "*If my doctor told me I had only six months to live I wouldn't brood. I'd type a little faster.*"
> — Isaac Asimov

starting your writing project or have been stalled for a while. If you are picturing your writing project as a huge hairy monster with an insatiable appetite, start out feeding it a diet of, say, 30 minutes a day.

To make this work, you will need to begin crafting your document with at least a week to spare. If you are working toward an established deadline, that should be easy to calculate. At each writing session, set your alarm clock to let you know when 30 minutes have passed. When the bell rings, decide if you have had enough or want to push forward a bit longer. You may find that you often want to stay on task, to hammer out a few ideas or paragraphs you have not yet settled on.

If you get into the habit of writing a bit of your piece every day—first thing in the morning, or during a lunch break, or after the kids go to sleep at night, for example—you will keep your creative juices flowing. You will find that whatever time you can shoehorn into your schedule will become very productive, and you will see progress on a daily basis.

Eventually you will hear your big scary document monster scream, "I'm melting!! I'm melting!!!" like the Wicked Witch of the West in *The Wizard of Oz*. Well, not quite, but I hope you get the picture.

What if a short deadline is breathing down your neck, or if it simply feels like your piece has been taking *forever* to get written? In that case, your writing rhythm is going to have to be quite different. You may need some time entirely devoted to it. Declare yourself "out of circulation," with no distractions or competing demands. Put up a "do not disturb" sign on your door and shut off your phone and email so they can no longer devour your time—even if only for a few hours. Chances are good that once you have worked hard to make that time and space for yourself, you will focus and take significant steps forward on your document.

The feeling of accomplishment will encourage you to carve out that room for writing again and again. As you see your piece come to life, the writing will get easier and more exciting—and proceed faster. Success attracts further success.

RECYCLE YOUR MATERIAL

You should almost never have to start a document from scratch. Gather every precious nugget you can find on your topic from other pieces you (or colleagues) have already written. Your word processor's "cut-and-paste" and "find" functions were born to do this! You might even develop a practice of indexing the contents of all major documents you write, so you can later borrow from them.

You can also use templates, also known as "boilerplates." That is, lay the groundwork for a certain type of piece that you are likely to write again and again, such as a newsletter, a grant proposal for a specific project, or a business letter. After you make this one-time investment, future editions or variations suddenly become a snap (relatively speaking).

> "*I love deadlines. I especially love the whooshing sound they make as they fly by.*"
> — Douglas Adams

Cutting and pasting can lead to laziness. Don't forget that, as in puzzle pieces you reuse to make a new picture, you always need to iron out any lumps or awkward disconnects. Tweak your transitions and watch for new flow and redundancy problems (topics I discuss later in this book).

Mind you, templates can get old and stale. Regularly go through them—perhaps during slower periods at your organization—and adopt the perspective of an editor. Freshen up the language, update the examples or facts you mention, and see if you can liven things up a bit.

PICK THE LOW-HANGING FRUIT FIRST

When you harvest an orchard you always go for the ripest, easiest-to-access fruit first. It makes sense. The sweet treats almost fall into your lap.

This same principle holds true for writing. Whatever bits of your document will flow the freest from your pen (or keyboard) should be the first parts you draft. Don't worry about where they will end up in the finished piece. Writing the easy parts first will get you going and convince you that yes, you *can* make a dent in the document—and fast. Then you proceed to the next easiest, and so on.

Soon you will have only the hardest parts of your piece left to polish. And with so much of the document already done, you just *have* to piece it together and finish it up. So much of it will be done, in fact, that you will not want to keep your readers waiting to benefit from what you have to say.

DON'T LET A MOMENTARY FEELING OF BEING STUCK SLOW YOU DOWN

What if you are proceeding along your merry writing way and you encounter a bump in the road that keeps tripping you up? Simply make a note to yourself to return later to that missing word, unknown specific data, or problem paragraph. I do this by simply inserting a blank space (_____), or by holding the spot with a bogus word or a series of options. I then highlight the area for later massaging. You can also write "FIX THIS" if you write something not quite right. You want to avoid losing any creative ideas that may just need a bit of fleshing out.

When you go back to the trouble spot, you will at least have something to work with. It is truly amazing how, after a little break, you return and can often solve the problem right away. This approach is especially effective if you are on a roll somewhere else in your piece, because the feeling of words flowing can carry over to the previously pesky sentence.

Of course, if you are the type who likes to get the hardest part out of the way and coast after that, go for it. But be ready to reconsider if you run into trouble.

EXAMPLE

In the passage on the previous page about the Wicked Witch of the West, I began by brainstorming about a few ways I could express my thought. I wrote: "you will eventually see your big scary document monster fade away, vanish, melt away, or disintegrate." I highlighted it to return to later, because I wanted a powerful visual but it was not coming to me. A friend later reminded me that the Wicked Witch of the West melted away before Dorothy's eyes, and I knew that was the comparison I wanted to make.

KEEP A "SWIPE FILE"

Why do artists and musicians of all kinds like to take in each other's work? It's no secret. Not only do they love to experience art, but they also are looking for ideas that can inspire their own creativity. Interviewers are always asking famous artists and musicians about their great influences; the answers are always interesting and sometimes surprising. You never know where that next spark of inspiration will come from.

You are also an artist, and you can also borrow from others. As you run across catchy, funny, or otherwise compelling word uses or phrases, add them to your collection. Keep an eye on the direct mail you receive, surf the web for eye-popping ideas, and take note of attention-grabbing billboards and ads you encounter online and offline. Savor them. Mull them over. And then let them inform your own work.

In the copywriting trade, this is known as a "swipe file." You can "swipe" ideas for titles, headlines, opening sentences, "About Us" boxes, and more. For instance, you might like the tone a particular writer adopts, or the rhetorical style she or he uses.

A swipe file is a handy reference of copywriting language that people in other organizations have used successfully. Whenever you need a little inspiration or perspective, your file can give you a nudge in the right direction. They say that there is nothing new under the sun—but creative reconfigurations are sure to get noticed! I am not suggesting that you copy others' work. Instead, notice what others are doing and put your own spin on it, making use of their approaches or style but not their actual material.

EXAMPLES

This swipe file of headline formats comes from the Internet. You can swipe other ideas for headlines from Chapter 9, "Start with a punchy opening."

1. Give Us [a short time period]—and We'll Give You [something great].

   Here you ask your reader to invest a bit and get an immediate return:

   ✑ Give Us a Single Day—and We'll Give You an Easy Way to Help Clean Up Our River.

2. The Lazy [type of person that your reader is]'s Way to [get something important done].

   Your readers are probably not truly lazy, but they do want to save time and money whenever they can:

   ✑ The Lazy Musician's Way to Get Great Gigs

3. Do You Recognize the [number] Early Warning Signs of [the problem you are addressing]?

   Help your reader avoid problems before it is too late:

   ☺ Do You Recognize the 3 Early Warning Signs of Skin Cancer?

4. Do You Make These [your issue or product] Mistakes?

   Everyone wants to know how to avoid preventable errors:

   ☺ Do You Make These Recycling Mistakes?

5. You Don't Have To Be [something challenging to live up to] To Be [desired result].

   Dispel a common myth or misconception about what it takes to succeed on your issues, and your readers will be interested:

   ☺ You Don't Have to Be a Masked Superhero to Make a Difference in a Child's Life.

   (Adapted from www.copyblogger.com/headline-swipe-file/)

By the way, graphic designers also make copious use of swipe files. For more about that, check out Chapter 20, "Make sure it *looks* right."

GET COWORKERS INVOLVED

Sometimes the most time-consuming part of writing is gathering all the information you need from your colleagues. We know that people are more likely to respond well to a request for input on an existing document than to a request to simply "write something."

Ask yourself: *What examples or starter info will jog your colleagues' memories or get their creative juices flowing?*

Take a first crack at your document, and leave blank spaces (like this: _____) for your colleagues to fill in. You might even want to use colored text or highlighting to make those sentences easier to spot. Most people will take a few moments to give you the information or ideas you want if they can simply fill in the blanks. This has worked for me for years and is something I do to substitute for—or follow up on—a full interview with a client.

For instance, you may want to list key words and ask them for more details. Perhaps you can provide subheadings for them to use as a structure for their thoughts. You can also ask for guidance about what copy they want to prioritize.

It is also wise to give your colleagues a deadline. After all, the document you are working on is not *their* priority. But if you tell them that you need their comments by a certain date, you increase your chances of getting timely feedback.

Once you have all the pieces you need, your task becomes much simpler and faster. Add to the existing text by applying your writer's magic. That is, apply the techniques I discuss in this book, plus any others you already use, to smooth out the rough edges.

KEEP THE WRITING BALL IN PLAY

Preparing anew each time you sit down to write can be tiring and time-consuming. It can also discourage you from continuing. So don't start cold. Finish each writing session by leaving yourself notes about where to pick up next time and what you want to cover or edit in your next session. Then, when you return, you will hit the ground running—or at least reduce your warm-up time.

Should you ever allow yourself a break when things are flowing? Some people find that they can bear in mind an energized, upbeat, and easy writing experience if they leave the party a bit before it ceases to be fun. When they return for the next session, they remain inspired and are again ready to roll. Others prefer instead to keep going until their daily writing momentum dissipates. Once it downshifts, they know it is time to wrap up.

Go ahead and try different methods for keeping your writing moving.

KNOW WHEN TO QUIT

Try not to obsess. If you have edited your piece enough to ensure that it is 100% accurate—though maybe only 99% polished—let it go. (Part IV helps you out with lots of editing tips.) If your edits are becoming extremely minor, your piece should be ready to share with the world. Take a bold step and declare it "done" so you can move on.

After all, it will never be perfect. Give yourself permission to stop trying to make it so.

Personally speaking

When I sit down for a writing session I often like to re-read what I wrote the previous time. It gets me in the right mindset and flow, and I can even edit a bit. Then I am ready to continue on my writing journey.

WRITING WORKOUT

Try this exercise as preparation for the techniques I share in the following chapters. Get yourself thinking in terms of how to be efficient as you tackle your writing projects.

STEP 1: Think about your average day and identify the places where your time seems to enter a black hole. For instance, do you get caught up in answering your email, making or returning phone calls, chatting on an instant messenger? Write down your thoughts and post the list in your writing space so you can refer to it often.

STEP 2: Once you know your time-theft culprits, make a commitment to change at least one of those behaviors for the next five working days. You might want to replace it with a positive habit described in this chapter.

STEP 3: Assess how difficult it was to make the change, as well as how effective it was. You are likely to see a significant improvement in your writing efficiency and may be motivated to try this little experiment again next week.

STEP 4: Does the Writer's Block Demon attack you regularly? If so, it is bound to slow down your writing. Make sure to read Chapter 7, "Break through your writer's blocks."

Section-at-a-Glance: Keeping the Golden Words Coming

CHAPTER 7: POWER THROUGH YOUR WRITER'S BLOCKS

Along your journey of **writing to make a difference** you will have to deal with the Writer's Block Demon. Why do I say that? Well, my friend, it happens to all of us.

- First, step back a bit and find out more about your readers.
- Consider your approaches.
- Prepare your writing area.
- Fight off the urge to procrastinate.
- Cut your task down to size.
- Listen to yourself.
- Use word association.
- Know that your first draft should *not* be perfect.
- Just start writing — about anything!
- Meet up with a writing buddy.
- If all else fails, take a break.

CHAPTER 8: SET UP FOR EFFICIENCY

Time. Everyone wants more of it, but it seems to slip away faster every year.

In community-benefit organizations, time is the one commodity that may be even scarcer than money. And even if you are rolling in dough, I am sure you want to be as efficient as you can be.

- Develop your writing rhythm.
- Recycle your material.
- Pick the low-hanging fruit first.
- Don't let a momentary feeling of being stuck slow you down.
- Keep a "swipe file."
- Get coworkers involved.
- Keep the writing ball in play.
- Know when to quit.

Section~ Hammering Out a Draft

These chapters cover all the essentials you need to keep in mind when you are moving through the first (or second) draft of your marketing or fundraising piece. In this section, you will learn how to:

- ◉ Grab your readers' attention with a fantastic opening
- ◉ Apply the cardinal rule of all great writing ("show, don't just tell")
- ◉ Get the most punch out of your verbs
- ◉ Make your writing as clear as you can
- ◉ Avoid losing your reader with jargon
- ◉ Guide your readers on a smooth—though adventurous—ride through your piece
- ◉ Use the sounds of language to your advantage
- ◉ Bring your piece to a close with your readers feeling good and eager to take the next step

Start with a punchy opening~

It really is true. In writing, as in life, you only have a few seconds to make a powerful first impression.

You can kiss your readers goodbye if you do not instantly grab their attention and set the tone for what is to come. You will not get a second chance.

In your headline and opening paragraphs, you need to pique your readers' personal interests enough that they will continue onward. You have to give your readers simple, believable, compelling images or ideas — compelling enough that their tired eyes will perk up in eagerness to find out more. They have to relate to your topic in a personally meaningful way.

Your opening should suggest why they should care about what you have to say and address their all-important question about your work: "So what?"

One of the three fundamental copywriting strategies I focus on is emphasizing the benefits you offer your readers (discussed in Chapter C, "Emphasize benefits more than features"). But while you focus on the benefits your organization offers your readers, don't forget about the benefits that your *specific document* provides. Tell your readers what they will get out of investing a bit of time with you. For example, they will learn about some cutting-edge information or recent research results, hear a well-thought out opinion or argument, encounter a new opportunity to make a difference, get to know an interesting person, laugh a little, etc.

Then start delivering on it immediately.

Your headline and opening lines carry so much importance that you need to spend extra time on them. Some copywriters even say that over half of your writing time should focus on these two components, no matter how long your document. Remember that headlines and openers go together, as your readers will encounter them virtually at the same time. Make sure they pack a one-two punch.

Here's how.

OBSESS OVER YOUR HEADLINE

Bonus Tip

The email equivalent of a headline is its "Subject" line. You would be wise to take it just as seriously.

Your headline should grab your readers' attention and refuse to let go. That word, phrase, or sentence has to be *extremely strong.* In fact, you might have the most powerful body copy (main text), but if your headline falls flat, you are doomed.

Go ahead and brainstorm to generate a lot of possibilities, and eventually choose the best one. You will probably end up with some great ideas that don't rise to the top. Consider those prime contenders for your secondary headline (see below). They can also serve as headlines you may want to test in the future.

Ask yourself: *If you were to come across your headline in a stack of papers, in your email inbox, or on a bulletin board, would it stand out enough to entice you to read on?*

Your headline should say: "Stop! This message concerns you! Right now!" It needs to emphasize the main benefit you offer, or at least hint strongly at it. Identify your subject and speak directly to your intended readers' concerns. Here are several common — and effective — types of headlines:

Ask a burning question that can only be answered by reading the copy

> **EXAMPLES**
>
> - Which of These 10 Energy Efficiency Mistakes Do You Make?
> - Which of These 5 Safety Tips Will Do the Most to Protect You and Your Family?
> - Want to Reduce Your Oil Dependency?
> - Do You Really Know How to Eat Right?
> - How Can You Benefit the Most From the Green Economy?
> - Think Biofuels Are the Answer? Think Again.
> - Can We Repair Our Broken Healthcare System?

Address an immediate need or concern

EXAMPLES

- ◈ What You Need to Know About Why Sunscreen May Be Bad for You
- ◈ The Climate Crisis: What We Can Do About It Right Now

Inspire curiosity with an unusual juxtaposition - the unlikely, the counterintuitive, or the unexpected

EXAMPLE

Finally…A Definitive Solution to the Cloth vs. Disposable Diaper Debate

Promise a meaningful benefit by commanding your reader to do something

EXAMPLE

Boost Your Creativity and Bring More Joy Into Your Life!

Present a special offer or deal

EXAMPLE

Sign Up for Our Free E-Newsletter — We'll Plant a Tree in Your Honor!

Tell "how to" achieve something

EXAMPLE

How to Write a Letter to the Editor That's Sure to Get Published

Provoke a smile, snicker, or ironic giggle

EXAMPLES

- ◈ How to Attract Eco-Investors Like Moths to a Compact Fluorescent Lightbulb
- ◈ Wake Up and Smell the….er…. Exhaust Fumes

Employ a sound bite or slogan

EXAMPLE

More Transit. More Convenience. More Savings.

Allude to a phrase in popular culture by slightly modifying it

EXAMPLES

- "And They _____ Happily Ever After" (lived)
- "A Long, Long Time Ago in a _____ Far, Far Away" (galaxy)
- "Just When You Thought It Was Safe to _____" (go back in the water)
- "7 Habits of Highly _____ _____" (Effective People)
- "To _____ or Not to _____: That Is the Question" (be, be)
- "The_____ Bill of Rights" (U.S.)
- "7 Wonders of the _____" (world)
- "It's 10 p.m. Do You Know Where Your _____ Are?" (children)
- "Friends Don't Let Friends _____ _____" (drive drunk)
- "_____ Cannot Live by _____ Alone." (man, bread)

Take note of especially intriguing headlines or attention-grabbing marketing words you come across, and keep them in a "swipe file" (as described in Chapter 8, "Set up for efficiency"). You will then be able to refer to them whenever you need a little nudge in a new direction.

Allow me to offer a few key copywriting words, to start you off:

Easy	Investment	Results	Value
Exclusive	New	Save	Yes
Free (of course!)	Now	Solution	You and Your
Gift	Proven	Special	

Other hot phrases feature numbers, as in 3 Secrets, 4 Steps, Top 10 Tips or Myths or Mistakes, 7 Deadly Sins, 10 Commandments, 25 Good Reasons, etc. Check out Appendix 4, "Additional Hot Marketing Words and Phrases," for a longer list.

If you are including at least one graphic with your copy — and I encourage you to do so — tie it to your headline. Your readers will get a quick and vivid understanding of what you are trying to say by scanning the headline and accompanying graphics. For more about graphics, see Chapter 20, "Make sure it *looks* right."

USE A SECONDARY HEADLINE IF YOU NEED IT

Often a secondary headline, or subtitle, comes right after a primary headline to further explain your message. The two pieces should work together to summarize the most important benefits you are offering or the news you are sharing. You want to present enough information so that skimmers can decide if they want to read closer.

> **EXAMPLES**
>
> - Which of These 20 Things Can Do the Most to Preserve Our Environment? (you might be surprised at the answers)
> - The Triple Bottom Line: our growing movement benefits the community, the environment, and profit margins
> - Local African-Americans Sue Over Alleged Voter Intimidation: citizens question legitimacy of two recent local elections
> - How You Can Help Fight Global Hunger (hint: it's not just by eating your vegetables)

Somewhere in your primary or secondary headline you should illustrate action by including at least one powerful verb (see Chapter 11, "Focus on the verbs," for more on what I mean by that).

BUILD ON THE MOMENTUM WITH YOUR "LEAD"

After you have intrigued your reader with a juicy headline, you want to immediately engage her or him personally. We often refer to these first few sentences (or paragraphs) as the piece's "lead." Some journalists spell it "lede," to make it stand out.

Your lead is your first opportunity to start showing your readers around your world, not just telling them what it is like (a concept I explore further in Chapter 10, "Show, don't just tell"). Fortunately, there is a vast number of great approaches to leads out there.

Narrative leads

Use a strong or controversial quote or bit of dialogue.

> **EXAMPLE**
>
> *Juan Romagoza Arce, a plaintiff in a legal case brought by The Center for Justice & Accountability against a perpetrator of human rights abuses, offered this testimonial. The organization has featured the quote in its materials:*

"When I testified, a strength came over me. I felt like I was in the prow of a boat and that there were many, many people rowing behind—that they were moving me into this moment. I felt that if I looked back at them, I'd weep because I'd see them again: wounded, tortured, raped, naked, torn, bleeding. So, I didn't look back, but I felt their support, their strength, their energy…"

(www.cja.org)

Tell a memorable anecdote or story that is bold, striking, unexpected, or controversial—and perhaps rebuts conventional wisdom.

EXAMPLE

The monograph Flipping the Script: White Privilege and Community Building, *co-authored by the Center for Assessment and Policy Development, opens with this story. It was adapted from an exercise at the Undoing Racism Workshop of the People's Institute for Survival and Beyond:*

A group of Native Americans is concerned about the well-being of a group of white children whose families live near the reservation. Several leaders of the Native American community feel the children are disadvantaged… This Native American group also thinks the white children are isolated and not benefiting from enough cultural experiences...

What steps do you think the Native American groups would have to go through before the parents of the white children would give them access to their children? Who would likely set the terms of the interactions? What safeguards might be put in place to protect the children from any unintended ill effects of the encounter?

Now imagine that the children needing assistance were Native American, or African American, or Latino/a. Imagine that the people who want to help these children are mostly white or, if they are people of color, they are employed by an institution established by white people of wealth… Where might white privilege and racism come into play, and what might be their impact?

(www.capd.org)

Focus on one person or thing and cite details and observations that symbolize a greater meaning.

EXAMPLE

From the Winter 2004/2005 newsletter of the Law Center for Families:

"Mario" thought he was buying a car at a dealer in his hometown of Hayward. He **was** pleased that he could negotiate with a salesperson who also spoke Spanish, **his** native language. The problems started, however,

when Mario tried to finalize the deal by signing a contract — which was written only in English. **Unbeknownst** to Mario, he was agreeing to a leasing arrangement that **included extra warranties, add**-ons and services that he had not discussed. The rental deal ended up costing him over $15,000 more than he had bargained for.

Unfortunately, Mario is far from alone… *(www.lcff.org)*

Briefly paint a striking word picture of the setting or situation.

EXAMPLE

Walk down the brightly lit main hall of Winchester Elementary School. Saunter past the children's cubbies and the music classroom. Look closely and there, nestled in this corner of suburbia, you'll find a treasure. A small sign in bold black letters marks this tiny window on the world: "Massachusetts Global Education Program."

Relay a flashback that quickly shifts back to the present.

EXAMPLE

It was 1991. Cindy Miller and Laura Ramirez had recently lost their newborns to SIDS. And they had no idea what they were about to create. For the next 15 years they would transform their family crises into a crucial resource for dozens of support groups of grieving parents all across the country.

Share a personal tidbit, internal monologue, or true confession.

EXAMPLE

I'm a mutt. I come from a long line of mixtures from all over the world: no purebreds here. Give me a moment and I'll tell you all about it.

Ask your reader to imagine a future scene that contrasts with the current situation, or with one that could have included her/him.

EXAMPLES

1. Imagine what it would be like to walk at a pace you really enjoy because you don't have to count steps or worry about what's in front of you. To have the freedom to think your thoughts, or carry on an engrossing conversation as you walk with a friend, because you don't have to think about how to avoid running into an obstacle or stepping off a curb. Just imagine it!

   And now, just imagine the joy of companionship, of feeling the comfort of having a trusted canine by your side — a beautiful animal that wins

> the admiration even of complete strangers. What a conversational ice breaker — what a friend-maker! *(www.guidedogs.com)*
> 2. *The following copy is accompanied by a photo of a crumpled up prescription for birth control pills.*
>   Imagine going to your pharmacist and getting this back instead of your medicine? It's actually happening today to women all across America.
>   *(www.plannedparenthood.org)*

Provide hints of a mystery unfolding with things not going quite as planned.

EXAMPLE

In the Ecuadorian Amazon the smell of gas hung heavy in the jungle air. Eager to find out what was going on, staff and volunteers from our research institute joined local health promoters and environmentalists on a little fact-finding mission. We found a situation that was much worse than we had expected.

Emotional leads

Ask provocative or loaded questions.

EXAMPLE

Having a hard time swallowing all this new technology? Does it seem like it's suddenly spread out before you in an impossible cyber-tangle? You're not alone.

Appeal to your reader's raw human instincts — such as survival, attraction, fear, sadness, thrill, or flight from danger.

EXAMPLE

I panicked.

I could hear my crazy heartbeat as I emerged from the tiny room where I had fumbled to stash my traveler's checks in my secret pouch. I tried to appear casual as I reached the luggage conveyor belt. But my lone suitcase was nowhere in sight.

"Come over here," beckoned an official-looking man. He led me to a locked cage at the end of a darkened hall. Images of headlines like, "American Lost Forever in Guatemala City Airport" flashed through my mind…

Convey a genuine sense of urgency by offering help to diffuse an acute hazard or pointing to a fleeting golden opportunity.

> **EXAMPLE**
>
> We don't have much time. Only until April 30 will the generous Foundation for Our City match the money we raise from our community (that's you). Each dollar you contribute means TWO dollars to us right now. That means you will double your impact! Please consider what this organization means to you and let us know before April 30. You can get in on this great deal if you act now.

LITZLER

"WITH YOU EVERYTHING STARTS WITH A HUMOROUS ANECDOTE."

Humorous or surprising leads

Tell a relevant joke.

> **EXAMPLE**
>
> *In a piece promoting gun control, you might open with something like this one-liner by the British comedian Eddie Izzard, in which he talks about the National Rifle Association:*
>   "The NRA says that guns don't kill people. People do. But I think the gun helps! You know?"

Define a word central to your piece in a witty or debatable fashion.

> **EXAMPLE**
>
> "ACRONYMS: Absurdly Contrived Representation Of Names Yielding Mass Stupefaction" *(www.businessballs.com/acronyms.htm)*

Juxtapose two or more opposing views or contrasting items or ideas.

> **EXAMPLE**
>
> Oty McGinnis may be a dummy, but few fourth graders in this town would ever call him stupid. For two years Oty has been a shining star at school, helping children learn to feel good about themselves.
>
> Oty's voice and movements are provided courtesy of a ventriloquist — and psychotherapist — named Jake Sills.

Relay a startling or intriguing fact or statistic.

> **EXAMPLES**
>
> 1. *This article, entitled "Racism Is Harmful to Health: 'Antiracism' Initiatives Needed, But Slow to Be Recognized, Say Experts," begins this way:*
>
>   You know about the dangers of smoking, obesity, fatty foods, unprotected sex, and environmental pollutants. Now chalk up another health hazard to that ever-growing list: Racism...
>
>   The health effects of racism are well-documented. One British study of 4,800 people finds that those who felt victimized by discrimination and forms of racism were twice as likely to develop psychotic episodes in the next three years. Meanwhile, a group of Harvard researchers documented that a mere 1% increase in incidences of racial disrespect translates to an increase in 350 deaths per 100,000 African Americans.
>
>   How? Being on the receiving end of overt or subtle racism creates intense and constant stress, say some experts, which boosts the risk of depression, anxiety and anger — factors that can lead to or aggravate heart disease. Some research also suggests racism can also manifest itself in respiratory and other physical problems.   *(www.webmd.com)*
>
> 2. Did you know that some HMOs only cover their "low-risk" women patients for a pap smear every three years? A lot can happen in three years.

Straightforward leads

Make a connection to something already on the reader's mind — a recent event in the news, time of year, anniversary, predictable holiday, or timely trend.

> **EXAMPLES**
>
> 1. The current economic downturn makes it clear: Income alone offers little protection again debt and poverty. But savings, a home, a small business, or other financial assets can offer the economic stability to plan for the

future with a financial buffer. *Closing the Wealth Gap*, a new report by the Women's Initiative for Self Employment, details the positive relationship between business development and a household's financial well-being.

(adapted from www.womensinitiative.org)

2. Every September, the poor state of U.S. public education makes headlines. But the problem is year-round and it's getting worse by the month.

Bluntly tell your readers the value they can gain from reading your piece.

EXAMPLE

Looking to extend your life expectancy? We have great news for you!

Go for the truly straightforward: Summarize the heart of the matter and give your conclusion.

Tell the most important parts of the story in a nutshell: who, what, when, where, and — of course — why (the big benefits to gain, or problems to avoid). If your readers only have time to read two or three paragraphs, what are their priorities going to be? Lead with those. (Journalists call this the "inverted pyramid" style.)

AVOID COMMON BUT MISGUIDED STRATEGIES

Want to know some mistakes to avoid in your openings? These are extremely common errors I am sure you have seen from time to time:

DON'T clear your throat

If you weigh your readers down with too much introductory information, you are going to lose them, bored expressions and all. Your readers are no dummies! They can spot wishy-washiness and stalling tactics in a moment. We all wrote student essays that contained at least *some* fluff; it fools no one. As adults, we get the goods or we are gone.

Some common throat-clearing devices include:

- ☞ Vague generalizations or stating the obvious
- ☞ Weak, irrelevant jokes or anecdotes
- ☞ Simple dictionary definitions
- ☞ Long descriptions with no action

DON'T start out too broad, with no focus

No doubt you know a lot about your topic and probably also about related topics. But that can be dangerous. Your readers have not turned to the encyclopedia to get the information you can provide — so don't write as if they have. It is fine to briefly outline the broad landscape of your topic, but be sure to move right into a focus on your specific point of view, attitude, or action item.

Your readers have come to your piece in search of specific answers or ideas. They will appreciate your help navigating all of the information out there. Long explanations, extensive narratives, and historical background do not belong in your lead.

DON'T skip the warm-up

At the same time, if you just dive into your piece without orienting your readers or gently inviting them to engage in a conversation, you have just lost a chance to build a relationship with them. If they have no reason to trust you, your expertise will not matter. Don't start off on the wrong foot by immediately launching into unexplained jargon or highly technical terms (see Chapter 13, "Avoid jargon"). Instead, begin by forging a personal connection with your reader (see Chapter 4, "Connect on a person-to-person level" for more on this).

I usually suggest that your first one or two paragraphs be extremely short and accessible to a wide range of potential readers. Once you have hooked them in with a strong lead and have established a rapport, then you can start in on the nitty-gritty.

DON'T beat a dead horse

Yes, that is a cliché, and I use it to remind you not to use them outright. Clichés with no twist or new dimension retain no heat and add no spice. It is okay to use a cliché as a memory trigger when explaining a new concept, but otherwise stay away (ahem…like the plague).

EXAMPLES

1. *Original:* A penny saved is a penny earned! Help us prove it during the Pennies from Heaven Fundraiser.

   Suggested revision: A penny saved is a penny…perfect for our Pennies from Heaven Fundraiser!

2. *Original:* Tired of "business as usual?" So are we.

   Suggested revision: It's time to do business as *un*usual. Live your social and environmental values every day! Here's how we can help…

DON'T start out with a focus on the "we" (your organization)

Your writing should center on your readers' needs and interests — and not your own. So don't start off with the spotlight on yourself. Instead, shift your starting point to talk about your readers' interests up front. Move from "about us" to "about you." (If you need a bit of help figuring out more about your readers and their interests, see Chapter B, "Engage your specific readers").

EXAMPLE

Original: We want to bring native plants back to our community. But we need your help!

Suggested revision: As you know, native plants bring many benefits to our community and help avoid eco-trouble down the line. With just a few simple steps, you can help improve our city's environment!

DON'T get too attached to your first try

Experiment with different openings. Always be on the lookout for ways to improve. Make it a habit to think of at least three ways you can open your piece and then choose the best one.

EXAMPLE

Here are two of my earlier attempts at leads for this chapter, both of which I ultimately rejected.

1. Your first paragraph should draw your readers in by piquing their interest so that they will stick around to hear the rest of the story (this is often called the "lead"). You want to get your reader thinking and engaging with you.
    (This is not very punchy.)

2. Yes, it's true. You only have a few seconds to make a powerful first impression.

    Don't do it and you are history. Don't grab your reader's attention and set the tone for what is to come, and you can kiss your readers goodbye.
    (This comes across as a bit too focused on the negative and might even be confusing.)

Bonus Tip

Do you recognize any of the common "DON'T" mistakes as ones you tend to make? If so, be sure to note them on your Personal Cheat Sheet (see page 12). And gently encourage yourself to find alternatives.

REMEMBER THAT WRITING OPENINGS IS A PROCESS

Even though this is the first chapter in the "Hammering Out a Draft" section of this book, keep in mind that the writing process for your headline and lead can start at any time. Don't worry if it becomes the last bit you write or finalize. In fact, that is often how it happens.

Your piece will take on a life of its own and may become somewhat different from your original idea — even if you have done great planning or outlining. Be prepared to tweak your headline and lead to fit the piece you end up with.

WRITING WORKOUT

This exercise will get you focusing on those all-important headlines and leads. After all, these two components embody some of the most important features of all good copy: They must be clear, simple, positive, action-oriented, and error-free.

STEP 1: Revise the following headlines, using the formats I suggest. Pay special attention to your tone and verbs. Feel free to add secondary headlines. You may need to invent some details as you draw out the main benefit you offer to your readers and/or their community.

A: *Original:* Let's Improve Nutrition in the School Cafeteria!
Suggested revision (as a question):

B: *Original:* Corporate Accountability Reports: A Look at Environmental and Social Impacts
Suggested revision (commanding your reader to act):

C: *Original:* Attention All Fixer-Uppers! Earth-Friendly Building Materials!
Suggested revision (telling your reader how and/or why to do something):

D: *Original:* Buying Fair Trade Is Easier Than You May Think
Suggested revision (using a number):

E: *Original:* A Shot in the Arm for the Anti-Poverty Movement
Suggested revision (twisting the cliché or eliminating it altogether):

STEP 2: Look through your organization's marketing or public education materials and write down three headlines you think could be improved. See what you can come up with, drawing on ideas from this chapter.

Original:

Suggested revision:

Original:

Suggested revision:

Original:

Suggested revision:

STEP 3: Check out the leads in those three pieces. Were they compelling enough to make your average reader want to read what came next? Why or why not?

STEP 4: Try your hand at producing three new powerful leads. Use any of the techniques from this chapter.

    If you need a bit more help, take a look at the beginnings of articles in any good newspaper, magazine, or online news story. Identifying solid leads will help generate some of your own ideas.

STEP 5: Take a look at the leads you just created. They should give your readers a sense of how you are approaching your topics and the benefits of what you have to say. They should also pick up where your headlines leave off. Do they?

STEP 6: If you come across any great headlines or leads in the next week or so, make sure to add them to your swipe file.

~Show, don't just tell.~ 10

Here is a major tip for producing great copywriting throughout your document: Show the reader what is happening. Don't simply tell.

Concrete images and specifics show your readers exactly what you are talking about. Vivid details help you build interest, add drama, and help your readers visualize the specific value your organization can bring to their lives. These words can transport them to the new reality you are creating. Vague storytelling or discussions do the opposite.

Turn anything abstract into visceral, tangible, personal impacts — otherwise known as benefits. For instance, think about the difference between *telling* your readers about "basic nutrition and affordable housing" and *showing* them "three solid meals a day and a safe roof over your head."

Most people best process new information if they can "see" it. Others want to "hear" the sounds behind the words. And still others want to smell, taste, or feel what they are learning. The more ways we experience something, the better we can integrate it into our personal knowledge base.

Your readers might need to notice the fleeting sparkle of a firefly at your summer camp for city kids. They might want to smell the fresh, nontoxic aroma of natural paint as your group refurbishes a schoolhouse, or of rich fair trade coffee at the senior citizen meeting you hold, or of honeysuckle after rain in your community garden.

They may need to hear the giggle of a newly adopted baby or kids chasing each other on the playground of your alternative health clinic. They might be interested in tasting the pure water running through the river you just cleaned up, or the organic watermelon at your mentor/mentee picnic. Or, they just might yearn to feel the soft fur of the sea otters your group recently rescued from certain death.

In addition, the more emotionally sensitive among us might want to know about the poignant moments, the compassion, and the personal challenges that are part of daily life at your organization. Families reunited, health restored, and hope established are only a few of the events you might draw your readers into.

"A scrupulous writer, in every sentence that he writes, will ask himself at least four questions, thus: (1) What am I trying to say? (2) What words will express it? (3) What image or idiom will make it clearer? (4) Is this image fresh enough to have an effect?"

— George Orwell in "Politics and the English Language"

How many times has someone said, "Do as I say and not as I do" — to no avail? That is because people need to be ***shown*** things. Realtors know they need to show a property before they can sell it. Car dealers know customers must test-drive a vehicle to get a feel for it. If you have ever tried to introduce a new technology to skeptical or resistant family members, you know that you need to demonstrate how the newfangled gadget will immediately benefit them and be worth the extra effort.

Another great example is the tip sheet (e.g., "10 Tips for Greening Your Home"), which I discuss in Chapter 18, "Cultivate conciseness." Tip sheets are like mouthwatering samples you taste at your local grocery store or farmers' market. Try it before you buy it! Your readers know that there is more where the initial sample came from, and they are now likely to seek it out.

Secondhand analysis and theory don't even come close.

The idea here is that you should not draw conclusions for your readers, telling them what to think or feel. Instead, use your writing to prompt their own sensory or visceral experiences. Think of yourself as their eyes, ears, hands, taste buds, nose — and heart.

This chapter suggests some ways to do that.

Bonus Tip

Tip sheets are even better than food samples. They are not perishable. They will not go stale, melt, spoil, or expire on a certain date. If your reader likes what he or she sees, your tip sheet is likely to stick around for a while. And with it, so do your name and contact info.

USE METAPHORS AND ANALOGIES TO CAPITALIZE ON FAMILIAR SIGHTS, SOUNDS, SMELLS, TASTES, TEXTURES, AND FEELINGS

Use figurative language to instantly convey new ideas or trends that may otherwise be difficult to grasp. Great ways to do this include using metaphors (comparing two things by saying that one thing *is* something more familiar) and analogies and similes (saying that one thing is *like* or behaves *as* something more familiar).

Best (Or Worst?) Ever Analogies from High School English Papers

1. He was as tall as a six-foot-three-inch tree.

2. The little boat gently drifted across the pond exactly the way a bowling ball wouldn't.

3. Her hair glistened in the rain like a nose hair after a sneeze.

4. The hailstones leaped from the pavement, just like maggots when you fry them in hot grease.

5. John and Mary had never met. They were like two hummingbirds who also had never met.

6. McBride fell twelve stories, hitting the pavement like a garbage bag filled with vegetable soup.

7. Long separated by cruel fate, the star-crossed lovers raced across the grassy field toward each other like two freight trains, one having left Cleveland at 6:36 p.m. traveling at 55 m.p.h., the other from Topeka at 4:19 p.m. at a speed of 35 m.p.h.

8. From the attic came an unearthly howl. The whole scene had an eerie, surreal quality, like when you're on vacation in another city and *Jeopardy* comes on at 7:00 p.m. instead of 7:30 p.m.

(urban legend on the Internet)

Figurative language helps your readers organize complex information into easy-to-relate-to images. Great quotes and sound bites are made of this stuff. Just be sure to choose comparisons that help advance your brand and point of view; obscure references will obscure your meaning. Your metaphors and analogies should shine a light on your subject, not cast a confusing shadow.

Ask yourself: *Can you liken your subject to a more familiar object, behavior, situation, or attitude?*

EXAMPLES

1. We know that 25% of whites and 75% of blacks can find the other race somewhere in their family trees. When those trees have become forests, sharing their seeds and shade, how can we even think about defining their branches as separate? Or declaring how and where they should grow and blossom?

2. *U.S. Senator Joseph Lieberman used this effective metaphor to describe the 2001 United Nations climate change conference in Bonn:*

   "[It] surprised people…The feeling was that if the United States took its football and left the field, the game wouldn't go forward. But the rest of the nations found their own football, and they completed the game. They left the United States on the sidelines." *(Source: The Los Angeles Times, July 25, 2001)*

3. Like a beloved symphony playing after years of anxious silence, the morning birdsong has once again returned to our open spaces. For the past several years, the only sounds we could hear in these parts were the rumbles of heavy machinery clearing the way for a new landfill. But our environmental conservation efforts have changed all that.

4. Many mountain bikers consider themselves not "motorcyclists without engines" but "hikers on wheels."

5. *Some popular science and technology metaphors and similes include:*

   The ozone hole in the atmosphere is like a hole in humanity's roof; the eye is a camera; a cell is a factory; the Internet is the information superhighway; rainforests are the lungs of the planet.

Personally speaking

By showing and not just telling, I find that I can better exercise my creativity in writing for community-benefit organizations. My poetic sensibilities often make an appearance when I conjure them up in this way. Although I am not much of a visual artist or musician, my computer keyboard and pen serve me well as virtual paintbrushes and musical instruments.

You can also create metaphors and similes that allude to history or popular culture: books, stories, slogans, rhymes, movies, television shows, websites, products, logos, songs, or well-known jokes or slang.

Although analogies can be quite memorable, they don't always get your message across in the way you intend. The Partnership for a Drug-Free America used the visual metaphor, "This is your brain. This is your brain on drugs," as an egg sizzled in a skillet. From the time this widespread ad campaign started in 1987, many people have used it as the butt of jokes. An example is the *Far Side* cartoon in which two chickens sit watching a television ad that says, "This is your egg. This is your egg covered with bugs."

EXAMPLES

1. That corporation's appetite for market share at any cost is like Homer Simpson's appetite for donuts: insatiable!

2. Let me tell you why I call him the Attila the Hun of our city.

3. Online social networking websites — such as Myspace, Facebook, Twitter, and LinkedIn — are today's town squares.

4. Are genetically modified organisms really Frankenfoods on steroids?

5. Reality grantmaking: Who will be the survivor?

6. It's an offer we *can* refuse.

7. Youth Radio and National Public Radio collaborate on a weekly series called *What's the New What?* Young reporters and commentators talk about ever-changing youth culture. Stories include, "Sex without a condom is the new engagement ring" and "Psychics are the new psychologists."

Another type of analogy you should consider uses the format: "saying or doing _____ is like saying or doing _____." This technique allows you to make an emphatic point by conjuring up a comparison your readers are sure to recognize as extreme.

EXAMPLES

1. Denying today's students a global education is like giving them bikes with flat tires.

2. Saying Stephen Hawking is just a physicist is like saying *A Chorus Line* is just a show or *The New York Times* is just a newspaper.

3. "Hypocrisy is like Idi Amin looking at Ghandi and going, 'You're too intense!'" — *Robin Williams*

Sometimes you would love to use a metaphor or simile, but nothing springs to mind. See if you can freshen up, tweak, or enhance any of these common ones found in U.S. culture:

- 20-20 hindsight
- all on the same page
- all the options are on the table
- backfire
- Biblical proportions
- bittersweet memories
- breath of fresh air
- bright idea
- carbon footprint
- chained to a decision
- cold & calculating, like a machine
- end on a high note
- feverish pace
- food for thought
- the genie is out of the bottle
- have your cake and eat it too
- icing on the cake
- life is jazz
- lift (or lower) the floodgates

- like a horse with blinders on
- meltdown
- money in the bank
- off the beaten path
- Pandora's box
- pulling yourself up by your bootstraps
- sea change
- shades of grey
- sink or swim
- sit on the fence
- sweet smell of success
- the bottom line
- the lights are on but nobody's home
- throw out the baby with the bathwater
- toxic cocktail
- two-way street
- warm or cold reception

Watch out for the two most frequent blunders in this realm: (1) Don't mix your metaphors (pair two completely different images), and (2) Don't overuse metaphors and analogies, as constantly drawing comparisons can overload and fatigue your reader.

(I list several others in Appendix 5, "Additional Common Metaphors and Similes.")

Try your best to use distinctively modified metaphors or similes; better yet, invent your own to evoke a specific image. Some metaphors are so heavily used that they have become ordinary speech or clichés. If you are used to reading or hearing a metaphor or simile that you are thinking of using, see if you can come up with a more precise, colorful, or updated one.

For instance, you might write about a "carbon crater" instead of a mere carbon footprint. Perhaps the "bottom line" is not that solid when the balance sheet does not account for all of the real social or environmental costs. Or, the choices might not be "sink or swim," but "sink or sink faster." Edible Love Chocolates, which makes organic fair trade truffles, uses the tagline, "Where you can have your LOVE…and eat it too!"

Bonus Tip

Values-based metaphors and similes have been widely used in political wordsmithing to encourage particular points of view. Called "rhetorical framing," this technique includes popular phrases such as: "welfare queens," "tax relief," "nanny state," "leveling the playing field," and "society's safety net." U.S. President Lyndon B. Johnson introduced the "War on Poverty."

Some theorists, such as linguist George Lakoff, posit that our brains actually develop throughout our lives by thinking in terms of metaphors. See the Recommended Resources section for more on this.

USE PERSONIFICATION TO MAKE THE ABSTRACT EASY-TO-UNDERSTAND

By giving inanimate objects human attributes, you can inject life into an otherwise desolate scene. It is also an easy way to help your reader relate to concepts or situations in a personal way.

EXAMPLES

- A file lives on your hard drive or server.

- The copy machine hates me.

- Your car dies suddenly.

- The office plants cry out for some water.

- The sun woke up and greeted me this morning.

- "The hills are alive with the sound of music" — *Oscar Hammerstein*

- Relief visited the hospital briefly as the fierce, howling windstorm generously allowed the staff an hour of calm — enough time to move the sick patients to safety.

- "Art is a jealous mistress." — *Ralph Waldo Emerson*

PRESENT THE STRIKING DETAILS

Even if you want to stick to literal language, you can convey a lot by carefully choosing a few outstanding representative details. Details not only help clarify your meaning, but they can also help set the scene or describe the people or things in your piece in a memorable way. Great fiction writers take advantage of this secret, and you can too.

Sparkling details also invite your readers to get involved in the creative process alongside you. You are encouraging them to imagine, to draw on their own keen powers of observation, and to fill in the blanks.

Zeroing in on concrete details can also help prevent another common writing problem in values-based organizations. We tend to talk in abstractions because we work with the big picture: trends, patterns, projections, systems, etc. However, writing that way is a sure-fire way to *repel* your readers.

Instead, I suggest that you take a microscope to your work. I am talking about seemingly trivial fine points, such as shades of color, exact numbers (e.g., 27 instead of "more than 20"), shapes, speech accents, clothing, decorations, etc. Even if you do not end up using all of them in your final piece, such details show how familiar you are with your subject. In turn, this encourages your readers to trust you as their interpreter.

Ask yourself: *What captivating details jump out at you that will help your piece come alive?*

For instance, you may be working with people whom you could simply talk about in the abstract: activists, neighbors, politicians, low-income families, or homeless veterans. Instead, share with your reader the unique details of particular activists, neighbors, politicians, low-income families, and homeless veterans. Create a snapshot in your reader's mind.

> **EXAMPLE**
>
> My daily walks around the Guatemalan town I was visiting meant that I constantly ran into indigenous women — from teenagers to grandmothers. I didn't need an academic lecture on their dismal economic status; I could see it for myself in their dark eyes. Some begged for jobs as underpaid and exploited domestic servants («muchachas» or "girls"). Others spent endless hours preparing and selling tamales, tortillas, or small fried snack foods on street corners. Once, at the end of the market day, I watched one dust-covered young mother work alongside her daughter, no more than four or five years old. They were gathering the family's dinner: any salvageable scraps the vendors had left behind in a huge heap of soggy, greenish-brownish vegetable rubbish.

Another great way to highlight details: Describe an odd juxtaposition, a stark contrast, or a surprising situation. Use this technique to interest your reader in an otherwise predictable story.

> **EXAMPLE**
>
> As a huge contributor to CO_2 emissions, jet travel has become a major concern of many travelers and scientists. Most estimates say that each air passenger is responsible for nearly 1 ton of emissions for every cross-country flight. According to the U.S. Department of Transportation's Center for Climate Change and Environmental Forecasting, air travel produces up to 10% of transportation-based emissions in the country. And this doesn't even include the incredible amount of waste generated by our nation's airports.
>
> You probably would expect environmentalists to be all over this issue, and they are. But some unlikely characters are also stepping up to the plate: airlines, airports, and travel agencies.

> Boston's Terminal A at Logan Airport opened in March 2005 as the first airport terminal in the U.S. to earn certification by the U.S. Green Building Council's LEED® (Leadership in Energy and Environmental Design) program. The entire new Indianapolis airport, opened in 2008, also abides by these tough sustainability guidelines.
>
> Continental Airlines claims to be nearly 35% more fuel-efficient in 2008 than it was in 1997. The company is also testing alternative fuels and fuel additives for its ground service equipment. Virgin Airlines is investing billions of dollars in energy-efficient aircraft. Boeing is working on a hydrogen-powered fuel cell airplane. And many airlines and travel agencies are offering customers carbon offsets or planting trees on their behalf.

If your organization deals with numbers at all — and that would include almost every organization — you can show your readers what those detailed numbers actually look or sound like.

For instance, millions or billions of dollars are not easy for most people to envision. We have no direct experience with that amount of money. But what if you compare the dollars Americans spend on cosmetics or SUVs to what that same amount of money could do to further your cause?

Or, perhaps the cost of an everyday item — such as a tank of gas or a meal in a restaurant — might be easy to compare with the cost (or savings) of investing in one of your services or products. Chapter 3, "Reflect your true numbers," shows you more about how to transform wonky numbers into user-friendly messages.

FOLLOW YOUR PRODUCT OR SERVICE THROUGHOUT ITS LIFETIME

Only the most Machiavellian among us believe that "the ends always justify the means."

As community-oriented organizations, we try to look at not only outcomes for our clients but also the processes we use to get there. These might include your organization's building or internal operations, materials suppliers, factory workers, contractors, consultants, distributors, vendors, and disposal systems.

By showing your readers your whole product or service cycle, they don't have to take your word for it that you are both socially responsible and effective: they can see for themselves. Presenting external certification also helps.

EXAMPLES

1. If your organization uses union-made or fair trade supplies, what does that say about the labor, environmental, and health practices you support?

How does it show your accountability to your community along the way of achieving your mission? And how does it show that you "walk your talk?"

2. If your organization uses its profits to support community-benefit projects, that is also something to show your readers. That is, after they buy your product or service the story does not end there. Profits from their purchases go on to give back to favorite causes your organization (and presumably your customers) believes in. Perhaps your product's packaging or components lend themselves to easy recycling or composting, thereby decreasing the environmental impact.

MAKE YOUR POINT MORE POWERFUL WITH UNDERSTATEMENT

This technique can work well when you are writing about something that is outstanding, fantastic, extremely emotional, or taboo. If you are familiar with British humor, you know what this can look like. Basically, you describe in a matter-of-fact manner a situation that obviously involves much more than the facts you present.

EXAMPLES

1. In Victorian England, Cleopatra's unorthodox behavior in her relationships with men was said to be "so unlike the home life of our own dear Queen!" That phrase is used to this day in Britain to describe scandalous, unconventional, or nontraditional arrangements.

2. In Monty Python's *The Meaning of Life*, the audience sees a soldier who has just lost his leg. When someone asks him how he feels, he looks down at the bloody remains of his leg and answers, "Stings a bit."

HELP YOUR READER "FEEL" THE ACTION

People experience the world not only through their five senses, but also through movement — physical or emotional. If you can involve your readers in the action, you will engage even more of their interest, understanding, and memory. We all have read things that move us enough to make us laugh, cry, smile, or feel angry, frustrated, thrilled, etc. Sometimes mere words can incite my heart to race, goosebumps to suddenly appear, or a chill to run down my spine. I am sure you have had similar experiences.

Bonus Tip

Where there is action, there are verbs. See Chapter 11, "Focus on the verbs," for more on making the most of them.

Ask yourself: *What kind of action takes place in your piece?*

That action does not have to be obvious to the naked eye (although it certainly can be). It can also include internal feelings, thoughts, or beliefs. It is your job to transport your readers into that action, so they can experience it alongside your characters. Show your readers what brings about feelings in the people you are describing.

EXAMPLES

1. Walls of Hope Art School and Open Studio recently packed the house when we screened the riveting documentary, *Artist of Resistance*, about our founder, artist Claudia Bernardi, and her experience of the exhumation of El Mozote, El Salvador. A huge massacre in 1981 had destroyed this rural Salvadoran town during the country's civil war. The film screening became a major healing event.

    In the audience sat Rufina Amaya, the sole survivor of the massacre. Rufina wept throughout the film. At the end, she spoke to thank the filmmakers and artists for being the carriers of the story of El Mozote. Many others also rose to speak — some for the first time in years — of the families, relatives, and friends they had lost. Many friends and neighbors cried and thanked the «internacionales», the people from outside, for remembering the tragedy and establishing an art school that helps heal the psychological wounds of war.

    As a member of a local religious and social base community said, "Art has accomplished what politics was never able to do."

    (www.wallsofhope.org)

2. Every week we see children like Andy. He shuffles into the school cafeteria for lunch with his head down and hands fidgeting. He looks like he doesn't belong here — or anywhere. But then he hears his name, he looks up, and spots his mentor waiting for him. A huge smile spreads across his face, and he suddenly stands taller and walks with a spring in his step.

But what if you, the writer, did not experience the story in question firsthand? No problem. Simply get as close to the action as you can in your telling of it — as if you *had* been there. That means gathering as much firsthand experience as you can from eyewitnesses, photos, recordings, and the like.

USE PHOTOS OR OTHER GRAPHICS TO COMPLEMENT YOUR WORDS

Do all you can to animate your words and then add the document equivalent of a cherry on top: a delicious graphic or two.

Just remember to write a strong caption that relates your text to the image. I hate to admit this, but sometimes readers only look at the pictures. So the caption should do the same job as a headline: Get at your point in a compelling way that grabs the reader's attention.

Don't forget to check out Chapter 20, "Make sure it *looks* right," for more on using graphic design to add to your words.

Bonus Tip

Now that it is easy to produce and broadcast video and audio online, you might want to consider adding moving pictures and sounds to your repertoire. For more information about doing that, check out Appendices 3, "Writing for Audio," and 6, "Writing for Video," as well as the Recommended Resources section.

WRITING WORKOUT

Here you will practice picking out the most gripping or persuasive parts of a story: the ones you will use to engage your readers.

STEP 1: Choose a document (your own or someone else's) that seems a bit lifeless, abstract, or bland.

Bonus Tip

If you have a real microphone or video camera, you might want to use this exercise to start planning a multi-media clip to use on your website or elsewhere.

STEP 2: Imagine that you have a state-of-the-art video camera or microphone. What images and sounds would you capture to illustrate the points the document makes? Would you stay in one place or move through different scenes? Would you do close-ups or survey the entire scene from afar? What or whom would you feature, or put off to the side, in the background, or outside the frame altogether? Think about examples you would use, and emotions or action you could show. What analogies could you draw? Take some notes.

STEP 3: Now imagine that your audience members are blind and deaf, and that they have a short attention span. It is your job to describe to them the most compelling things about what you just recorded. Grab your keyboard or a pen and start writing down these descriptions. Draw on the tips in this chapter.

⌐Focus on the verbs⌐ 11

The title of this chapter is one of my favorite mantras. But why do I love verbs so much?

These little engines drive the English language. They show action, movement, feeling, and drama. They bring ordinary scenes or descriptions to life. If you conceal or neglect your verbs, you are likely to end up with a snoozer of a document.

Verbs are especially important as you write to inspire your readers to act in ways that will benefit your community. You want to encourage a sense of participation in a living, breathing organization or movement that accepts and embodies social responsibility with fairness, integrity, professionalism, and creativity. Using strong verbs can go a long way in that effort.

Check out my tips to highlight the verbs in your writing and put them to work for you.

FAVOR THE ACTIVE VOICE

Verbs in the passive voice are, well, passive. They connote an unresponsive state of affairs, with not much action or movement. They leave out the subject (who or what is performing the action) and focus on the object (the recipient of the action). In essence, the supposed actor or character is simply lying there passively — like a wet rag — receiving action but not doing a thing.

One easy way to spot passive constructions is to check for verbs that come after a helping form of "to be," and/or before the word "by." These sentences leave a lot of questions unanswered with their vague, lifeless descriptions.

EXAMPLES

1. Hundreds of women in the U.S. are physically or sexually abused every minute. *(We don't know who is abusing the women, or how or why.)*

2. The United States is seen as a land of opportunity. *(By whom? Why?)*

3. Jobs were lost by thousands of local factory workers. *(The factory workers may not have "done" anything, but do you want to make them passive here?)*

On the other hand, verbs in the active voice state what is happening and *who* or *what* is doing the action. They create a more robust sentence and allow you to describe the situation more powerfully and, often, more honestly.

Active verbs pack a serious punch. They can:

- ◉ clarify your meaning;

- ◉ engage your readers in your work;

- ◉ pinpoint causes of problems and hold appropriate parties responsible for their actions;

- ◉ maintain the identity, activity, and efficacy of your characters;

- ◉ bring a human face to the issue;

- ◉ allow you to convey well-chosen details;

- ◉ eliminate excess words, especially prepositions and "to be" verbs (which I discuss later in this chapter).

Yes, verbs really can do all that.

Ask yourself: *Would you rather act (with a verb in the active voice) or be acted upon by someone or something unspecified (in the passive voice)?*

Look at how you can boost your impact by changing passive verbs into active verbs:

EXAMPLES

1. *Original:* Hundreds of women are physically or sexually abused every minute.

   We add much more information about the responsible parties, and avoid focusing only on the women as victims, when we write:

   Suggested revision: Romantic partners, friends, relatives, and even strangers physically or sexually abuse hundreds of women every minute.

2. *Original:* The United States is seen as a land of opportunity.

   Decide whom you are talking about and declare:

   Suggested revision: Immigrants from around the world see the United States as a land of opportunity.

3. *Original:* Jobs were lost by thousands of local factory workers.

   Although we know who lost their jobs, to emphasize the people (not the jobs) write instead:

   Suggested revision: Thousands of local factory workers lost their jobs.

   Do you see how verbs in the active voice clarify and strengthen these sentences?

Here is another example focusing on the people involved:

EXAMPLE

Original: The issue will be voted on in Iowa's 2010 election.

Suggested revision: Iowans will vote on the issue in their 2010 election.

Sometimes writers intentionally use the passive voice to distract, confuse, or mislead by glossing over the subject (the person or group who did the action) and focusing on the object. This strategy is popular among those who would rather not assign responsibility, accept blame, or detail the situation.

EXAMPLE

Original: An indication of industrial waste has been detected in the groundwater.

Suggested revision: Several independent groups of prominent scientists have detected industrial waste in the groundwater.

Even if you are not trying to obscure anything, use passive verbs only when you have a particular reason to do so. For instance, passive verbs are fine to use if:

- a sentence sounds too awkward with active verbs;
- the people or things doing the action are less important than the objects;
- the actors are assumed;
- you don't know who the actors are;
- you are doing it for effect.

EXAMPLES

1. The organization was founded in 1975 by three public-interest attorneys.

2. The federal CAN-SPAM Act was passed in 2001.

3. The community arts center renovation has been completed.

4. Mistakes were made — but they were corrected!

Bonus Tip

Some online copywriting intentionally uses the passive voice to place search engine-friendly keywords at the beginnings of sentences. Again, this should be the exception rather than the rule.

USE VIVID VERBS

 Ask yourself: *Even if your verbs all use the active voice, are they as strong as they can be?*

Replace everyday verbs, including those that require adverbs or prepositions, with more potent or unusual single-word verbs that convey your precise meaning. Try to paint a picture so your readers see the scene in their mind's eye.

> **EXAMPLES**
>
> 1. *Original:* "walked slowly"
>
>   *Suggested revision:* trudged, wandered, tiptoed, crept, dawdled, ambled, shuffled, strutted, promenaded
>
>   *See how vivid verbs evoke distinct images and precise meanings?*
>
> 2. "Tip over" can become topple; "take out" becomes delete. For "look at," use: stare, gaze, view, or glare.
>
> 3. *Original:* She collaborated with another dancer, Katie Green, who did the choreography.
>
> 4. *Suggested revision:* She collaborated with another dancer, Katie Green, who choreographed the piece.
>
> 5. *Original:* I worked well within the cross-cultural environment at my previous job.
>
>   *You can say more than that! How about:*
>
>   *Suggested revision:* At my previous job, I developed extensive cross-cultural communication skills through daily work with colleagues from Asia, Africa, and Latin America.

And definitely, positively, by all means: Feel free to use a thesaurus.

WATCH OUT FOR UBIQUITOUS CONJUGATIONS OF THE VERB "TO BE"

Major offenders in this area include: "there is," "there are," and "it is." Academic semanticists like to use the term "E-prime" (i.e., a slight variation of the English language) to describe the intensified style of writing and speaking that eliminates forms of "to be."

That vaguest of verbs often tops the list of common verbs, and its third-person version ("is") often ends up on lists of the ten most frequently used English words. Clearly, minimizing these run-of-the-mill verbs will help your work stand out.

To help eliminate them, focus on optimizing your description of the action involved.

EXAMPLES

1. *Original:* There are only a few community-building efforts that explicitly name and address institutional or structural racism in their work.

    Suggested revision: Only a few community-building efforts explicitly name and address institutional or structural racism in their work.

2. *Original:* The emergency food pantry is helpful to hundreds of individuals and families in times of crisis.

    Suggested revision: The emergency food pantry helps hundreds of individuals and families in times of crisis.

3. *Original:* David is a doctor who works in several community clinics in Zimbabwe.

    Suggested revision: David practices medicine in several community clinics in Zimbabwe.

Nixing "to be" usage can also produce more concise sentences. You may even find that some of them function as extraneous "throat-clearing," as I described in Chapter 9, "Start with a punchy opening."

Using E-prime often helps clarify your writing. In particular, E-prime can encourage you to write from your own rich experience, and refrain from making sweeping statements or implying that your opinion represents the absolute truth.

EXAMPLES

1. *Original: Illusions* by Richard Bach is a great book.

    Suggested revision: I truly enjoyed reading *Illusions* by Richard Bach.

2. *Original:* This enchilada is fantastic!

    Suggested revision: This enchilada looks, tastes and smells fantastic!

Remember President Clinton's remark during his testimony before the federal grand jury on August 17, 1998? He tried to muddy the waters about his relationship with Monica Lewinsky by arguing that, "It depends on what the meaning of the word 'is' is," referring to whether there is (or had been) a sexual affair between them. That little verbal dodge was meant to distinguish between a nonexistent current affair and a very real past affair. Clinton could honestly attest to the former and had tried to conceal the latter.

(I wonder what would have happened if everyone had been speaking in E-prime that day. We might have gotten a bit more clarity and accountability.)

But remember that even though using E-prime often strengthens our writing, that technique can sometimes sound stilted, artificial, strange, or downright silly. Use your best judgment.

EXAMPLES

1. *The famous soliloquy in Shakespeare's Hamlet:*

   To be or not to be,
   That is the question.

   Would become:
   To exist or not to exist,
   That must I decide.

   (This seems rather more scientific than philosophical!)

2. *The old poem:*

   Roses are red
   Violets are blue
   Honey is sweet
   And so are you

   Would turn into:
   Roses appear red
   Violets appear blue
   Honey seems sweet
   And so do you

   (Not nearly as flattering!)

TEASE OUT THE CONCEALED VERBS

Often a verb finds a comfy hiding place in a long phrase and ends up diluting the sentence. To avoid this fate, try using a single-word verb instead of a wordy construction containing one or more words.

Likely hiding spots for interesting (but diluted) verbs come right after forms of *give, have, make, do, provide, perform,* or *take.* Another way to uncover hidden verbs is to search for words that end with "-tion" or "-ment." Too often, we writers "give an explanation" instead of "explain," and "make a choice" instead of "choose." It is a nasty habit that suffocates our good friends, healthy verbs.

EXAMPLES

1. *Original:* We made the decision to hire new staff for the program.

   Suggested revision: We decided to hire new program staff. *or,* We will hire new program staff.

The main action here is not making a decision, but deciding. Actually, you may not even need to say that you decided because there is an even more powerful verb involved: will hire.

2. *Original:* The mission of our organization is to give inspiration to thousands of people in our community and to give them encouragement to take action for the environment.

   Suggested revision: The mission of our organization is to inspire and activate thousands of people in our community on behalf of the environment.

USE SIMPLE VERB FORMS

Simple verb tenses and constructions add more punch to your sentences than complex ones do. They are easier to immediately understand, are more concise, and they do not need helping verbs (from the "to be" or "to have" family) to make their point.

Minimize your use of "-ing" verb forms (i.e., participles and gerunds), by changing the verb to the simple form or the infinitive (preceded by "to").

EXAMPLES

1. *Original:* He is feeling sick because of the polluted air in his office.

   Suggested revision: He feels sick because of the polluted air in his office.

2. *Original:* Getting revenge by resorting to armed conflict leaves us with the reputation of being thugs.

   Suggested revision: If we resort to armed conflict to get revenge, we earn a thug's reputation.

3. *Original:* After having researched endangered species in the wild for decades, Dr. Yang is currently touring the country giving presentations.

   Suggested revision: Dr. Yang's national speaking tour concerns his decades of research on endangered species in the wild.

   This third example is a more subtle revision. I turned the unnecessarily complex verb forms ("having researched" and "is touring") into nouns and pulled out the implied verb ("concerns") to re-organize the sentence.

(For more pointers on verbs, refer to Chapter 21, "Reach agreement on your subjects, verbs, and pronouns.")

WRITING WORKOUT

These exercises give you practice breathing new life into your verbs — and thus your sentences.

STEP 1: Try your hand at recasting these verbs in the active voice. Remember that passive sentences often do not mention the actors, so you may need to supply new information in your revisions.

A. *Original:* If the planned action is decided upon, and facilitation services are requested of our firm, a bid will be developed for those services.

Suggested revision:

B. *Original:* As a result of recent events in our community, we were invited to create a neighborhood policing program.

Suggested revision:

C. *Original:* Reduce, reuse, and recycle, the three Rs of waste management traditionally referred to, should be supplemented with a fourth R: rethink.

Suggested revision:

D. *Original:* Our organization was founded by local activists who were told by an angry mob to "love it or leave it."

Suggested revision:

E. *Original:* Women were finally given the vote in 1920.

Suggested revision:

F. *Original:* Many precious books in the Iraq National Library and Archives were burned in 2003.

Suggested revision:

G. *Original:* A decision was made that we would start ignoring the unjust law.

Suggested revision:

H. *Original:* When was America discovered by the Europeans?

Suggested revision:

STEP 2: Revise these sentences to feature more vivid verbs.

I. *Original:* The income of the average working family in our city has gone down a lot during the past three decades.

Suggested revision:

J. *Original:* The board wants to do a CEO search, but there are many barriers in the way.

Suggested revision:

K. *Original:* She was doing a comparison of five different electric bicycles.

Suggested revision:

L. *Original:* The website article provided clarification and explanation of the new city ordinance.

Suggested revision:

M. *Original:* The scientists looked carefully at each specimen with a microscope.

Suggested revision:

N. *Original:* Our grantmaking emphasis is given to projects that encourage citizen participation and are models for other initiatives across the country.

Suggested revision:

O. *Original:* It is interesting to note that public radio is becoming more popular now. But it is also true that funding it is harder than ever.

Suggested revision:

STEP 3: Replace the following phrases with single-word verbs.

- arrive at a conclusion
- be in attendance
- come to a complete stop
- extend an invitation
- give encouragement
- have the capability to
- hold a discussion
- make simple
- take into consideration

STEP 4: Simplify and enliven the verbs in these sentences.

P. *Original:* Giving a briefing to the staff on the new policy is on the Director's agenda.

Suggested revision:

Q. *Original:* The two agencies will be merging soon and that will lead to them being able to leverage their strengths.

Suggested revision:

Get crystal clear. **12**

LITZLER

"SORRY. YOUR INSTANT MESSAGE WASN'T CLEAR AND NOW YOU HAVE TO TALK TO ME."

Any time your readers have to fish through your document to find the essential points—or have to read your sentences more than once—you have wasted their time. And they will not be happy for it.

As a writer, you have to make sure that your readers never have to stop to wonder what you are trying to say. You cannot expect them to work too hard to decipher your words. They may have generous souls, but even the most patient reader has limits.

You want your writing to be easy to understand and remember. The simpler the better. (But not simplistic!) Choosing uncluttered, elegant, and clean words should be your goal. Clear, efficient writing makes for satisfied readers.

You will be glad to know there is no shortage of techniques you can use to clarify your writing. Here are a few of them, and you will find several more throughout this book.

> *"Those who write clearly have readers; those who write obscurely have commentators."*
>
> — Albert Camus

CLARIFY WORD MEANINGS IF THERE IS ANY CHANCE OF CONFUSION

English lends itself to mix-ups (and wordplay) because it is full of words with more than one meaning.

EXAMPLES

1. "Terminal" means something different to a doctor (deadly), office worker (workstation), and an airplane pilot (spot to land or take off).

2. "Critical" can describe something extremely important, a very serious medical condition, or someone that analyzes by finding weaknesses.

3. You may be "interested" in something or someone in any number of ways: financially, academically, personally, sexually, professionally, etc.

4. In public-benefit organizations, we often use "development" to mean fundraising, programmatic growth, or socio-economic improvements.

Ottoman or ottoman?

Comedian Eddie Izzard uses wordplay in his monologue about European history: "In Europe, everyone had empires…Turkey had the Ottoman empire, full of furniture for some reason."

Headlines sometimes end up having some clarity problems because of double meanings. Here are a few funny, pun-ridden, and supposedly real ones:

EXAMPLES

I have underlined the words most in question.

- Safety Experts Say School Bus Passengers Should Be Belted
- Drunk Gets Nine Months in Violin Case
- Farmer Bill Dies in House
- Iraqi Head Seeks Arms
- Prostitutes Appeal to Pope
- British Left Waffles on Falkland Islands
- Eye Drops off Shelf
- Stolen Painting Found by Tree
- Teachers Strike Idle Kids   *(www.e-writers.net/jokes2.html)*

So when the context does not make your meaning absolutely clear, find a more precise word, or at least clarify the existing one.

EXAMPLES

1. *Original:* The headline "Teachers Strike Idle Kids" sounds pretty brutal.

   Suggested revision: "Teachers on Strike; Kids Idle" clarifies the situation.

2. Sometimes a misinterpreted word can make the difference between life and death. Psycholinguist Steven Pinker cites an incident in New England, where a rescue crew came to save a woman who had fallen "on the ice." While she definitely had fallen on the ice, she also had fallen *through* the ice. Because she was submerged, and the rescuers were looking for her on the surface, she was not found before she perished in the frigid water.

Remember that many words have different connotations to different communities. Be aware of how your readers might interpret your words in ways you may not intend. Emotions, experiences, or different communication styles may come into play here. If there is any chance that you will be misunderstood, rethink your word choice.

Personally speaking

A few years ago, I gave a workshop to a group of grantseekers from Russian nonprofit organizations. They questioned me about my meaning when I kept saying the word "community." They noted how often we Americans use it and how it means different things all the time. They wanted to know: Did I mean a local neighborhood, a national or global group of like-minded people, an online gathering space, or what? It was a reminder that while we may all speak English, we may not truly speak the same language.

Let me be clear: I do not advise that you avoid issues or concepts that may be controversial. I simply mean to encourage you to pay close attention to the terms you use. (See Chapter 6, "Write with reader diversity in mind," for a deeper discussion of this issue.)

EXAMPLES

1. The word "police" might connote protection and safety in a wealthy neighborhood that just experienced a rash of car thefts or break-ins. But the same word may arouse terror, anxiety, or anger in a neighborhood where police brutality reigns.

2. "Moral values," "abortion," and "racism" are often hot-button words on many levels.

3. Men and women may tend to understand or use words such as "emotional" or "sorry" in different ways.

In addition, make sure that the word you use is *actually* the word you mean to use. If you think you might be confusing it with similar words, be sure to double-check. Examples may include: accept/except, allude/elude, everyday/every day, and continuous/continual. (Check out Chapter 23, "Sort out confusing words," for more info.)

BE SPECIFIC

Vagueness and wishy-washy descriptions help no one.

EXAMPLE

There may be dozens of results from services and activities implemented through investment in our Eco-Zone strategy. The strategy could impact multiple systems and multiple issues in a number of ways. The total impact could be much greater than a focused strategy that impacts only one or two results in a measurably significant way.

If you can use a number, name, or other specific reference, go ahead and do it. Avoid generalizations and unsubstantiated opinions.

Remember to include enough background information to support your claims—but don't go overboard. It is a fine balancing act. You want to give your readers enough information to draw their own conclusions, but not so much that they drown in data. If appropriate and necessary, you might even want to use a footnote or two.

Bonus Tip

Double meanings can also yield some clever copy. The phrase "it's about time" can refer to how fast and convenient your product or service is, while also suggesting that we have been waiting for it for ages. The popular title format "_____ Matters" (e.g., "Health Matters") also relies on a double meaning: "Matters" refers to both the importance of the topic and the variety of issues relating to the topic at hand.

EXAMPLES

1. *Original:* The tutoring program was very successful!

   (What do you mean by successful? Shouldn't the reader be the judge of that?)

   Suggested revision: We are thrilled to report that 60 out of the 70 young readers in our tutoring program demonstrated a reading-skill increase of at least one full grade level—in just 4 months.

2. *Original:* Many of our employees participated in community volunteer projects on company time. They loved the experience!

   (Can you be any more specific?)

   Suggested revision: This year, over 200 of our employees participated in community volunteer projects on company time. Over 95% of them described the experience as "very" or "extremely" positive, often using words such as "empowering," "enriching," "meaningful," and "valuable."

3. *Original:* The Kids Love Art program is for students in Monroe County schools who are in need. In our first year, we reached over 1300 elementary school children, and we are pleased with the program's positive impact.

   Suggested revision: The Kids Love Art program involves students in Monroe County schools who live in socioeconomic crisis (based on poverty indicators such as the percentage of children eligible for free lunch). In our first year, we reached over 1300 elementary school children, and we have already seen the program's positive impact. Students and their parents are now interested in local performing arts events, and teachers have asked us to help them integrate performance art into their classroom lessons.

You may have noticed that in the above examples, the original sentences relied on forms of the verb "to be." This construction often crops up in vague sentences; using a more specific verb will often lead to increased clarity. For more information about that, see Chapter 11, "Focus on the verbs."

Of course, you need to make sure that everything is accurate. If you do not know the exact fact or detail you need, look it up or leave it out. Don't try to gloss over it or (worse) hope to slide by with errors. (Leave a note to yourself in the draft to fill in the data later.)

EXPLAIN, USING LOTS OF EXAMPLES

Complex ideas or trends are much easier to illustrate with juicy examples than with worn-out descriptions. How many times have you asked for an example when you were trying to understand a new concept? All good teachers and journalists know that an illustrative or symbolic example is worth far more than a long-winded explanation.

An example or anecdote that makes your point will often stick in your reader's mind.

> **EXAMPLE**
>
> *To explain this assertion:*
>
> If evaluators want to get accurate data, they must consider the situations, values, and cultures of the people they are evaluating.
>
> *you can provide an example, such as:*
>
> We found that when we first evaluated the Neighborhood Family Initiative in an area of the city where many new immigrants live, we were asking inappropriate questions. When we asked respondents, "Is your family well?" and presented options ranging from "strongly disagree" to "strongly agree," many respondents expressed their frustration and confusion. They did not know if we were referring to their family here or back home or both, and what we meant by "well."

Make sure your examples draw upon the realities of as many of your readers as possible. Use names, places, and other details that represent many different cultures and life choices.

But don't worry if good examples are not coming to you very easily as you hammer out your first or second draft. Mark the spots where you would like to include them and continue on your merry way. Don't let roadblocks such as this interrupt your writing flow.

BREAK DOWN PROCESSES & SYSTEMS STEP-BY-STEP OR COMPONENT-BY-COMPONENT

Your readers are looking to you for simple ways to understand your topic, and all the more so as the topic becomes more complex.

Imagine an extremely useful (but, alas, rare) "do-it-yourself" instruction booklet that explains what pieces you will find in the box and how to assemble your new bookcase, backyard barbecue set, or new audio equipment. It will prevent you from building odd-looking and nonfunctional contraptions with extra screws, holes, or other random parts jutting out of the wrong spots or ending up in the leftover pile.

Your writing needs to feature just that sort of lucidity. And, either before or after you break it down for your readers, show how all of the components work together to form a larger, heartier whole.

Personally speaking

If you grew up in the 1970s or 80s, you may recall the *Schoolhouse Rock!* series of television spots. These short cartoons taught grammar, history, science, and other subjects with entertaining examples and songs. I still love watching them on YouTube and singing along.

Personally speaking

This book would fall on its metaphorical face without the copious examples I feature in every chapter. Just think how much lower the value would be to you without them.

Bonus Tip

Do you prefer to move through your points organically, with less of a linear structure? "Mindmapping," popularized by Tony Buzan, is one alternative. In this technique, you draw relationships between and among key words or images to show relationships. You can start with an idea in the center and then branch out into different facets or threads. To use mindmaps in your written documents to enhance your clarity, you will need to include a well-labeled diagram. For more about how graphics can help clarify your words, see Chapter 20, "Make sure it *looks* right."

Personally speaking

I must confess that I am a compulsive list maker. Lists help me track and organize my thoughts. I then break out the spreadsheet software (faster than you can say "out of control") when my list gets too difficult to keep straight in my head.

EXAMPLES

1. Wikipedia, the Web-based free encyclopedia written by over 75,000 volunteers around the world, offers an excellent example of components working together marvelously. This huge collaborative writing project compiles more than fourteen million articles in more than 260 languages (as of early 2010). Each entry begins with an overview and goes on to include a clear breakdown of many facets of the topic at hand. It also links to a number of related articles within the Wikipedia system, as well as outside sources. *(www.wikipedia.org)*

2. Each of the Writing Workouts in this book begins with a brief introduction to tell you what to expect, or what you will get out of the exercise (i.e., how it all fits together). I then break down the exercise into a few easy-to-follow steps.

GIVE A QUICK RUNDOWN IN A LIST

One handy way to share your thoughts is in an outline or list. That is, use a bulleted or numbered sequence. While this technique may or may not thrill you as a writer, lists often help readers get a quick and clear—and comprehensive—sense of your message. Just make sure that you also provide any explanation, annotation, or embellishment that your list may need.

Here are several things to remember about building a list (yes, I am using a list in this explanation):

1. Make sure it is complete and not redundant. Readers often see a list as a checklist that covers what they need to know or do. Keep in mind that they might even lift your list and use it as a stand-alone piece.

2. Introduce your list with background information and solid labeling, so it actually makes sense to your reader. Content without context is of limited value and can instead confuse.

3. An overgrown list does not benefit your reader as much as a concise one. Carefully prioritize and prune yours to identify both the essentials and any side points you want to make. (See Chapter 18, "Cultivate conciseness," for more about brevity.)

4. Make list items complete sentences whenever possible.

5. Keep your list items parallel in structure. (For more information on that, check out Chapter 22, "Get a handle on your sentence structure.")

IN GENERAL, STAY AWAY FROM DOUBLE NEGATIVES

I am not just talking about grammatical double negatives as in the classic phrase, "Don't use no double negatives." Dig a little deeper and you will find that by saying something is "not" something that is already stated in the negative, you can whip up a lot of confusion. After all, writing should not be akin to an algebraic expression, where you painstakingly cancel out as many negative signs as possible to finally arrive at the solution.

 A Lecture About English

A linguistics professor was lecturing to his English class one day. "In English," he said, "a double negative forms a positive. In some languages, though, such as Russian, a double negative is still a negative. However, there is no language wherein a double positive can form a negative."

A voice from the back of the room piped up, "Yeah, right." *(www.ahajokes.com)*

If you can state something directly, and in the affirmative, do so. Doing this will take the guesswork out of having to unravel what you mean when you say things like, "We will not refrain from calling for changes in the policy if we notice that they are not lacking in obscurity." (Say that three times fast!)

EXAMPLES

1. *Original:* We did not choose to discontinue the online marketing campaign.

   Suggestion revision: We chose to continue the online marketing campaign.

2. *Original:* They did not remember that they were not to unlock the doors.

   Suggestion revision: They forgot to keep the doors locked.

3. *Original:* (From the British politician Boris Johnson) I couldn't fail to disagree with you less.

   Suggestion revision: I disagree with you.

But on an occasion when you want to be extremely diplomatic, intentionally nebulous, or rhetorical, you can employ a dash of double negatives. For example, you might say, "The Director did not dislike the decorations at the fundraising gala."

MAKE SURE YOUR PRONOUN REFERENCES ARE CLEAR

You probably have some kind of memory of this one from English class. But here it is again: Pronouns (she, he, it, this, them, we, etc.) should refer to the closest noun in your sentence (the pronoun's antecedent).

> "*Don't write merely to be understood. Write so that you cannot possibly be misunderstood.*"
>
> — Robert Louis Stevenson

EXAMPLES

1. *Original:* The hiring manager and the jobseeker knew that she was not getting her needs met.

   (Who was not getting her needs met? The director? The jobseeker? Both of them?)

   Suggested revision: The hiring manager knew that she was not getting her needs met, because the jobseeker kept repeating irrelevant information.

2. *Original:* I agree that a unanimous vote by the board to change the bylaws is a bit extreme. I am not sure why they instituted this in the first place.

   (Whom are we referring to as "they": the current board or some other entity? Are we questioning the requirement of a unanimous vote to change the bylaws, or something about the bylaws themselves?)

   Suggested revision: I agree that the requirement of a unanimous vote by the board to change the bylaws is a bit extreme. I am not sure why this voting policy exists.

Another pronoun clarity problem may show its face when you use the same pronoun to refer to two different groups in the same segment of your piece.

EXAMPLE

Original: Our family is blessed with plenty of money, real estate, and bright ideas. We now need to figure out how to use those resources to benefit our community. One trend we found several times in our research was an interest in investing in social entrepreneurs: people who are starting businesses to address today's most pressing social problems.

Here, "we" refers to both the entire family and a subset that did some research. Let's clarify the paragraph:

Suggested revision: Our family is blessed with plenty of money, real estate, and bright ideas. We now need to figure out how to use those resources to benefit our community. A few of us—one person from each of the three living generations—spoke with our peer family members. One trend that kept cropping up was an interest in investing in social entrepreneurs: people who are starting businesses to address today's most pressing social problems.

WRITING WORKOUT

STEP 1: Here are a few sentences similar to those I have helped clients clarify in their pieces. Now you can take a stab at them! Edit so that the reader can more easily understand—and act upon—the information. Feel free to invent any missing data to add specifics and examples.

A. *Original*: We are working with our team to identify various marketing strategies, and this can be a specific question we discuss with the Board.

(What exactly is the question you will be discussing?)

Suggested revision:

B. *Original:* We have made great progress in building effective partnerships with parents in our in-home educational services program.

(What, specifically, do you mean by "great progress"? What kind of effective partnerships are you referring to?)

Suggested revision:

C. *Original:* At my previous position I coordinated fundraising events and participated in the strategic planning process.

(Are we talking about black-tie receptions or car washes and bake sales? What was your role in the strategic planning process—and why was that process important to your organization at the time?)

Suggested revision:

D. *Original:* It is not infrequent that the director does not budget accurately.

(What does this sentence mean to convey?)

Suggested revision:

E. *Original:* After losing her teenage sister in a drunk driving accident, she wanted to get involved somehow.

(What did she want to get involved in, exactly?)

Suggested revision:

F. *Original:* I except the idea that our trucks could reduce their greenhouse gas emissions, but the steps to take to make that happen continue to allude me.

(Check for confused words here.)

Suggested revision:

G. *Original:* The boy and his father knew that he was in trouble.

(Whom did the writer mean to say was in trouble? The boy? His father?)

Suggested revision:

> " *The most powerful factors in the world are clear ideas in the minds of energetic men [and women] of good will.* "
> — J. Arthur Thomson

STEP 2: Now look at a piece that you—or one of your colleagues—has recently written. See if you can find any spots that could use a little clarifying, particularly in light of the lessons in this chapter. For instance, if you described a process or system, did you give enough detail to clarify how it works? Can you separate out any vague or confusing language into a concise list? Would an example help illuminate a new concept? Use a colored pen to mark your suggested changes in the piece.

If you chose to edit a colleague's piece, think about whether he or she would appreciate your edits. If so, go ahead and share them.

~Avoid jargon~ 13

LITZLER

"THE AGENDA IS COUNTERFEIT IF YOU HOLD IT UP TO THE LIGHT AND THE B.S. SHOWS THROUGH."

I confess. I succumb to shoptalk just as easily as the next person.

Community-benefit organizations are notorious for using jargon or unexplained acronyms for even the simplest ideas. Sometimes we get so used to talking in verbal shorthand that we end up doing the same thing in writing. We can swim in jargon so much that we don't even realize that we are dripping with it when we come up for air. In addition, we all like to feel like insiders, and sometimes speaking an insider language can contribute to that feeling.

That is fine—or even necessary—for the workplace. But when you are trying to reach beyond your particular office, organization, or close-knit group of collaborators, you have to watch out.

Let's face it: Words wield great power. You can use them to demystify your work and engage your readers, or to confuse and alienate them. The last thing you want to do is provoke them to throw up their hands in frustration and disgust.

Ask yourself: *When was the last time you attended a meeting, read a piece, or heard a conversation that was full of jargon unfamiliar to you? How did this make you feel?*

You probably felt some combination of lost, bored, overwhelmed, and anxious— or that you had just been stranded on another planet. You might have been curious about what was going on, but unless you had a lot of extra time and special motivation, you most likely lost interest in a hurry.

Please don't do that to your poor readers! Instead, strive to make all your words easy to understand at a glance. Here's how.

USE WORDS THAT YOUR READER USES

Ask yourself: *Would your readers use the term you are considering?*

We best understand a word or concept if we can use it ourselves. Remember all those vocabulary drills in school where you had to "use the word in a sentence"? If you cannot imagine your intended reader using your terms in their sentences, rephrase.

> *"The purpose of writing is to inflate weak ideas, obscure pure reasoning, and inhibit clarity. With a little practice, writing can be an intimidating and impenetrable fog!"*
>
> — Calvin in Bill
> Watterson's
> *Calvin & Hobbes*

EXAMPLES

1. *Original:* Our organization promotes food security for all.

   (An artist friend of mine once told me that she visualized a carrot shackled to the floor when she first heard this term.)

   Suggested revision: Our organization works to ensure that enough nutritious food is always available and affordable to everyone.

2. *Original:* With the LOHAS market booming, you stand to lose a lot of customers if you don't adopt socially responsible business practices.

   Suggested revision: More and more of your customers are leading lifestyles of personal health and planetary sustainability. You stand to lose out if you don't adopt socially responsible business practices.

3. *Original:* At our research institute, we study women's transition away from pink-color jobs and into nontraditional jobs.

   Suggested revision: At our research institute, we study women's transition away from low-paying jobs traditionally held by women (such as secretary, housecleaner, waitress, and daycare provider) and into higher paying blue-collar jobs (such as electrician, plumber, and firefighter).

Also, your organization may be using a familiar term in a way that differs from its use in everyday English. If so, you need to explain that difference to your reader.

Ask yourself: *What does it mean to your organization? And is that the most common understanding of the word or phrase?*

EXAMPLE

An organizational client of mine used the term "supportive community" to describe what they offered teens and young adults. Do you think they meant: a therapy support group, an emotionally close-knit group of friends and mentors, a religious cult, a cheerleading squad, or adults who can financially underwrite the young people?

Your readers, like all of us, surely use slang from time to time. Slang can also be a type of jargon, as it is only for the "in" group. Use it only if you know exactly how and when your readers use it. But avoid appropriating words or phrases from one culture to use in another just to sound hip or cool. When in doubt, skip it.

Another place jargon or unexplained terms love to hide is in your budgetary information. While some line items are self-explanatory (such as "office rent"), special procedures you undergo or unusual costs you incur need some explaining. You may label certain items in a way that makes sense to your organization internally, but leaves your outside reader in the dark. A little extra effort goes a long way.

EXAMPLE

Common budget line items that could use a bit of clarification include:

- Any brand names specific to your work that outsiders might not know
- Fundraising expenses
- Marketing and outreach
- Professional services fees
- Program materials
- Staff development
- Board expenses
- Communications
- Equipment
- Evaluation costs
- Events
- Media
- Transportation

My final point about using the same words as your reader uses: Unless you have a special reason not to—such as specific knowledge of your readers' demographics, culture, or linguistic background—stick with the English language. Words from other languages might sound impressive, but the common language in the U.S. remains English. While this state of affairs is changing in today's globalized world, non-English phrases still tend to alienate some readers. You may want to make exceptions for a few common Latin abbreviations (such as: i.e., e.g., and et al.); turn to Chapter 24, "Nail down your punctuation," for more information about those.

EXPLAIN YOUR THOUGHTS AS IF YOU WERE SPEAKING TO A NEWCOMER

Ask yourself: *If you were trying to use the simplest and most accessible terms possible to describe your subject or advocate for your idea, what would they be?*

Have you ever tried to explain something to someone whose first language is not English? Or introduce a new concept to someone who is not very familiar with it? Both exercises are great practice for ensuring that you are as clear as possible. Often, when we are too close to our topic we lose our perspective. (By the way, good editing can help with this problem, and you will find much more on that in Part IV of this book.)

Personally speaking

I like the George Carlin routine on euphemisms that have sprung up in the English language in recent decades. He notes how "dump" has become "landfill," being "broke" is now referred to as having "a negative cash-flow position," and "fired" has been replaced with "management wanted to curtail redundancies in the human resources area, so many people are no longer viable members of the workforce." It can be very tempting to sterilize the sticky issues a bit—I cannot lie to you (or, as Carlin says, "engage in disinformation").

Personally speaking

I frequently work with non-native English speakers. To be effective, I have to consider where they are coming from and make sure not to use words that have multiple meanings, are very informal, or are what I call "GRE words": words only spoken in graduate school or at think tanks.

Keep it simple! Fancy words and jargon tend to obfuscate, not elucidate (as in this sentence). Instead of impressing your reader, complicated words can backfire and make you appear detached from reality.

You might try to write your piece so that it would fit well in your hometown newspaper or *USA Today*. By simplifying or being direct, you are likely to stick to welcoming language that most of us will actually want to read. I generally recommend words with three syllables or fewer. A reader whose eyes glaze over is a reader lost.

A wonderful side effect of shaving your words for clarity's sake is that your sentences also become more concise (a central feature of effective writing, discussed in Chapter 18, "Cultivate conciseness").

PREPARE IF SOMETIMES YOU JUST *HAVE* TO TALK SHOP

You might feel an absolute need to use certain technical terms or acronyms. For instance, you may want to promote the use of a specific term or redefine one that is often misused. That is fine on an occasional basis; just make sure that you explain your terms the first time you use them, and/or create a brief glossary for your readers' reference. Repeating new terms throughout the piece will introduce them to your readers. However, avoid using more than a few new terms at once.

Bonus Tip

Check out Appendix 7 for a fun (and popular) formula for measuring how difficult your words are to understand: the Gunning Fog Index. Once you arrive at a general sense of your clarity (or lack thereof) you can adjust accordingly.

EXAMPLES

1. *The United Way of the Bay Area's 2004 report,* The Bottom Line: Setting the Real Standard for Bay Area Working Families, *focuses on issues related to the technical term "economic self-sufficiency." So, they immediately define it on the first page:*

   Achieving economic self-sufficiency means not having to choose between the most basic needs—choosing between housing and healthcare, or between childcare and food.   *(www.uwba.org)*

2. Give Something Back Business Products, Inc. prides itself on being a "green" company, offering green office supplies. But they don't just toss that term around. Their website features a glossary that outlines exactly what they mean. Among the words they define are:

   - Chlorine-free
   - Compostable
   - Recycled paper
   - Sustainability

   (www.givesomethingback.com)

Of course, if you are writing for colleagues in your field, you can feel free to use the generally accepted lingo. The good news: If you clear out the jargon, you can often recycle or reuse parts of your internal documents (e.g., grant proposals or reports) in the marketing or fundraising materials you write for a broader readership.

CHECK YOUR USE OF ACRONYMS

But, you may ask, what about using acronyms that refer to your organization or programs, especially when they have long names? Your primary concern here is to avoid alphabet soup that confuses or alienates your reader. See if you can abbreviate the names so that you retain the essence but provide smaller mouthfuls in your repeated references.

EXAMPLES

1. Your organization is The Center for Improved Infancy and Child Development, and you operate the Alliance for Quality Adoption Program, the Babies Are Beautiful Program, and the Childcare Workers' Rights Program.

   Instead of referring to yourself as the CIICD, you can refer to your organization as "The Center." Your programs—AQAP, BBP, and CWRP—can become the Adoption Program, the Babies Program, and the Workers Program. Of course, the first time you refer to these programs you would spell them out in full.

2. You might refer to the "Coalition of Writers Focused on Accessible, Jargon-Free Language" as CWFAJFL. But who can remember that—especially if it appears in a document with five other acronyms, all competing for space in your poor reader's attention span? You will do far better if you refer to the group as "The Coalition of Writers."

Bonus Tip

When naming organizations, programs, services, or products, think about the acronym or abbreviation that you would be stuck with. This is similar to naming a child and considering the nicknames that might spring forth. Also, great acronyms can actually add to or reinforce their own meanings. A couple of great examples are WOW (Wider Opportunities for Women) and ECO (Environmental Careers Organization).

WRITING WORKOUT

STEP 1: Take out a red pen and go through a document your organization recently produced. Mark any words that might make an outsider — such as your hair stylist, your grandfather, a coffee shop clerk, or your dentist — look at you with a puzzled expression, ignore you, or just walk away. If you need help, ask for it directly from such folks.

In the unlikely event that you have no red marks on your document, take a look at these frequently used jargon-y words from public-benefit organizations of all types. (I spell out meanings of acronyms in parentheses.)

- 501(c)(3) or (4) (tax identification numbers)
- Above or below the poverty line
- At-risk young people
- Benchmarking
- Capacity-building
- CBO (community-based organization)
- Change agent
- Civic participation
- COB (close of business)
- Consensus
- Continuum of care
- Cooperative learning
- Core competencies
- Cost center
- CRM (contact relationship management)
- CSR (corporate social responsibility)
- Deliverables
- Disincent
- Driver of change
- Empowerment
- Enable

- Facetime
- Grassroots/grasstops
- Learning-based feedback
- Leverage
- Logic model
- LOHAS (Lifestyles of Health and Sustainability)
- LOI (letter of inquiry/intent)
- Meaningful jobs
- Metrics
- Modality
- NGO (non-governmental organization)
- Paradigm
- Parameter
- Proactive
- Process-oriented
- Professionally supported
- Prospecting
- Results-oriented performance measures
- Risk assessment
- ROI (return on investment)
- Scalable
- Shrink reduction
- SRI (socially responsible investing)
- Stakeholder
- Stewardship
- Supply chain
- Synergy
- Touch point
- Value-added
- Working poor

STEP 2: Try your hand at "de-jargonizing" the words you identified above. (Yes, I just coined a new term, but we are all insiders here, right?) Pretend you are writing a casual letter to a friend or a typical reader who is not a specialist in your field. How would he or she say the same thing?

STEP 3: For the next few days, be on the lookout for jargon or technical buzzwords that jump out at you during staff meetings or in everyday memos and conversations around your organization's office. Take note of them. Send the list to coworkers and get their additions (and maybe share a chuckle or two).

STEP 4: Now see if you can translate the terms (from Step 3) into language that your readers, including newcomers, would use. For technical terms that you simply have to use, think of ways to break them down.

STEP 5: Post your list of jargon (and their translations) in a prominent place in the office, or circulate it by hand or email. Leave some room at the bottom for later additions. The list will serve as a handy reminder of terms to try to avoid—and more accessible alternatives to use—when writing for any readership beyond yourselves.

Keep your piece flowing smoothly 14

A good writer guides readers as they travel together on the journey of a piece. It is your job to help your readers avoid speed bumps, hazardous curves, and dead ends. And as the tour guide, you are responsible for the nitty-gritty logistics of getting from point A to point B.

Reading works from mission-driven organizations can and should be a pleasant, rewarding experience. While your readers might initially come to your organization for your mission or the benefits you offer, they will stay for the way you treat them.

Assure your readers they are in good hands, and they will want to participate. You want your writing to provide an enjoyable and memorable ride.

You want to be easy to follow, without hesitation or distraction. Your readers should not have to worry about the details of the voyage. Instead, they should be free to contemplate the meaning of the information you are offering, how it makes them feel, and (eventually) how they will act on it.

But that kind of trust has to be earned. You have to show them that you do, indeed, know the smoothest route—that you have a roadmap and know where you are going—and that you will keep their best interests at heart. You have to assure them that you know exactly what you are doing.

So how do you do that? Let's look at some options.

ARRANGE YOUR INFORMATION INTO A SENSIBLE SEQUENCE

You have gathered your most important puzzle pieces (i.e., your content). Now you have to assemble the puzzle.

Ask yourself: What do your readers want or need to know first, second, and third (and so on) for your piece to make sense to them?

Think about how you can logically arrange your points to help build your argument toward your conclusion. For instance, you may want to tell your story or

Bonus Tip

Sometimes you will have to stick to a predetermined sequence. This is common for some formats, such as grant proposals or press releases. Even if the prescribed sequence seems to be redundant or makes little sense to you, just start plugging in your messages, making use of the set structure as best you can.

explain a process chronologically. That way, your piece will have a built-in flow, and your readers will understand how step one leads to step two.

But what if you want to try something different? Some options:

1. Start out by sharing the bottom line (a clear conclusion), and fill in background information along the way.

2. Move from simple ideas to more complex ones.

3. Divide your material by category or theme, and follow each one in turn.

4. Establish a predictable pattern to your piece that your readers can count on, similar to the way newspapers and magazines always include the same standard sections.

My main point here is to find an engaging yet understandable route to take. You might need to experiment with a few possibilities before you arrive at the best one.

USE SUBHEADS AS SIGNPOSTS

Go ahead and start grouping your messages according to your chosen sequence. The most essential messages in your copy should lend themselves to subheads, which tell your story for you. Subheads help your readers stay on track and focused on your main points.

Ask yourself: *If your readers were to read only your headline and subheads, and not the body text, would they come away with your main messages? Would they understand and remember the importance of working with you?*

If so, you are doing well. If not, go back and identify the weak spots.

> **EXAMPLE**
>
> An Annual Report from the Global Greengrants Fund tells its essential story in the first few pages using subheads, beginning with these:
>
> ⚭ Tapping the energy of communities around the world
>
> ⚭ An incubator of grassroots initiatives
>
> ⚭ Return on investment
>
> ⚭ Grantmaking on a personal scale
>
> ⚭ A new model for grantmaking   *(www.greengrants.org)*

You might also want to ask others what they expect to find in the body of your piece after reading only your headline and subheads. Ask them if these few phrases or sentences (sometimes called "micro-copy") are easy or hard to grasp at a glance.

And don't try to be overly pun-filled, cutesy, or obscure with your subheads. If you make them too vague or uninformative, they can do more harm than good.

EXAMPLE

In a piece about the fictional Aviary Consortium, the writer might have wanted to play with words in a subhead that introduces a section about the organization's ties to its community:

Original: Not just "for the birds"

But does that subhead truly give the reader any new information?

Suggested revision: Connecting Ohioans with local birds

Each subhead will signal that you are taking your readers down a slightly new but related trail. They will appreciate the alert. What may otherwise seem like abrupt directional shifts will now be indicated with landmarks and outlined by frames-of-reference.

Subheads also help your reader skim a long document. With more and more readers skimming—and never really reading—writing for that reality is essential. This is especially true online. For more about maximizing your piece's visual appeal to skimmers (and others), see Chapter 20, "Make sure it *looks* right."

LEAD YOUR READERS FROM ONE SIGNPOST TO THE NEXT

This is not as hard as it might sound. Try out different transition words and phrases that might help your readers follow your train of thought. For example, unless you are writing something especially formal, it is usually fine to start a sentence with "And," "But," or "So." These words can add a conversational flow to your piece because they mimic how people connect ideas when they speak.

Here is a list of some other useful connective words and phrases:

◉ after all	◉ in addition
◉ also	◉ in contrast
◉ another	◉ in conclusion
◉ consequently	◉ in fact
◉ despite	◉ in other words
◉ earlier	◉ in short
◉ finally	◉ indeed
◉ for example	◉ initially
◉ furthermore	◉ meanwhile

Bonus Tip

I know, I know. Your grammar school English teacher probably forbade starting a sentence with a conjunction. But the rules have become much more lenient in recent years, given the widespread use of email and blogs, as well as the drive toward increasing the accessibility of our language. This is particularly true for marketing copy. You will find more on such linguistic changes in the section titled "Picky, Picky, Picky" (Chapters 21 through 25).

✐ moreover	✐ similarly
✐ nevertheless	✐ speaking of
✐ next	✐ still
✐ not only…but also	✐ that is
✐ now	✐ that's a great segue to
✐ of course	✐ the fact remains
✐ on the contrary	✐ then
✐ on the other hand	✐ therefore
✐ once again	✐ unfortunately
✐ otherwise	✐ yet
✐ regardless	

If you want to emphasize certain points, try words and phrases such as "especially," "particularly," "most importantly," and "above all" to give your readers a heads-up.

You can also show a close relationship between two related thoughts by repeating a concept, word, or phrase—or pointing out a clear contrast—as you connect two paragraphs. This technique provides structure or rhythm to your piece. One approach is to set up a metaphor and guide your readers along it (as I do with the idea of travel throughout this chapter). See Chapters 15, "Make sure it *sounds* right," and 19, "Eliminate unintended, accidental, repetitive redundancies," for more information about intentional repetition.

ASK—AND ANSWER— GOOD QUESTIONS ALONG THE PATH

As your curious readers allow you to lead the way, they are bound to come up with ideas. By giving voice to their questions—and following up with answers—you can show that you are right there with your readers at every turn. Well-written questions and answers engage your readers in a virtual dialogue with you, the writer, and can also liven up your piece with a personal touch.

In addition, you may have some questions you would like your readers to think about. Particularly if you are introducing questions that may not have occurred to your readers to ask, be sure to provide solid explanations or sample answers to set things in motion.

EXAMPLES

1. But how does all of this relate to your everyday life? Allow me to give you some examples…

2. What if you notice a problem a month after you purchase our product? No problem. Our lifetime guarantee has you covered!

3. We have all had experiences that have taught us about other races and ethnicities. What did you learn in school? On the playground? In your place of worship? What did family and friends teach you?

   You are likely to have learned to adopt derogatory attitudes toward one or more groups along the way. But did you pick up those attitudes from times and places that no longer exist? Is it time to re-examine them and possibly make a change?

(For more information about this technique, refer to Chapter 4, "Connect on a person-to-person level.")

USE FOOTNOTES WISELY TO AVOID SLOWING DOWN YOUR READER

Your sentences and paragraphs can become cluttered with background information, often known as "backstory," that is not central to the here and now of your main story. This is where footnotes can come in to save the day. However, you will want to avoid contributing to reader anxiety with too many little numbers scattered all over the page. Moderation is key here.

 Ask yourself: *Do you truly need to include all of the details in the main body of your piece, or can you delete or footnote the supporting facts or background?*

EXAMPLE

In a piece about a retreat center for women recovering from drug addiction, we might read:

Our participants come from the Essex County area of New Jersey, a severely drug-infested area of the state.

That may be enough information to provide context in the main copy; more specific or additional details or citations could then appear as a footnote.

But first, before considering footnotes, I suggest that you take a good hard look at your material. You may do better to simply cut (or save for a later document) a lot of the content you are thinking about mentioning in footnotes. Most often, only

If you think something is taking too long to say, you may have conciseness issues bogging you down. Check Chapter 18, "Cultivate conciseness," for more on this issue.

the long or formal/technical pieces you write require the sorts of information that would warrant the hassle of footnotes!

VARY YOUR PACE

No one ever said that flow must always be straight and narrow, or uniform. And it definitely should not be boring. You don't want your readers to wander away for lack of variety or adventure.

We all know what it is like to have to endure (or simply stay awake during) a seemingly endless, dull monologue. You might remember the scene in the film *Ferris Bueller's Day Off,* where the high school teacher drones, "Bueller, Bueller, Bueller......Anyone? Anyone?" and the entire class ignores him. This principle applies to reading any document. As the writer, you must keep your piece moving along at a lively and interesting clip.

If your virtual "airwaves" only carry one sound, your readers will eventually tune out. One way to avoid this fate is to use different sentence and paragraph lengths. In copywriting, this means varying from short to really, really short. A well-placed sentence fragment (discussed in Chapter 22, "Get a handle on your sentence structure") can be just one word. Right? Or you can go as long as twenty words (you will begin to lose your readers if you go too much longer). An occasional dramatic pause—caused by paragraph spacing or punctuation—can also adjust the tempo.

Another way of varying your pace: Take short detours or side trips by including particularly compelling or useful special features. For instance, you can insert client profiles, facts-at-a-glance, checklists, or pull-out boxes. You can also quote others, point to quick examples, or intersperse your straight narrative with tangential—yet relevant and important—observations. I have used many of these techniques throughout this book.

A FEW OTHER IDEAS:

1. Throw in an unexpected twist on a familiar story (refer to Chapter 5, "Share stories," for a list of common storyline types).

2. Give your readers a fun diversion: a snappy joke or cultural reference.

3. Keep your readers anticipating the next step on your journey by dropping hints (also known as "foreshadowing").

Personally speaking

This flow stuff can be hard! I am often tempted to "brain dump" all of the information I want to share—and my readers want to know—and I forget to smooth out the lumps. But smooth out we must if we want to keep our readers by our side. I know I would not want to feast on something that is only half-baked or not blended properly. Neither should I ask my readers to.

WRITING WORKOUT

In this exercise you will practice fitting together some pieces of copy.

STEP 1: Read through this text to identify some of the spots that don't flow smoothly. You might want to jot down some notes in the margins.

Organization X was founded in 1989. Our mission is to rebuild the lives of severely at-risk youth and young adults.

Disadvantaged youth in our city face significant barriers to achieving economic independence and well-being. They must deal with poverty, substance abuse, educational underachievement, lack of skills, and family instability.

Youth are looking for a path to self-sufficiency: now. It is extremely difficult for them to find paid employment-based learning opportunities that also involve the critical supportive services they need. They are searching for a place where they are valued and receive encouragement to identify and reach their own goals.

We accomplish our mission by operating four community-benefit businesses that employ and train our young clients, as they recover from homelessness, substance abuse, and related problems.

Without opportunities and a positive experience designed for their risk factors, it will be nearly impossible for these young people to attain higher education, stable employment and, ultimately, self-sufficiency as adults. Costs to society — related to public assistance benefits and incarceration alone — are enormous.

Compared to the national averages for disadvantaged adults, Organization X has yielded much *higher* rates of: sustained employment, living wages, movement from welfare to economic independence, and acquisition of stable housing.

We have also seen much *lower* rates of criminal activity.

We use a model focused on the specific needs and goals of the individual, supported by mentors and peers. Over several months and up to two years, we teach disadvantaged young people how to realize their potential and become economically independent members of their communities.

(Adapted from the work of New Door Ventures, www.newdoor.org)

STEP 2: Now rearrange the text, using a sequence that makes sense. Write subheads that guide your readers through that sequence.

STEP 3: Think about transition words or phrases you might use to bridge your paragraphs or sentences. Remember that you can also use conversational techniques, such as asking your reader questions.

STEP 4: Consider some options for varying the pace a bit to keep the piece moving along with an interesting rhythm.

STEP 5: Now rewrite the copy to integrate your flow choices.

STEP 6: Check out a few paragraphs of a document that you are working on. See if you now can smooth out some of the choppy parts of it.

Make sure it *sounds* right 15

How does your piece sound? This may seem like a strange question, given that we are focusing on the written–not spoken–word. But most people, including yours truly, hear words as they read them. You may have similar experiences.

We take for granted phrases such as "sounds good" and "I hear ya." They remind us that part of the way we understand and relate is through what we hear. As a writer, you want to always sound your best.

Second only to sight is our sense of hearing in telling us information about the world. In fact, some of us prefer learning in auditory fashion. Consider the popularity of lectures and teleseminars, or recordings of them. Audiobooks—books read aloud—are also on the rise. A phone conversation still conveys far more than an email can, and a movie or television show with no soundtrack is just not the same.

Educators, salespeople, marketers, neuroscientists, and multi-media artists all know that if you can both see and hear a message, you are more likely to remember it than if you only see it *or* hear it (the phenomenon of "multi-sensory learning"). This is important for writers to know, too.

For instance, consider the widespread use of slideshows accompanied by narration. When carried out well, this type of presentation takes full advantage of complementary modes of communication. And most successful marketing campaigns involve at least a small component of "I heard it somewhere."

But even if you do not have music, sound effects, or rich accents at your disposal, your words themselves should also have the right pitch and phrasing. Here are a few ways you can adjust your writing's musicality.

> "*Every writer is a frustrated actor who recites his lines in the hidden auditorium of his skull.*"
> — Rod Serling

LISTEN TO YOUR TONE

Ask yourself: *What kind of impression do you want to leave your readers with?*

The tone you adopt in your pieces reflects your organization's overall image and brand. It should embody a specific attitude or perspective toward your material. That is, your reader is most interested in hearing your organization's take on your topic. Be sure to offer that perspective within the tone of your writing.

EXAMPLE

Below is an excerpt from the Insight Center for Community Economic Development's organizational communications brief. It helped guide work on a major re-branding effort, reminding staff members of the agreed-upon impression the organization wanted to convey to the public. The ideal tone is:

accessible	experienced	positive/hopeful
collaborative	inclusive	professional
creative	innovative	resourceful
dedicated	insightful	strategic
effective	knowledgeable	visionary

Their website contains the following copy. Do you think it conveys their intended tone?

> We work in collaboration with foundations, nonprofits, educational institutions, government and businesses to develop, strengthen and promote programs and public policy that:
>
> - Lead to good jobs—jobs that pay enough to support a family, offer benefits and the opportunity to advance
> - Strengthen early care and education systems so that children can thrive and parents can work or go to school
> - Enable people and communities to build financial and educational assets
>
> The goal of our program work is to help families, seniors, and the communities in which they live, become and remain economically secure. We define economic security as not only having enough money to take care of yourself and your family, but also having the ability to save and develop assets. *(www.insightcced.org)*

Someone (or a group of people) at your organization should decide on what you want to sound like.

Here are a few other possibilities:

Authoritative and well-documented

> **EXAMPLE**
>
> The dearth of affordable housing in the New York City area has escalated to crisis proportions.
> *(You would back up this statement with research findings and/or quotes from outside experts.)*

Friendly, conversational, and approachable

> **EXAMPLE**
>
> We want to serve you better! Please answer our five questions in the online survey and enter to win a fabulous prize for you and a loved one. If you'd like to talk to someone instead, please call our new toll-free number with your questions and comments.

Humorous and light-hearted

> **EXAMPLE**
>
> We thought you might like to check out our human resources manual and insurance policy...a little light reading for the weekend.

Patient and polite

> **EXAMPLE**
>
> Thank you for taking the time to visit our website. We appreciate your interest in our work and look forward to continuing to serve you—and our community—in the near future.

Modest and hard-working

> **EXAMPLE**
>
> We have tried to be thorough in this report, and hope you find it useful.

Personal and intimate

> **EXAMPLE**
>
> I want to share with you an experience I had...

Satirical or ironic

> **EXAMPLE**
>
> *Pick up* The Onion *newspaper. This publication holds no sacred cows and even makes fun of the traditional newspaper writing style.*

Personally speaking

I know some people think that adopting a tone designed to encourage readers to feel afraid, guilty, ashamed, or embarrassed is actually a wise move, but I have to say that I disagree. While this strategy may translate into short-term alarmed participation, I recommend a positive tone of empowerment, of "doing one's part." For instance, instead of a purely charity mindset, I prefer promoting more of a "hand up" than a "hand out" attitude about long-term positive change. The idea here is to both teach people to fish (if they do not already know how), and stop taking away their fishing poles or access to the waterways.

And a few more:

- ◈ Youthful and hip
- ◈ Participatory and nonhierarchical
- ◈ Cutting-edge and newsworthy
- ◈ Supportive and inspiring
- ◈ Practical, problem-solving, and do-it-yourself
- ◈ Firm and decisive, but respectful

You might also need to choose between opposites:

- ◈ Serious or whimsical
- ◈ Calm or wild
- ◈ Celebratory or somber
- ◈ Accessible to all, or exclusive to a few
- ◈ Radical or traditional

EXAMPLE

ING Direct, an online bank that is also quite involved in promoting and supporting financial literacy, has a playful, casual brand. It deals with a traditionally boring and complex topic, but the tone makes it accessible.

In an article in a recent newsletter about phishing entitled "Don't get hooked," the bank explains that, "phishing is when scammers (the bad guys) send fraudulent emails to look legit." The article entitled "What's with the Fed rate cuts and how do they affect you?" encourages the reader to "let rates go up and down (you can't stop 'em anyway!)" but to rest assured that ING Direct "will be your lap-bar on the rate roller coaster."

Its outdoor ad campaigns also speak in the same lightweight, friendly tone, with one-liners such as: "Oh my, what big pockets you have!", "Bank fees are like financial wedgies," and "Still paying bank fees? You masochist, you." *(www.ingdirect.com)*

A few tones you surely want to avoid:

- ◈ Downtrodden, whiny, and wimpy
- ◈ Desperate and melodramatic
- ◈ Holier-than-thou and condescending

- Fanatical and alienating

- Monotonous and frustrating

- Curmudgeonly, snide, and cynical

- Cliché and outdated

- Overly simplistic or contradictory

As public-interest organizations become savvier about marketing—both in print and online—we tend to favor a direct, informal or even conversational tone to draw in our readers. Think about it: If you feel that you can easily relate to, talk to, and listen to a writer, you are more likely to remember and eventually act on her or his words.

Decisions you need to make about your brand's tone include:

- Are you going to refer to your organization as "we" or as "the organization"?

- Is it all right to use "I," or should you favor a more collective or formal stance?

- Should you address your readers in the second person (you), or refer to them in the third person ("he," "she," they," or "clients")?

I usually suggest an "I" or "we" point of view, which makes your tone personal and approachable. But any decision is fine, as long as you stick to it. If you want to draw attention to a special segment of your piece, you can temporarily depart from consistency by sporting an entirely new tone. Examples might be a quote from an outside source, an excerpt from a featured document or speech, or an individual's personal message to the reader.

My final word of advice about establishing your tone is to know how your readers talk. Make sure your language is not inappropriately hard-sell, too informal, too high-falutin', too bureaucratic, or otherwise a likely turn-off. For instance, when your readers are officials or are unfamiliar to you, your best bet is to use a formal tone, at least at first.

Make sure that while your writing veers confidently from the King's English, you do not stray too far afield. Avoid sounding amateurish: sloppy, incompetent, or naïve.

STAY POSITIVE

Your pieces should present an upbeat, inclusive orientation, as people find positive thoughts and feelings much more appealing than critical ones. If you think about the implications of your words, you can usually find a way to frame your message in positive terms.

Emphasize what you *can* and *will* do, rather than what you cannot. Stress what something is, rather than what it is not. Talk about the satisfying outcomes your organization achieves, rather than the negative outcomes that you seek to avoid. Lead with affirmative, empowering information.

EXAMPLES

1. *Original:* In an attempt to make data collection <u>less onerous</u>, our staff will collect evaluation forms on a quarterly basis at the advisory board meetings.

   Suggested revision: In an attempt to make data collection <u>more convenient and smooth</u>, our staff will collect evaluation forms on a quarterly basis at the advisory board meetings.

2. *Collaborating Agencies Responding to Disasters of Alameda County does a nice job of casting its topic of emergency preparedness in a positive light. A few phrases from the organization's materials for parents:*

   ◉ "Learn disaster preparedness and response skills and empower yourself to protect yourself and your family. Be a responder, not a victim!"

   ◉ "You can decide what your children will see and experience: Hope, determination, gratitude, and people pulling together? Or fear, anger, bigotry, and people being victims? Optimism is a learned behavior."

   ◉ "Fear is not sustainable; love and the desire to keep everyone safe and healthy are enduring motivators."

   By evoking life-affirming feelings, and avoiding fear-mongering, this organization encourages public participation instead of apathy or rejection.
   (www.FirstVictims.org)

Sometimes we can become a bit too enthusiastic about our organization's ability to deliver results. Remember to only encourage expectations that you are sure you can live up to. Dashed hopes benefit no one. And if you end up over-delivering, your organization will be a hero!

By positioning your organization as a problem-solver with a can-do attitude, you encourage your readers to have high expectations and to want to be part of your team. For a list of positive, encouraging words, refer to Appendix 4, "Additional Hot Marketing Words and Phrases."

BUT WATCH OUT FOR SPIN THAT MISLEADS

Some writers intentionally apply their own spin to popular terms or buzzwords in ways that sound good, but may be less than completely ethical or accurate. I encourage you to be honest and transparent with the words you use. Deliberately masking your meaning by using deceitful framing, speaking in code, or "greenwashing" may call into question your organization's integrity.

EXAMPLES

Some terms currently floating around that sound right but may or may not mean what they appear to mean:

1. Environmental or health-related:

   - 100% natural
   - fat-free
   - green
   - sustainable
   - biodegradable
   - eco-friendly
   - non-toxic
   - healthier

2. Political or economic:

   - family values
   - patriotic
   - security
   - privatization
   - free trade
   - progressive
   - terrorist
   - subsidies

 ## Being Creative with Troublesome Kin

You are working on your family genealogy and let's say that your great-great uncle, Remus Starr, a fellow lacking in character, was hanged for horse stealing and train robbery in Montana in 1889.

A cousin has supplied you with the only known photograph of Remus, showing him standing on the gallows. On the back of the picture are the words:

"Remus Starr: Horse thief, sent to Montana Territorial Prison, 1885. Escaped 1887, robbed the Montana Flyer six times. Caught by Pinkerton detectives, convicted and hanged, 1889."

Pretty grim situation, right? But let's revise things a bit. We simply crop the picture so all that shows is a head shot. Next, we rewrite the text:

"Remus Starr was a famous cowboy in the Montana Territory. His business empire grew to include acquisition of valuable equestrian assets and intimate dealings with the Montana railroad.

Beginning in 1885, he devoted several years of his life to service at a government facility, finally taking leave to resume his dealings with the railroad. In 1887, he was a key player in a vital investigation run by the renowned Pinkerton Detective Agency. In 1889, Remus passed away during an important civic function held in his honor, when the platform upon which he was standing collapsed." *(www.ahajokes.com)*

CULTIVATE YOUR PERSONAL WRITER'S VOICE

Although you probably have to represent the voice of your organization, you still are an individual. You bring your own set of experiences, perceptions, emotions, and personality to your writing. As such, you are (I hope!) allowed to be puzzled, thrilled, frank, and reflective from time to time. Your personal point of view can add juice to your reader's experience of your organization's message.

Acknowledging—even encouraging—the writer's voice forms the backbone of what is known as "creative nonfiction" or "literary journalism." We in community-benefit organizations can apply this technique too.

You should not have to try to make your work sound like what others have told you good writing *should* sound like. A unique person is writing your words; that self should shine through.

Of course, you need to stay within the limits your organization sets. You want to be thoughtful, respectful, and professional. But this does not necessarily translate to dry, dull, or lofty.

We most often see this personal touch in short pieces, such as blog postings or "Notes from the Director" in a newsletter or annual report. But anyone can use this technique, in virtually any context. Simply decide what amount of voice is appropriate—given your topic, intended readership, and organizational expectations—and inject some of yourself into your piece.

To get started, try one of these three techniques to make your piece sound authentic and personable:

1. Transcribe what you would say to a respected friend about a topic that is familiar to you and close to your heart.

2. Pretend you are meeting up with an acquaintance on the subway ride home. Talk about the project you just worked on at the office.

3. Act the part of a host giving your readers a tour of your "home"—in this case, a topic you know a lot about and want to share.

Take your readers into your confidence. Trust them to understand and be curious, and they will trust you to be honest and share only the most important and interesting ideas and information. Feel free to reveal your sense of humor—and your humility.

In addition, because you work in a values-driven organization, you probably have great personal passion for your work. Use this to your advantage! Let your genuine voice convey what matters most about your organization.

But, don't alienate your readers with endless details that interest only you, or references to what may seem strange when taken out of context (i.e., "you had to be there to understand"). Remember that you are your readers' advocate, always searching for the information they want and need, and cutting through the clutter. Balance your enthusiasm and idealism with a reality check: Solicit feedback about the tone of your document from people outside your organization.

EXAMPLE

As Irma Herrera, former Executive Director of Equal Rights Advocates in San Francisco, opens a recent newsletter's Message from the Director, you can hear her voice clearly:

> I am surprised by what still surprises me. It would be logical to assume that after ten years at Equal Rights Advocates I would be unfazed by the hostility and discrimination women face in the course of earning a living. Or the assumption made by so many people that discrimination against women and girls is a societal problem from the past: one we solved long ago. But I am still dumbfounded from time to time by ERA clients' situations... [and] nothing gets the attention of employers like a lawsuit. In a recent Bar Association seminar I attended, a distinguished professor who studies discrimination in corporate America explained that the single most important factor in creating equal opportunity at places of work was—surprise, surprise—discrimination lawsuits.   *(www.equalrights.org)*

ESTABLISH A RHYTHM

Another way to sound right is to get a good rhythm going and run with it. This is similar to what happens in a good poem, song, or chant. Look for patterns in your language that you can emphasize, such as key words, repeated or parallel phrases or sounds, or simply sentence structures that have a nice ring to them. Sometimes you will discover interesting words that are catchy and memorable.

EXAMPLES

1. *I scream, you scream, we all scream for ice cream.*

2. *"This is what democracy looks like."* (the chant heard in the 1999 "Battle of Seattle" and subsequently used as a rallying cry in many other political protests)

You can also establish rhythm in a longer piece by repeating similar segments or structural features. For instance, you can begin or end each section with a relevant quote, or repeat a unifying phrase throughout.

EXAMPLES

1. *At an 1851 women's rights convention, Sojourner Truth delivered this famous speech containing the widely quoted refrain, "Ain't I a woman?":*

   "That man over there says that women need to be helped into carriages, and lifted over ditches, and to have the best place everywhere. Nobody ever helps me into carriages, or over mud-puddles, or gives me any best place! And ain't I a woman?

   Look at me! Look at my arm! I have ploughed and planted, and gathered into barns, and no man could head me! And ain't I a woman?

   I could work as much and eat as much as a man—when I could get it—and bear the lash as well! And ain't I a woman?

   I have borne thirteen children, and seen them most all sold off to slavery, and when I cried out with my mother's grief, none but Jesus heard me! And ain't I a woman?"

2. *Winston Churchill also had a gift for language and often used repetition, as in this famous speech from 1940:*

   "...we shall fight on the seas and oceans, we shall fight with growing confidence and growing strength in the air, we shall defend our Island, whatever the cost may be, we shall fight on the beaches, we shall fight on the landing grounds, we shall fight in the fields and in the streets, we shall fight in the hills..."

Another type of rhythm focuses on a single sound. Alliteration strings together two or more words that begin with the same consonant sound.

EXAMPLES

- Great Grants
- First Fridays, Third Thursdays
- Top Ten Tips
- Dialing for Dollars
- Mailing for Moolah
- Cultivating Conciseness

Related to this is assonance: repeated or similar vowel sounds that create rhyme, echo, or harmony.

EXAMPLES

1. The rain in Spain stays mainly in the plain (*from the famous song in the musical,* My Fair Lady)

2. R-E-S-P-E-C-T—find out what it means to me! (*famous lyric by Aretha Franklin*)

3. "Hear the Mellow Wedding Bells" (*from "The Bells," by Edgar Allen Poe*)

4. *Gene Kelly popularized this traditional English tongue twister in the film* Singing in the Rain:

> "Moses supposes his toeses are roses,
> But Moses supposes erroneously;
> Moses he knowses his toeses aren't roses,
> As Moses supposes his toeses to be!"

Alliteration and assonance are techniques that, while entertaining to the writer, can annoy a reader if overused. They also can draw attention to themselves, which may not be your intent.

USE WORDS & PHRASES WITH HIGH SOUND QUALITY

"Snap," "crackle," and "pop" are three of the many words in the English language that actually sound like what they describe. As a three-word phrase, this marketing marvel still speaks to us long after the Kellogg Company first used it in 1933 (accompanied by three sprightly elves with these names). The technical term for this is "onomatopoeia," and such words can contribute to your writing's sound quality.

Other fun examples include cuckoo, ring, slush, sizzle, garble, splash, drip, ooze, crack, boom, whoosh, flap, creak, shush, and squeak.

READ YOUR PIECE OUT LOUD

Yes, really do this—even if only to yourself. You might get a colleague to listen to alternate versions of a troublesome passage and tell you what sounds better, but most often you will have to rely on your own judgment.

Close the door and mumble under your breath, or pretend you are speaking to someone on the phone. Whatever you do, your words should roll off your tongue. If they don't, try rephrasing.

Many great writers have used this technique. French novelist Gustave Flaubert is said to have yelled out his sentences to hear them. This may sound a bit extreme, but it certainly worked for him!

Reading your work out loud helps you feel the rhythm, flow, and pace of your piece. It also gives you a direct sense of what your readers will hear in their mind's ear when they read your work. When you are ready to refine your piece, this

Watch out for words that sound alike (or very similar) but are spelled differently. These critters, called "homophones," can creep into your writing and may sound fine to the ear, but convey the wrong message in print. Check out Chapter 23, "Sort out confusing words," for more information.

Bonus Tip

If you can find a willing colleague, ask her or him to read some of your work back to you. Not only will you get to hear what your piece sounds like, but you will also hear it after being filtered through another person's eyes, brain, and mouth. It might not sound quite as you intended it to!

method will also help you catch awkward phrases and abrupt tone changes (more on that in Chapter 25, "Proofread—and then proofread again").

IF YOU ACTUALLY WILL BE HEARD, TAKE THAT INTO ACCOUNT

Today's technology makes it easy to create audio segments for use on your website or to send to radio stations. Monologues or interviews are good examples. But even if you are not planning to record, you may be preparing a live speech, a presentation, or a webinar.

Of course, it is always best to think about what you are going to say before you speak. A script or at least a page of talking points is in order here. While the techniques listed earlier in this chapter also apply to the spoken word, I would add a few pointers:

1. Use short sentences with straightforward structures. Make sure all words are easy to grasp the first time around. In addition, watch out for unintended tongue twisters (those sentences with parenthetical phrases, too many commas, or long clauses that get lost in the telling). Writing for listeners should sound even more conversational than writing for readers.

    (If you need help tightening your sentences, see Chapter 18, "Cultivate conciseness" and Chapter 22, "Get a handle on your sentence structure").

2. Check out the dialogue in your favorite novels or radio ads. You want to simulate that same conversational feeling.

3. Experiment with different tones of voice, accents, etc. When you perform your writing orally, you have a lot more tools at your disposal than simply what appears on the page. Use them all.

4. Read, listen to, or watch outstanding speeches by great orators and notice their presentation styles. Consider Martin Luther King, Jr., Susan B. Anthony, Dwight Eisenhower, John F. Kennedy, Molly Ivins, Franklin D. Roosevelt, Frederick Douglass, Arundhati Roy, Nelson Mandela, Golda Meir, Thurgood Marshall, and Christopher Hitchens—as well as your own personal favorites. Think about what makes their words come alive, and notice how so many of these people have given us pithy quotes that live on well past their original usage.

(To learn more, see Appendix 3, "Writing for Audio," and the Recommended Resources section.)

WRITING WORKOUT

This exercise will help you begin to hear the sound you are projecting.

STEP 1: Fill in these blanks according to what your organization does and whom you serve:

The _____[your organization's name]_____ is integral to

our community. Our _____[product or service features]_____

brings _____[your main benefit]_____ to _____[clients]_____

in the _____[geographic]_____ area. Our work is important

because _____ .

(If you need a refresher, check out Chapter C, "Emphasize benefits more than features." Chapter 1, "Spotlight your mission repeatedly," will also help if you get stuck.)

STEP 2: Now rephrase the above paragraph in several different ways, keeping in mind a few readers your organization is trying to reach. They might differ by education level, lifestyle, age group, or other categories (refer to your Reader Inventory from Chapter B, "Engage your specific readers," if necessary). Try using three of the different tones suggested at the beginning of this chapter. If you prefer, look through a favorite newspaper, website, or novel to identify additional tones and rhythms. See if you can use any words and phrases that "snap, crackle, and pop." And make sure to keep things positive.

STEP 3: Now read each version aloud. Which one sounds the most like your organization? And which sounds most like your personal voice? Think about how a tone change might help your message reach new readers, given your organization's existing brand. If necessary, try rewriting the paragraph in the tone that you think would be most effective. Ask a colleague or two for feedback, or consider asking some outside constituents for their opinions.

> " *It's easy to be a writer. You just open a vein and bleed over every page.* "
>
> — Willa Cather

Go out with a bang. 16

Second only to its beginning, the ending of your piece packs the most punch. Why is that true?

People often remember best what came last: the grand finale. Think back to the most recent fireworks show, television sitcom, or stage performance you watched. What stood out for you then and sticks in your memory now? Chances are good that it has something to do with how the production finished off.

Your ending is literally your last word, your final chance to drive your point home and express your organization's perspective. Plan for it, build up to it, and you can take full advantage of its power. The challenge is to leave your readers with a solid sense of your main messages, something to think about, and—in most cases—some kind of spur to action. If the ending falls flat then your overall piece, in the final analysis, is likely to follow.

But keep in mind that, as with the beginning of your piece, the right ending may not materialize at the exact time you want it to. Below are some suggestions for bringing that moment of inspiration closer.

> *You have to hold your audience in writing to the very end—much more than in talking, when people have to be polite and listen to you.*
> — Brenda Ueland

SUM IT ALL UP

In public speaking, the standard advice is to "tell 'em what you're going to say, say it, and then tell 'em what you just said." Writing for community-oriented organizations is very similar.

People appreciate tidbits of information that jog or consolidate their memories. One-liners, stark word images, analogies, and the like are always popular ways of summing up. Quotations, anecdotes, and jokes that symbolize your thoughts might also be quite helpful.

From the moment you start planning a piece, start keeping an eye out for these treasures. You might find them in your interviews, your journal, your dreams, chats with friends, an overheard conversation, an advertisement, on the web, or somewhere you least expect it.

As you begin to create your document, some of these precious snippets may come to you. Prepare yourself by setting up a file for them. Try reserving one of the best, juiciest, or most dramatic lines for your ending; as you build your piece, see if you can lead up to it. Your ending should be like the perfect dessert that rounds out a satisfying meal.

Even if your piece is not trying to be particularly inspirational, you can leave your reader with a new way of looking at your topic. End with a surprise that communicates that. Try a little-known, poignant, funny, or telling fact that puts it all into perspective.

> **EXAMPLE**
>
> *At the end of a piece detailing issues of domestic violence, you might write something like:*
>
> Tragically, many battered women have nowhere to go. In the U.S., we have fewer battered women's shelters than animal shelters. We can do better.
>
> *If you are able to do this, your copy will continue to resonate for your readers well after they finish your piece.*

SPELL OUT THE BOTTOM LINE

By the end of your document, your readers have heard all of the details. You have said your piece and expressed your views. Now you want to remind them what it is all about and why they just spent time with you—and perhaps reveal their next step.

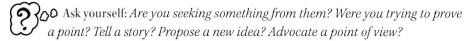 Ask yourself: *Are you seeking something from them? Were you trying to prove a point? Tell a story? Propose a new idea? Advocate a point of view?*

As you wrap up, hit the highlights. But instead of just the facts, you also want to show what your thoughts mean—to your organization, to your community, to the environment, and (above all) to them, your readers. Spell out the moral of the story: How does it affect their lives or the lives of others they care about? What benefits, in the end, does your organization offer concerning the issue at hand?

You will find great bottom-line statements in organizations' requests for investments, particularly in their conclusions and executive summaries.

> **EXAMPLES**
>
> 1. Women's funds tackle our greatest global challenges: economic security, access to healthcare and education, family and community violence, sex trafficking and human rights violations. Your investment helps the Women's Funding Network empower our members to find the most strategic and focused women-led solutions to these challenges.
>
> *(www.womensfundingnetwork.org)*

2. *Spark, a youth development program, lists three bottom-line results on its website. Each one is accompanied by brief explanatory facts, stories, quotes, and examples:*

- Spark inspires middle-school youth by connecting their interests to their education.
- Spark facilitates positive learning relationships between youth and adults, turning local workplaces into educational spaces.
- Spark teaches students how to access resources and support, in order to be effective self-motivated learners in high school and beyond.

(www.sparkprogram.org)

TIE BACK TO YOUR BEGINNING

Run a quick test: Re-read your opening followed by your closing.

Ask yourself: *Do they match up and even flow into one another?*

If your message got derailed somewhere along the way, the problem will probably show up here. Like bookends, your ending and beginning should frame your piece and give it integrity. You might need to mirror some of the same words, themes, or images you explored at the outset.

Remember: Your opening got your readers interested in your work in the first place. You guided them through the body of your piece. Now your ending should at least echo that original gleam of inspiration. For instance, if you started with a metaphor, follow it through. If you began with an anecdote, deliver its conclusion.

By coming full circle, you complete your reader's journey with you and provide a sense of closure.

EXAMPLE

A few years ago, a fundraising booklet by the Independent Press Association opened with a series of questions, including:

- Why has the poverty rate increased 12.5% since 2000?
- Why do 44 million Americans have no health insurance?
- Why are 50% of America's rivers too polluted to provide drinking water?

And that led to the headline:
Why have so many of us stopped asking tough questions?
Flip the page and we found the answer:
Because mainstream media stopped asking them long ago...
The twelve-page piece ultimately ended with a reference to the headline:
Together, we can start asking tough questions once again.

Clearly, openings share several common features with endings. Feel free to refer back to Chapter 9, "Start with a punchy opening," as some of those ideas are also suited to using here.

TELL YOUR READERS WHAT TO DO NEXT

Imagine that a reader has read the rest of your piece, turns to face you, and says, "Well, I need to think about it. Right now I'm just looking around."

What do you say?

Yes, it is true that most people are great procrastinators. "Why do today what I can do tomorrow?" is the refrain. But—as we know too well—that "tomorrow" may never come.

Give them reasons to act now! This is the marketer's "call to action" or "the ask," and should include three things:

1. *An absolutely clear request to act:* This is the time—after you have explained the value of the benefits you offer—to mention the money, time, effort, or other resources you request of your reader in exchange. Or course, you should not wait until the end to start encouraging your reader to act. Start as early as possible, and then make your closing the final push.

2. *All the details your readers need to easily and quickly respond in the way you want them to:* Provide phone numbers, website addresses, and perhaps even a self-addressed stamped envelope.

3. *A limited-time offer, deadline, or other implication of urgency:* Any document is simply too easy to put down and forget about. The best time to activate your readers is while they are engaged with your piece.

> **EXAMPLE**
>
> Try a phrase such as "time is running out," "while supplies last," "limited availability," "introductory offer," "early-bird bonus," "act now," or "help us meet our deadline."

Here you are finding ways to overcome hesitation or even rejection. Remind your readers of the key benefits they and their community will enjoy, if they take immediate action. Keep in mind that even though most people say that they make decisions based on logic, emotions also play a huge role. For more about this psychology, see Chapter 4, "Connect on a person-to-person level."

SIGN OFF WITH A SIGNATURE LINE

You may be able to recite great lines others have used to sign off. Walter Cronkite's "And that's the way it is" comes to mind. Looney Tunes used "That's all folks!" Mine is "Happy writing!"

Come up with your own, and you can carve out a little niche for yourself.

WRITE A POSTSCRIPT

Most people will skim a letter or other document but read every last word of the P.S. (postscript). If your format allows it, attach one to your piece and use it to:

1. repeat your main point;

2. restate an outstanding offer;

3. reiterate the request for your readers to take a certain action;

4. remind readers of the context, importance, or urgency of your message.

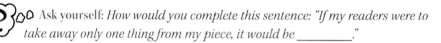

Ask yourself: How would you complete this sentence: "If my readers were to take away only one thing from my piece, it would be _____."

The answer to that question is the content of your postscript.

Notice how the idea I am talking about is a bit different from the traditional casual "P.S." I am suggesting one that is far from just an afterthought that can easily be overlooked, or that is of tangential importance.

This last word of your document is more akin to the "P.S.: I love you" reminder in the 2007 movie of that title. That line is repeated at the end of each of the ten letters that a young widow receives unexpectedly from her recently deceased husband. In each letter the familiar postscript uses three little, but potent, words to re-establish the bond between the two lovers. This is the "core message" of each letter, expressing its deeply felt importance.

DON'T DRAG IT OUT

This is analogous to the problem of "clearing your throat" when trying to get your piece started (see Chapter 9, "Start with a punchy opening"). Dragging out the ending can be as annoying to your reader as taking a long time to get started. Go ahead and let that fat lady sing. When the action is over and you don't have anything else to say, gracefully exit the stage.

Your ending should not introduce a new and unexplored thought. Doing that would definitely not clarify or strengthen your message. If you find that your piece missed the boat on any piece of priority information, go back and integrate it into your body. Don't simply tack it onto the end and hope for the best. (An exception might be if you just received some updated information that you cannot fit neatly into the pre-existing structure of the piece.)

WRITING WORKOUT

This exercise will give you a bit of practice punching up your ending to make a more powerful final impression on your readers.

STEP 1: Choose a two- to five-page piece you worked on several months ago. Take out a highlighter, and read through it with fresh eyes. Mark the things that stand out in your mind, such as quotes or stories, summary statements, or action steps.

STEP 2: Now look only at the highlighted sections and see if any of those ideas made it into the ending. Even if some of it did, is there a way you could have gone out with a bigger bang, using any of the techniques outlined in this chapter? If so, spend a few minutes rewriting. Even though the document may not be current any more, the changes you make are likely to be useful to you in your next document on a similar subject.

Section-at-a-Glance: Hammering Out a Draft

CHAPTER 9: START WITH A PUNCHY OPENING

It really is true: In writing, as in life, you only have a few seconds to make a powerful first impression.

You can kiss your readers goodbye if you do not instantly grab their attention and set the tone for what is to come. You will not get a second chance. In your headline and opening paragraphs, you need to pique your readers' personal interests enough that they will continue onward.

- Obsess over your headline.

- Use a secondary headline if you need it.

- Build on the momentum with your "lead."

- Avoid common but misguided strategies.

- Remember that writing openings is a process.

CHAPTER 10: SHOW, DON'T JUST TELL

Here's a major tip for producing great copywriting throughout your document: *Show* the reader what is happening. Don't simply tell.

Concrete images and specifics show your readers exactly what you are talking about. Vivid details help you build interest, add drama, and help your readers visualize the specific value you can bring to their lives. These words can transport them to the new reality you are creating. Vague storytelling or discussions do the opposite. Turn anything abstract into visceral, tangible, personal impacts - otherwise known as benefits.

- Use metaphors and analogies to capitalize on familiar sights, sounds, smells, tastes, textures, and feelings.

- Use personification to make the abstract easy-to-understand.

- Present the striking details.

- Follow your product or service throughout its lifetime.

- Make your point more powerful with understatement.

- Help your reader "feel" the action.

- Use photos or other graphics to complement your words.

◦Section-at-a-Glance: Hammering Out a Draft◦

CHAPTER 11: FOCUS ON THE VERBS

The title of this chapter is one of my favorite mantras. But why do I love verbs so much?

These little engines drive the English language. They show action, movement, feeling, and drama. They bring ordinary scenes or descriptions to life. If you conceal or neglect your verbs, you are likely to end up with a snoozer of a document.

Verbs are especially important as you write to inspire your readers to act in ways that will benefit your community. You want to encourage a sense of participation in a living, breathing organization or movement that accepts and embodies social responsibility with fairness, integrity, professionalism, and creativity. Using strong verbs can go a long way in that effort.

- Favor the active voice.

- Use vivid verbs.

- Watch out for ubiquitous conjugations of the verb "to be."

- Tease out the concealed verbs.

- Use simple verb forms.

CHAPTER 12: GET CRYSTAL CLEAR

Any time your readers have to fish through your document to find the essential points — or have to read your sentences more than once — you have wasted their time. And they will not be happy for it.

As a writer, you have to make sure that your readers never have to stop to wonder what you are trying to say. You cannot expect them to work too hard to decipher your words. They may have generous souls, but even the most patient reader has limits.

- Clarify word meanings if there is any chance of confusion.

- Be specific.

- Explain, using lots of examples.

- Break down processes and systems step-by-step or component-by-component.

- Give a quick rundown in a list.

- In general, stay away from double negatives.

- Make sure your pronoun references are clear.

⌒Section-at-a-Glance: Hammering Out a Draft⌒

CHAPTER 13: AVOID JARGON

I confess. I succumb to shoptalk just as easily as the next person.

Community-benefit organizations are notorious for using jargon or unexplained acronyms for even the simplest ideas. Sometimes we get so used to talking in verbal shorthand that we end up doing the same thing in writing. We can swim in jargon so much that we don't even realize that we are dripping with it when we come up for air. In addition, we all like to feel like insiders, and sometimes speaking an insider language can contribute to that feeling.

That is fine — or even necessary — for the workplace. But when you are trying to reach beyond your particular office, organization, or close-knit group of collaborators, you have to watch out.

- Use words that your reader uses.
- Explain your thoughts as if you were speaking to a newcomer.
- Prepare if you just *have* to talk shop.
- Check your use of acronyms.

CHAPTER 14: KEEP YOUR PIECE FLOWING SMOOTHLY

A good writer guides readers as they travel together on the journey of a piece. It is your job to help your readers avoid speed bumps, hazardous curves, and dead ends. And as the tour guide, you are responsible for the nitty-gritty logistics of getting from point A to point B.

Reading works from mission-driven organizations can and should be a pleasant, rewarding experience. While your readers might initially come to your organization for your mission or the benefits you offer, they will stay for the way you treat them.

- Arrange your information into a sensible sequence.
- Use subheads as signposts.
- Lead your readers from one signpost to the next.
- Ask — and answer — good questions along the path.
- Use footnotes wisely to avoid slowing down your reader.
- Vary your pace.

Section-at-a-Glance: Hammering Out a Draft

CHAPTER 15: MAKE SURE IT *SOUNDS* RIGHT

How does your piece sound? This may seem like a strange question, given that we are focusing on the written–not spoken–word. But most people, including yours truly, hear words as they read them. You may have similar experiences. As a writer, you want to always sound your best.

- Listen to your tone.

- Stay positive.

- But watch out for spin that misleads.

- Cultivate your personal writer's voice.

- Establish a rhythm.

- Use words and phrases with high sound quality.

- Read your piece out loud.

- If you actually will be heard, take that into account.

CHAPTER 16: GO OUT WITH A BANG

Second only to its beginning, the ending of your piece packs the most punch. Why?

Your ending is literally your last word, your final chance to drive your point home and express your organization's perspective. Plan for it, build up to it, and you can take full advantage of its power. The challenge is to leave your readers with a solid sense of your main messages, something to think about, and — in most cases — some kind of spur to action.

- Sum it all up.

- Spell out the bottom line.

- Tie back to your beginning.

- Tell your readers what to do next.

- Sign off with a signature line.

- Write a postscript.

- Don't drag it out.

Part IV

Editing Your Own Work

Part IV is all about taking your work from draft to finished piece. Many people skip the necessary steps of editing and end up with sub-par results. But you, dear reader, are not one of them!

I will accompany you as you revisit, polish, and fine-tune your work. But note that editing comes only after the initial creative process of writing your draft(s). As I mentioned in Chapter 7, "Power through your writer's blocks," the drafting process should be as unencumbered as possible, free of your "internal editor." The editing process—a separate animal—is where you can (and should) get more analytical and self-critical.

Section A, "Revising and Polishing: The Next Level," begins with important macro-level editing issues that you can learn to recognize and address in your own writing. If you do indeed have a writing buddy (which I highly recommend) you will find some tools for maximizing that relationship.

We will also discuss commonly overlooked ways to strengthen your piece by working to achieve conciseness and remove redundancy. Finally, I will offer some thoughts on making your piece pleasing to your reader's eye.

And because I just cannot let you go without giving you some advice on tidying up the fussier details of grammar, Section B, "Fine-Tuning: Picky, Picky, Picky," serves that purpose. But alas, this is not a grammar book (see the Recommended Resources section for that). My intention here is to briefly remind you of the most common nagging (or worse) errors I have encountered in my work with community-oriented organizations.

Details can mean a lot to your reader and can contribute to—or detract from—the professionalism of your copywriting and branding. Why not eliminate errors that are easy to fix? That way, your reader can concentrate on your content, and not so much on the mechanics of your writing. Nothing better exemplifies this truth than a cover letter/resume package or a grant proposal. You want to be judged on the quality of your work, and not rejected just because of stray punctuation marks, typos, messy sentence structures, etc.

Section *IVa* — *Revising and Polishing: The Next Level*

I n this section, I let you in on some comprehensive editing secrets — both large- and small-scale. You will learn how to:

- ◉ Transition from writer to editor
- ◉ Hone your wordsmithing craft
- ◉ Start imagining your piece as visually appealing

Edit the big picture — 17

T he time has come to separate from the part of yourself that knows what you *meant* to say when you crafted the early draft(s) of your copy. You must now pose as an editor, seeing the piece for the first time. Wearing your new hat, your first job is to scrutinize the big picture — from the perspective of one of the author's (well, your) intended readers.

If you have trouble getting that hat to fit, recall other times in your life when you have adopted another person's point of view. If you have ever acted in a play, done character imitations for your friends, or read lines of dialogue from a storybook to a child, you have some experience pretending to be someone else.

Even though you are extremely close to the material, you can still spot missing pieces and other glaring problems. These often spell the difference between a quick and dirty piece, and one that comes across as a little more carefully crafted.

This chapter will give you some practical tips to help you edit on a macro-level (technically called "developmental editing"). This process is at the other extreme from precise proofreading. You may want to continue to review these general editing ideas as you get further along in your editing work.

"Why do we write? To get it right the next time."
— William Faulkner

TAKE TIME AWAY BEFORE RETURNING TO YOUR LATEST DRAFT

Sorry — no last-minute cramming. Get some sleep if you can during this down period. But even if you only have time to take a break from your piece between morning and afternoon, it will be well worth it.

By giving yourself some time to reflect and gain a little distance, you will be quicker to spot problem areas in your first draft, such as:

- The piece is missing some important information your readers need to know.

- Your points are not clearly presented.

- It is not as accessible to your intended readers as it should be.

- The flow of the piece is not yet smooth, and/or the sequence and organization don't make sense.

- The tone you use throughout (or in certain spots) is a bit off.

- The piece contains unnecessary or distracting concepts.

Once your ideas start flowing, your unconscious mind needs time to contribute to the creative process. I recommend keeping a notepad and pen on your nightstand or in your purse or pocket as you go about your day. You invite ideas to visit you at any time if you are ready to greet them.

Writing down your ideas tells your brain to "keep 'em coming," by keeping the most active idea space in your mind clear and available. When you return to your piece, you will have your list of new thoughts ready to go.

CHECK FOR CONTENT HOLES

Ask yourself: *Does the piece serve its purpose — convincingly?*

You want to make sure that the content seems clear, compelling, and correct. Here is a basic checklist:

1. Your piece helps create or advance your brand (Chapter A).

2. Your document is reader-centered, not writer-centered, consciously aimed at engaging your intended readers (Chapter B).

3. You include all of the priority information your readers want and need, especially the key benefits you are offering (Chapter C).

4. You cast your organization's work in the best light and position it as vital to your community and your readers (Chapters 1-6).

5. You integrate at least some of the "Hammering Out a Draft" techniques (Chapters 9-16).

Personally speaking

Do you often get nighttime inspirations — sometimes at 3 a.m.? So do I. Searching for a way to avoid fumbling with a flashlight or having to readjust my eyes to the bedroom light, I found a great lighted pen. I use it regularly to capture my illuminating ideas. Learn more about it on my website (described at the end of this book).

You might come across parts of your piece that you could improve by using graphics or a good design. Note those ideas for future follow-up. You will want to go back to them in light of Chapter 20, "Make sure it *looks* right."

DON A THICK SKIN AND GET SOME BLUNT FEEDBACK

Believe me, I know this can be tough. At this point, you may feel quite attached to your piece. It is, after all, something you brought into this world: your baby.

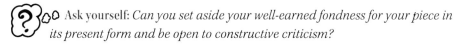 **Ask yourself:** *Can you set aside your well-earned fondness for your piece in its present form and be open to constructive criticism?*

Once you are reasonably happy with your work — or if you just feel stuck and need some input — try running it past at least one or two members of your intended audience. This will help whether you need confirmation that you are indeed on the right track, or you think you might need a slight course correction.

No matter how careful you may have been in drafting your piece, a second or third perspective will improve it.

Your reviewers should preferably be no more than acquaintances — or good friends outside your organization whom you can trust to give honest opinions, not sugar-coated comments. If you have serious concerns that your reviewers will try to avoid ruffling your feathers, ask them to provide suggestions anonymously.

If you only have time to consult with your colleagues or supervisor, that is okay too. Ask them to play the role of your intended readers. Here too, request that they forget about sparing your feelings.

Show, in advance, appreciation and respect for your reviewers' time and honesty. Assure them that you really do want to hear what they have to say. You can handle it — you are a professional. (If you need to vent a bit after receiving particularly harsh comments you can always do so in private.) That said, ask them to try their best to be: 1) objective (i.e., downplay their own personal biases); 2) specific in criticism (i.e., say exactly what is wrong and how they might change it); and 3) consistent (i.e., maintain the same standards and approach throughout the piece).

People always respond better to specific prompts than they do to vague ones. So instead of asking, "What did you think?" try a targeted approach.

First, tell them your piece's specific purposes and intended readers. Then, ask them to address at least the following questions:

- Does the piece effectively achieve its purposes?

- Does the piece speak to its intended readers?

- What are the two or three most important points they take away?

Bonus Tip

You may find yourself frequently working electronically, with little face-to-face contact with coworkers or supervisors. If so, the questions you ask of your critics become even more important. I suggest submitting your piece for editorial comment by email or snail mail, while asking to receive the feedback in a phone or in-person conversation. By connecting orally with your critic, you engage in a dialogue that is often more useful than written advice alone.

◉ What worked well?

◉ What could use improvement?

I like to add another crucial question to the mix:

◉ How do they *feel* after reading the piece?

Your reviewers might feel confused, unconvinced, dissatisfied, frustrated, disappointed, overwhelmed, or hopeless — as opposed to inspired, motivated, encouraged, or generous. As a writer for a socially responsible organization, you are not only out to share facts and figures, but also perspectives and solutions.

If a critic can give you even more time and attention, ask the more detailed questions you will find in the Editing Checklist (Appendix 8).

Unsure of the logistics of the feedback process? Many word processors allow your critics to track or highlight their suggestions and comments — from document-wide ideas to line-specific editing. Make sure you understand the details of that system before asking your critics to use it. An alternative is to develop a color or number code to indicate different types of comments, such as: "great," "clarification needed," "add an example here," "check for accuracy," etc.

Some prefer to review and comment the old-fashioned way: with paper and pen in hand so they can scribble in the margins. Offer your critics that option too.

However, despite all of your guidance, sometimes your critics will give you vague or inconsistent comments — or raise their own questions about issues you may not have considered. If that happens, and you have the resources, seek clarification by probing a little deeper. Sometimes your reviewers just need a little extra help or time to put their thoughts together.

But — and this is important — always remember that *you* are the writer. You are the final judge of what stays in and what gets deleted. You need to decide what criticisms and suggestions are legitimate, given your resources, and which will have to wait or get tossed. You should also consider the vantage point of each reviewer to understand her or his comments, especially if you get conflicting feedback.

Given a little time, you will probably find that even the harshest comments feel less like attacks, and instead feel simply genuine and constructive. Having a sympathetic friend listen to you talk about the criticism you received may also help you process it.

If you think you could benefit from help beyond what you can find within your own circles, consider working with a writing coach or professional editor. If you think your piece could benefit from a co-author (or –authors), consider writing it collaboratively (see Chapter 2, "Maximize your collaborations," for more on that).

Bonus Tip

When you find yourself providing feedback on someone else's work, apply these same techniques. Your job as an editor is to preserve the writer's original intent and style, while helping to clarify, complete, and correct the piece.

WRITING WORKOUT

In this exercise, you will practice giving and receiving constructive criticism on pieces of writing during your lunch break.

STEP 1:   Find a friend or colleague who is willing to swap documents with you — any reasonably brief pieces you wrote recently will do. You will be each other's editors.

STEP 2:   Now tell each other what purposes and intended readers you had in mind while writing the documents under review. Share with your colleague the list of feedback questions above (under "Don a thick skin and get some blunt feedback"). Take out colored pens and mark up each other's paper for five to ten minutes.

STEP 3:   Then, engage in a friendly discussion about your suggestions. Notice what you are thinking and how you feel while receiving (and giving) feedback.

STEP 4:   What did you learn or get reminded of by doing this exercise? Jot down some notes to yourself on your Personal Cheat Sheet.

> *"If you want to appear expert, your writing must be expert: professional and clear...Words matter. Craft, sand, and polish your words religiously...Assume everyone in your company could communicate more clearly—and invest in learning how...Most people write just a little better than they draw."*

— Harry Beckwith in
*What Clients Love:
A Field Guide to Growing Your
Business*

Cultivate conciseness. 18

Don't you hate wading through mounds of information to find what you want?

Most people will take a pass rather than spend much time or energy trying to sort things out. In fact, the more you can use meaningful sound bites the more effective you will be as a copywriter.

One of my favorite phrases about writing is rather Orwellian: Less is more.

But it is not doublespeak—it's true. Concise statements are powerful. Accessible words and phrases get read. Your readers are on the go, in the real world or online, grabbing a few nuggets of data or insight along the way. You, the writer, are responsible for mining, filtering, and delivering that gold in an eye-catching package. Your challenge is to keep your piece as brief as possible, without compromising your meaning. See how tight you can write.

Conciseness helps put punch — and precision — in your prose. Think of it this way: If you saw a single brilliant painting displayed in an art gallery, would it attract your attention more than several mediocre ones cluttering up the wall right beside it?

In school, you may have learned to "pad" your writing to make sure your papers reached minimum word or page number requirements. And you may have used polysyllabic words to impress your instructors. But concise writing demands the opposite.

By the way, did you notice that we are focusing on conciseness only after progressing through the creation stages of writing, and even after the initial editing phase? Cultivating conciseness should not overly preoccupy you until this late in the game.

EVERY WORD SHOULD WORK; DELETE FREELOADERS

Stray words or phrases clutter up your meaning — if they are not doing their fair share. If you suspect you have some freeloading words, sentences, or even

Brevity comes at a price. Be prepared to spend serious time distilling your messages.

"I didn't have time to write a short letter, so I wrote a long one instead."
— Mark Twain

paragraphs, put them to the "So what?" test. That is, check to see if any words leave your reader wondering, "So what? Did I *really* need to read those words?" Passages that do not pass the test weigh down your piece.

Ask yourself: *Does every word, phrase, sentence, and paragraph advance your argument, contribute important information or insight, or help paint a picture in your reader's mind?*

If the answer is no, start deleting. This goes beyond cleaning up for its own sake. Extraneous words or concepts can distract or bog down your readers, and that can spell disaster.

I came across some wise advice a while ago: Pretend you have to pay for each word in your piece — as if it were a classified ad. Are you getting your money's worth?

> **EXAMPLES**
>
> 1. *Original:* I had the opportunity to interact with the youth and understand different issues they were facing within their lives as well as to observe different aspects of the correctional facility and how that environment affected them.
>
>   *Suggested revision:* I interacted with the youth and understood their unique life challenges. I also observed how the environment at the correctional facility affected them.
>
> 2. *Original:* She is a person who focuses on the minute details that each of our programs is comprised of.
>
>   *Suggested revision:* She focuses on each of our programs' minute details.

Other freeloaders include introductory phrases that add little or nothing to your sentences.

> **EXAMPLES**
>
> 1. It has been found that…
> 2. It can be said that…
> 3. It is a fact that…
> 4. It is evident that…

Do you tend to use a lot of long sentences or paragraphs? They are likely offenders when it comes to freeloading. Think about dividing them up or shortening them to become more readable.

Personally speaking

Wordiness creeps infectiously into the English language. Almost every client I have had fights this condition. In fact, I still often find myself wallowing in a circuitous, excessive, unnecessary, irrelevant, extraneous multitude of quicksand-like mountains of verbiage (like this). Word proliferation is an occupational hazard for all writers. But if you find ways to moderate that situation, your readers will reward you. That is why this chapter on conciseness is, ironically, one of the longest chapters in this book.

EXAMPLE

Original: As you move forward in your thinking and your planning, I would hope that before you jump into trying to resolve the major issues we have discussed — in terms of identity, autonomy, and governance — you spend at least a little more time and energy exploring the perceived benefits of the discussed arrangement, and seriously asking if those benefits can be attained in other ways.

Suggested revision: I hope you continue to work to resolve the major issues we have discussed — in terms of identity, autonomy, and governance. As you further explore the perceived benefits of the potential arrangement, seriously ask yourselves if you can get those benefits in any other ways.

In fact, long sentences may also be run-ons (discussed in Chapter 22, "Get a handle on your sentence structure").

A rule of thumb is to keep your sentences to no more than about twenty words. Most newspapers aim for a sentence length of about fourteen words, and so should you. Also, the more complex your subject or idea, the shorter the sentences need to be to attain clarity.

On the other hand, if you think you may be using too many sentences to make your point, consider how you could collapse two or three choppy sentences into a single more elegant one.

> " *Say all you have to say in the fewest possible words, or your reader will be sure to skip them.* "
> — John Ruskin

EXAMPLE

Original: The current digital divide situation is far from ideal. It has been improving somewhat in the past few years. But despite that fact, the problem persists.

Suggested revision: Today's digital divide situation is far from ideal, despite recent improvements.

Remember that paragraphs can be anywhere from one brief, pithy sentence to five or six closely related sentences. Aim for an average of three or four, all focused on the same topic.

INCLUDE ONLY AS MUCH DETAIL AS YOUR READERS WANT OR NEED

Not everyone wants a play-by-play of how your organization accomplished its goals and objectives — or all of the background that went into decisions. The inside story ("backstory") might be important to, well, insiders, but think about what your readers truly need or want to know. Most likely they are simply looking for a solid summary of final results — and a few well-chosen details to illustrate your points and to forge a personal connection.

As people become more interested in your work, many of them will want to know more and more information. That is only natural, and you should prepare for it. But not all of your readers will fall into that camp.

Along these same lines, avoid digressions and eliminate irrelevancies. If you take your readers on a side trip that detracts from their main reading experience, you are likely to lose them.

LITZLER

"THERE'S A FINE LINE BETWEEN FULL DISCLOSURE AND TOO MUCH INFORMATION."

CHECK PREPOSITIONAL PHRASES FOR WORDINESS

These pesky little critters can single-handedly bog down any sentence. Prepositions show a relationship in time or space between two things or concepts — their "positions" — but often do so in a roundabout way. Look for prepositional phrases in your piece that begin or end with words such as: about, at, by, for, in, of, on, to, and with. Then see if you can get rid of them.

EXAMPLES

1. *Original:* Many funders in today's marketplace want to see the participation of beneficiaries in the design and implementation of the project.

   Suggested revision: Many funders today want to see beneficiaries participating in the project's design and implementation.

2. *Original:* At the meeting, we improved our internal operations in order to fulfill our vision of becoming an agile learning and advocacy alliance.

   Suggested revision: At the meeting, we agreed on several internal operations to help us become a more agile learning and advocacy alliance.

Here is a short list of common prepositional phrases — and their more concise versions. I bet you can add to this list.

LENGTHY PHRASE	CONCISE VERSION
With the exception of	Except
Despite the fact that	Although
At the present time	Now/today
In the event that	If/when
The question as to whether or not	Whether
Pursuant to our agreement	We agreed that
Due to the fact that	Because

(See Appendix 9 for a longer list of wordy phrases and their concise versions.)

There is another simple reason to minimize your use of prepositions. If you use too many of them — especially back-to-back — you may end up confusing your reader. Instead, cut out as many as you can and put the remaining ones as close as possible to the words they should actually refer to.

EXAMPLES

1. *Original:* I just visited the website of our local credit union in a layout accessible to visually impaired customers.

   (What is laid out in a special way: the website or the credit union?)

   Suggested revision: I just visited our local credit union's website, which is accessible to visually impaired customers.

2. *Original:* The survey suggests that most parents want a review of existing private school policies about children with disabilities, with or without wheelchair access, with an eye toward improving educational outcomes.

   (Do most parents want a review of private school policies in terms of how they affect children with disabilities? Or is this sentence actually concerned with how private schools do or do not provide wheelchair access?)

   Suggested revision: The survey suggests that most parents want a review of existing private school policies concerning wheelchair access. How do these policies affect educational outcomes for children with disabilities?

(For more information about misplaced modifiers, see Chapter 22, "Get a handle on your sentence structure.")

SHORT, SIMPLE WORDS ARE ALMOST ALWAYS BETTER THAN LONGER, MORE COMPLICATED ONES

Traffic signs are great examples of conciseness used well. A red octagonal sign carries one word to enforce its meaning: "STOP." It's a good thing, too. No one would react quickly enough — or perhaps at all — to a sign that reads, "Bring your vehicle to a full and complete cessation of motion."

Of course, in most cases you probably do not want to strip down your piece quite that far. But the lesson is well-taken.

 Ask yourself: *Are you using words and phrases that are short and accessible enough for your intended readers?*

Put your vocabulary on a diet: Slim down most of your words to only one or two (at most three or four) syllables. This is not dumbing down your language, but simplifying it to reach the widest possible readership. While you may be required to use certain formal words, I suggest livening them up as much as possible to sound less bureaucratic and more user-friendly. Eliminate words and phrases that may confuse or annoy. Opt instead for the words that your readers would use themselves and thus prefer to read.

Instead of the following dry or unnecessarily complex/technical words, consider alternatives:

Bonus Tip

Every once in a while, you may want to throw in a particularly weighty (or even nerdy) word for emphasis or for a special stylistic reason. That is fine, as long as you keep it to a minimum and make sure that it speaks to your intended readers.

COMPLEX/TECHNICAL TERM	USER-FRIENDLY TERM
Diminutive	Small
Utilize	Use
Accordingly	So
Heretofore	Until now
Dialogue	Talk
Operationalize	Start working
Fortuitous	Lucky
Optimal	Ideal, best
Substantiate	Prove
Terminate	End, finish
Ascertain	Learn
Quantify	Measure
Cognizant of	Aware of
Desirous of	Want
Endeavor	Try

(To learn more about how to be free of jargon, the nemesis of direct language, see Chapter 13, "Avoid jargon.")

Speaking of complicated constructions, sometimes the most concise way of saying something is to turn a long-winded negative sentence into a straightforward, positive one. See Chapters 12, "Get crystal clear," and 15, "Make sure it *sounds* right" to find out more.

USE VERBS THAT DON'T NEED ADVERBS OR LONG PHRASES

In Chapter 11, "Focus on the verbs," I share a lot of ideas about what I call "vivid verbs": powerful verbs that say plenty on their own. By replacing weak verbs, you can cut excess words and breathe new life into your sentences.

EXAMPLES

1. *Original:* They decided to drive the pickup truck very dangerously down the freeway.

   Suggested Revision: They careened down the freeway in a pickup truck.

2. *Original:* I currently agree with you.

   Revision: I agree with you.

   (Here, the adverb saps the power of the vivid verb "agree.")

DON'T OVERDO IT WITH LENGTHY LISTS OR TOO MANY EXAMPLES

Some people are list makers. (Yes, I definitely include myself!) While lists can help clarify and organize our thoughts, after we brainstorm we may forget to narrow the list to make it less overwhelming. The secret is to find ways to group our brilliant ideas into compelling, prioritized categories that are at once thorough and streamlined. A condensed but comprehensive list will support your point quite nicely.

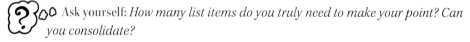 Ask yourself: *How many list items do you truly need to make your point? Can you consolidate?*

First, make sure that the items in your list are not simply different ways of saying the same thing (i.e., redundant, as described in the next chapter). Then, try to cover the entire terrain with a list of three or four items or examples. More than that could be overkill; use your best judgment.

Bonus Tip

The cutting room floor often is littered with great stuff that almost made it in. If you find yourself attached to a great line or image that is clobbering your attempt to be concise, save it for another project where it might be more on target. Add it to your running swipe file, as described in Chapter 8, "Set up for efficiency."

EXAMPLES

1. *A workers' rights empowerment project might list its activities like this:*
   - Ensures that injured workers know their rights to medical care for on-the-job injuries
   - Stops companies from abusing workers' rights on a daily basis
   - Addresses hazardous workplace conditions by educating workers about workplace health and safety issues
   - Prosecutes employers for illegal retaliation against workers who speak up
   - Increases workers' understanding of the legally mandated workers' compensation system
   - Stops rampant racial discrimination and sexual harassment on the job

   We can tighten that list like this:
   - Ensures that injured workers know their rights concerning workplace health and safety issues, including how to access the legally mandated workers' compensation system
   - Stops rampant racial discrimination and sexual harassment on the job
   - Prosecutes employers for illegal retaliation against workers who speak up

2. Look at the lists I use in this chapter. I carefully chose each item to encompass a variety of examples. Could I have done better?

TRY OUT A NEW FORMAT DESIGNED FOR CONCISENESS

We have already discussed three good examples of concise writing: strong headlines and compelling leads (see Chapter 9, "Start with a punchy opening") and subheads (see Chapter 14, "Keep your piece flowing smoothly"). But you also may need to think beyond the document formats you usually use.

For instance, many socially responsible organizations produce one-page tip sheets, fact sheets, FAQ's, at-a-glance briefs, or "cheat sheets." Other concise formats include the time-tested "DOs" and "DON'Ts," and "Myths vs. Realities." A Top 10 list or compilation of pithy summary quotes from well-known people can also do the trick.

These bite-size pieces convey that you not only know your stuff, but you also want to benefit your readers and community right away with that knowledge. In addition, brief documents provide a quick look at what you can do.

EXAMPLES

Here are a few titles of excellent tip sheets I have picked up recently:

1. "Seafood Watch: Sustainable Seafood Guide": This handy wallet-size card from the Monterey Bay Aquarium lists which seafood to choose and avoid when making "choices for healthy oceans."

    (www.montereybayaquarium.org)

2. "6 tips that will improve your nonprofit's performance": *The Stanford Social Innovation Review* included this insert in a marketing mailing, along with citations for the relevant articles in their recent issues. They also reminded readers: "For full access to the archives, subscribe now!" *(www.ssireview.org)*

3. "Are You a Working Teen? Protect Your Health! Know Your Rights!": This piece from the U.C. Berkeley Labor Occupational Health Program uses FAQs and tips to cover all the basics their readers might need to know. It also includes information about where to get help from caring individual adults, nonprofits, and government agencies. *(www.lohp.org)*

4. "10 Tips for Working with Transgender Individuals: An information resource publication for heathcare providers": This brochure by the Transgender Law Center in San Francisco provides an introduction to the transgender community and offers specific suggestions based on real-life experiences for how to improve provider/patient relations and outcomes.

    (www.transgenderlawcenter.org)

Bonus Tip

You can also use these concise bits as sidebars or attachments to your larger pieces, such as newsletter articles, appeal letters, presentations, web postings, or even thank-you notes.

Personally speaking

I am a huge fan of public libraries. My mother introduced me to these treasure chests as a young child, and I will never shake the habit. Libraries have long known the value of turning a bookmark into a handy tip sheet!

COME UP WITH A SNAPPY TAGLINE

Another fantastic way to distill your message is with a concise tagline (i.e., slogan or motto). These explanatory phrases — ideally ten words or fewer — appear with your organization's name or logo. Eric Swartz, president of Tagline Guru, calls tagline development the "haiku of branding."

In one powerful phrase, you can advance your brand by expressing your: (1) impact or value to your community; (2) core values and beliefs; (3) unique problem-solving approach; and (4) overall attitude and tone. A memorable tagline exemplifies several of the writing techniques I have explored in this book. That is, it is focused on benefits to your intended readers in a punchy, clear, distinctive, motivational, emotional, and demonstrative way. And, of course, a tagline should promise exactly what you deliver.

A tagline is especially important if you have a name that does not itself explain who you are or what you do. That goes for your entire organization, but also for individual programs, departments, services, or products that you may seek to "tag."

EXAMPLES

I think these taglines work well. Do you agree?

These have been in use for several decades:

- "A mind is a terrible thing to waste."® *(UNCF, United Negro College Fund)*
- "The toughest job you'll ever love" *(U.S. Peace Corps)*
- "Take a bite out of crime" *(National Crime Prevention Council)*

These use colloquial language or twists on clichés:

- "We tell it like it was" *(Black American West Museum and Heritage Center)*
- "When you can't do it alone" *(Jewish Family & Children's Service of Sarasota-Manatee, Inc.)*
- "Wheels when you want them" *(Zipcar)*
- "Less waste in the first place"® *(Flexible Packaging Association)*
- "Whatever it takes to save a child" *(U.S. Fund for UNICEF)*
- "Because the earth needs a good lawyer" *(EarthJustice)*
- "Unleashing potential. One girl at a time." *(GirlSource)*
- "Climate change is not a spectator sport" *(Celsias)*

These clarify a vague or potentially misunderstood name:

- "Economic action for a just planet" *(formerly Co-op America, now Green America)*
- "Getting things done" *(AmeriCorps)*
- "Where mission meets the marketplace" *(Social Enterprise Alliance)*

These are central to media campaigns:

- "There's no excuse for domestic violence" *(Family Violence Prevention Fund)*
- "Save the crabs, then eat 'em" *(Chesapeake Bay Program)*

WRITING WORKOUT

These exercises will encourage you to identify and then trim the fat from your piece.

STEP 1: Try to make these sentences more concise.

A. *Original:* The workshop to improve our website lasted for three hours.
Suggested revision:

B. *Original:* The institution insisted that information based on surveys administered in standardized ways to large numbers of people was far more accurate than stories told in the community.
Suggested revision:

C. *Original:* Due to the fact that we are no longer using that old letterhead, you can recycle it.
Suggested revision:

D. *Original:* In the event that you have food left over after your event, please let us know so we can promptly bring it to the homeless shelter.
Suggested revision:

E. *Original:* It can be said that these copywriting tips are not difficult to remember, with the exception of that one.
Suggested revision:

F. *Original:* Foremost among the reasons for this is that the composition and metabolism biology of women's bodies more easily absorb and store fat-soluble chemicals.
Suggested revision:

G. *Original:* African NGOs are working to operationalize a collaborative effort with their U.S. counterparts, and when they begin to work together they will have to start all over again from the very beginning of the entire decision-making process.

Suggested revision:

STEP 2: If your organization has a tagline, review it in light of what you learned in this chapter. If you are not satisfied with what you have, start from scratch and see if you can write a more effective one.

STEP 3: Think of at least three topics you could write about in a one-page tip sheet. To get started, try filling in these blanks:

- "10 Tips for _____"

- "Know the Facts about _____"

- "5 Things Every _____ Needs to Know About _____"

- "_____: Myths vs. Realities"

STEP 4: Take out a highlighter and look through a brief piece you have written lately. Mark any instances of:

- Freeloading words, phrases, sentences, or paragraphs

- Inappropriate details or backstory

- Wordy use of prepositional phrases

- Unnecessarily long or complicated words

- Watered-down verbs

- Overly long lists

  Now spend a few minutes editing those sentences.

Eliminate unintended, accidental, repetitive redundancies. 19

You do not want to be redundant. Careless repetition is a sure-fire way to bore your readers and give them reason to question your competence and professionalism. It also needlessly bulks up your documents and makes them less of a quick, fun, essential read.

There are actually several ways you can be redundant. Kind of ironic, don't you think? Rid your piece of all of the redundancies, and the streamlining effect may amaze you. As you might have guessed, this technique is another great way to cultivate conciseness.

Did you notice that the title of this chapter contains two redundancies (unintended/accidental and repetitive/redundancies)? Dramatic or humorous effect is the main reason that occasional repetition can be a good thing, if used well (more on that later). In most cases, however, purging your document of redundancies helps a lot.

 Stop Redundancy

The Committee for the Reduction of Redundancy and the Antiproliferation of Repetition has decided not to meet until they have their first meeting and thus will not be meeting until the first time.

Their Pre-meeting Statement wanted to make this clear before they had their first meeting, so that it would not be confusing.

So their first meeting will actually be their first meeting and they will not have a meeting before the first meeting.

This should avoid having people show up for their first meeting before it is held, since to do so would be confusing to those who did so and this is what they want to avoid by reducing the confusion and lessening the repetition.

(www.ahajokes.com)

DON'T REPEAT YOURSELF, USING IDENTICAL OR SIMILAR WORDS

This garden-variety redundancy often results from assembling material via cutting and pasting without re-reading the final product. It is especially likely to crop up if two or more people work on a single piece, or if you do not group similar ideas as you write. When drafting several revisions of your piece over time — especially if it is lengthy — you may lose track of similar segments and introduce redundancy problems.

Be on the lookout for redundancies that are likely to creep into your sentences, whole paragraphs, or larger units. Redundancies often represent attempts to clarify, but they can leave you sounding like an amateur.

> **EXAMPLE**
>
> *I have underlined the especially redundant phrases in the second paragraph (note how information-packed the first paragraph is on its own).*
>
> Organization Builders specializes in working with community organizations. The expertise of our unique consulting firm is helping clients navigate the complex realities of their organizational development. We provide services to help clients clarify their organizational mission, build capacity and infrastructure, manage risk, and reach out to new constituencies. Organization Builders delivers results by integrating business proficiency with principles of excellence, innovation, and exceptional professional service.
>
> Organization Builders helps clients clarify and define vision and mission, manage risk, and implement clear solutions by utilizing solid internal systems. We work with clients to strengthen organizational infrastructure and enhance long-term effectiveness by infusing principles that improve organizational effectiveness and competitive advantage. Throughout our work, Organization Builders demonstrates a deep understanding of each client's mission, culture, and context, forming a true partnership for success.

DON'T REFER TO FACTS AND DEFINITIONS WITH CIRCULAR REASONING

Failing to give any real substance or meaning to what you are saying can frustrate your reader to no end. Although many politicians get away with stating the obvious, I encourage you to refrain from picking up the habit.

> **EXAMPLES**
>
> 1. Our socially responsible business focuses on the values of social responsibility.

2. The classic definition of death in Western culture is "the permanent cessation of the flow of vital bodily fluids." But what makes a fluid vital? It is necessary for life.

Instead, ensure that your sentences illuminate the concepts you are writing about.

EXAMPLES

Let's revise the above examples to avoid redundancies.

1. Our socially responsible business focuses on the values of high-quality products and services, environmental conservation, living wages for our workers, a fair trade supply chain, ethical marketing, and affirmative action.

2. The classic Western definition of death is "the permanent cessation of the flow of vital bodily fluids." To Hippocrates, those fluids included blood, yellow bile, black bile, and phlegm. But modern physicians point to blood, lymph, and cerebrospinal fluid.

DON'T OVERDO ATTEMPTS TO GET YOUR POINT ACROSS

Ask yourself: *Do you need to use more than one word to describe your thought?*

Very often a single word will suffice to convey your entire meaning. In those cases, the noun or verb you are using cannot mean anything other than what you intend. But sometimes we tack on a superfluous adjective, adverb, or other modifying word to try to further strengthen our point. The results can be a bit funny — so enjoy a smile or laugh, and then eliminate the redundancy.

EXAMPLES

1. Serious crisis *(a crisis cannot be non-serious)*

2. I personally reviewed your case *(thank goodness you did not review it with an impersonal touch)*

3. I made a conscious decision *(we are glad you did not decide while sleepwalking!)*

4. *Yogi Berra is famous for his intentionally redundant one-liners:*

   "It's like déjà vu all over again."

   "It's tough to make predictions, especially about the future."

5. *In* When Will Jesus Bring the Pork Chops? *George Carlin began his short essay, "Count the Superfluous Redundant Pleonastic Tautologies," like this:*

"My fellow countrymen, I speak to you as coequals, knowing you are deserving of the honest truth…"

Take a look at these other common ones — you might be so familiar with some of them that you need a moment to catch the redundancies:

- Important essentials
- Final outcome
- Future plans
- Effectively explain
- Where were you born originally?
- General consensus
- Past history
- Original founder
- Expert specialist
- The general public
- Shrugged his shoulders
- Owns his own electric generator
- He thought to himself
- True facts

Then, of course, there are redundant pairs. Many of these persist from our linguistic history, in which words from other languages piled on top of each other to form the creole we now call "English":

- Simple and easy
- Dull and boring
- First and foremost
- Full and complete
- So on and so forth
- Null and void
- Aid and abet
- Part and parcel
- Hopes and dreams

Want an easy way to spot a prime opportunity for redundancies to invade your piece? Watch out when you use more than one adjective, verb, or noun in a row — usually joined by "and" or "or." Check to see that you are not simply using two or more synonyms!

DON'T OVERUSE FAVORED WORDS OR PHRASES

Ask yourself: *Do you tend to overuse certain words?*

This tendency afflicts many of us in public-benefit organizations. We become so accustomed to discussing certain topics, that we lose sight of how repetitive our writing can become. Examples of these sneaky words include: **work, help, project, program, service, issue, donor, gift, investment, community, green, agency, and stakeholder.** Reading aloud is one technique that can help you notice when you use a word too frequently.

Challenge yourself to think of other ways to refer to the same things — or, use a thesaurus. Your readers will stick around if you keep your writing fresh: Avoid the staleness of rehashed words.

EXAMPLE

Original: Our organization employs over 200 young adults in our Green Jobs Program. The program keeps newspapers, cans, and cardboard out of the county landfill, extending the life of the landfill. In the last five years, our program has kept over 1,500 tons of recyclable materials out of the landfill.

Suggested revision: Our organization employs over 200 young adults in our Green Jobs Program. In the last five years, our work has kept over 1,500 tons of newspapers, cans, and cardboard out of the county landfill.

(Note that the revision both eliminates repeated words and is more concise.)

You do not need to bend over backward just to avoid repeating words. If a substitute sounds too awkward, it can distract your readers and dilute your message. For example, don't convolute "the girls' after-school program" into "the adolescent females' extracurricular gathering."

On a similar note, check your work for unnecessary repetition of the words "we" and "us." Yes, you do want to write in a personal, conversational way, and using the first person pronoun can help. But if you keep running into self-references in your writing, you are probably straying from one of the fundamental copywriting strategies: Keep your piece reader-centered, not writer-centered (described in Chapter B, "Engage your specific readers"). See if you can reframe your sentences to focus less on your organization and more on the community you work with.

EXAMPLE

Original: We provide essential services to homebound seniors in our city. For example, we work with hundreds of volunteers who deliver healthy vegetarian meals on a weekly basis. And we are always looking for new folks to get involved in our programs.

Suggested revision: Homebound seniors in our city enjoy weekly visits and healthy vegetarian meals from our hundreds of volunteers. And we are always looking for new folks to get involved!

Now is also a great time to consider the accessibility of the words or phrases that repeatedly pop up in your writing. You may find them to be a bit jargon-y after all. If so, consider more reader-friendly alternatives. (Refer to Chapter 13, "Avoid jargon," for more ideas.)

BUT, ON SPECIAL OCCASIONS, YOU *SHOULD* REPEAT FOR EMPHASIS

However — and this is important — working to be concise *should not* hold you back from emphasizing your main messages by intentionally repeating them throughout your copy and in your ending. In fact, good marketers know that messages take up to nine repetitive exposures ("impressions") to sink in. You want to remind your readers of your main points and how to act on them right now (your "call to action").

EXAMPLES ～～～～～～～～～～～～～～～～～～～～～～

1. Edit, edit, edit. Then edit again.

2. Definitely, positively, by all means: Feel free to use a thesaurus.

3. Our organization's annual report uses the same, identical, monotonous template year after year. Hey — at least it's consistent!

4. P.S.: Act now to take advantage of this special offer!

You may also repeat phrases, words, or sounds as a rhetorical device to create a rhythm, as Martin Luther King, Jr. did in his famous "I Have a Dream" speech. Chapter 15, "Make sure it sounds right," goes into more detail about the effective use of repetition.

My point here is that whenever you choose to be redundant, you should be clear on your strategy. This is quite different from allowing redundancies to slip in unnoticed.

Repetition only works if used sparingly. If you hit your readers over the head with the same thing too many times, too quickly, they will probably flee in disgust.

At the risk of redundancy, I want to remind you: Make sure that you say what you have to say the first time around. If it bears repeating, do so intentionally and elegantly.

WRITING WORKOUT

Try your hand at spotting and fixing redundancies. Notice how much stronger the writing becomes.

STEP 1:   Come up with inventive ways to make the following sentences less redundant.

A.   *Original:* The children are homeless because they do not have a place to live.
Suggested revision:

B.   *Original:* Although our coffers are not as full as they once were, I wouldn't say that this implies a regression and backward movement away from offering scholarships. We will simply get more creative in our financing arrangements, as our commitment to making higher education affordable is unquestionable and unwavering.
Suggested revision:

C.   *Original:* We are having a drought and have not had rain in months; we are extremely low on water.
Suggested revision:

D.   *Original:* We continue to uncover and find socially responsible investment opportunities that we feel have great potential. Going forward, our firm is focusing on alternative energy research and development, as well as green chemistry and appropriate technology stocks going forward.
Suggested revision:

E.   *Original:* Children with parents in prison often must endure traumatic and detrimental consequences for years and years.
Suggested revision:

STEP 2: Eliminate the redundancies in these common phrases.

- difficult hardship
- entirely surrounded
- very unique
- general principle
- customary practice
- new beginner
- past experience
- positive growth
- plan in advance
- assemble in a group
- cooperate together
- up above
- bits and pieces
- safe and sound

STEP 3: Go back to the first example in this chapter and try to eliminate the redundancies by rewriting the passage in a single paragraph.

STEP 4: Jot down three sentences that contain words or phrases that you overuse at your organization. Can you think of other ways to say the same thing, without sounding awkward? Keep a list of alternatives on your Personal Cheat Sheet for future use.

STEP 5: Find at least one effective instance of intentional, elegant repetition in a recent piece produced by your organization. What made it work so well?

Make sure it *looks* right 20

At this point, your piece is really shaping up. Your draft has gone through several rounds of painstaking writing and editing. The process may have even involved some late nights and unhealthy doses of caffeine.

I am quite certain that you would agree: Such a fine specimen deserves a great visual presentation.

Ask yourself: *When was the last time someone said, "Yes, I can see what you're saying"?*

People need to be able to picture your message, both figuratively and literally. Our culture is extremely visual; it behooves you as a writer to not only notice this, but to also let that knowledge help you find more readers. Some simple layout and design choices can make a huge difference.

A clean, consistent, and provocative design is an essential ingredient of any well-produced message. Visual appeal grabs your readers' attention and keeps them around long enough for your words to inform, inspire, and activate. And nowhere is this truer than on the Internet.

Although I never claim to be a professional designer, I know a few things that make words "pop" — a marketing graphics term for "leap off the page." Without the right look, your carefully crafted piece can end up like an overlooked flower lost in a field of weeds. If a reader happens to stumble upon your beautiful words, a poor design could mark it as not worth the hassle to untangle. Your forget-me-not becomes a "remember-me-not."

Solid graphic design techniques make readers take words more seriously. Why not enhance your strategy of ***writing to make a difference***? Although I have positioned this chapter at the end of the editing process, I suggest that you begin as early as possible to plan your document's look. Consult often with your document team (i.e., any other writers or editors, plus your graphic designer).

Personally speaking

I have the good fortune to know several outstanding graphic designers. Over the years I have become convinced that — even though I love most the sound and meaning of words — I also have to consider how copy is presented. In fact, I worked closely with this book's designer from nearly the beginning of the process. Doing this helped me envision the final product and influenced some of my writing decisions.

ORGANIZE YOUR PIECE INTO READABLE CHUNKS

Categorize, categorize, categorize. Think about how you can divide up your piece into bite-size groupings that fit together. For instance, clients often come to me to assemble a resume, starting with lots of high-priority information that is all over the map and hard to grasp easily. We make the material easier to skim simply by "chunking" the content, and refining from there.

Each information chunk in your piece needs a subhead that explains its contents at a glance. These subheads help readers go with the flow of the piece and transition among your various ideas and subtopics (refer to Chapter 14, "Keep your piece flowing smoothly," for more on this). Once you have your chunks laid out before you, consider how to make them appealing to the eye. The goal is to draw in the casual reader to inspect your piece more closely.

A super-long, dense block of text is a huge turn-off; even many academics try to avoid them. "White space" (i.e., area without text or graphics) lets your readers rest their eyes a bit so they can focus better on your words. One simple approach is to separate each paragraph with a blank line.

EXAMPLE

These are the subheads on the inside of a classic six-panel brochure by Environment California. The piece contains enough white space to make it user-friendly.

> *On the left inside panel:*

Wanting a clean environment isn't enough

The copy that follows is just two paragraphs, followed by a quote from their Legislative Director about the organization's mission.

> *On middle and right inside panels:*

- Our Threatened Environment
- Standing Up to Powerful Interests
- Tough-Minded Advocacy
- A Focus on Results

A photo accompanies each chunk, consisting of two short paragraphs of explanatory copy. *(www.environmentcalifornia.org)*

Another idea is to use bullets or numbering to:

- separate distinct but related thoughts;
- break down complex ideas into simple, digestible pieces;
- transform any list of three or more items from a daunting mess of a sentence into an inviting segment.

If you have details that your reader needs to know — such as juicy quotes, colorful case studies, special reminders, or to-do lists — set them off distinctly. You can use a bordered, shaded, or colored box (a "call-out" or "sidebar") off to the side, in the margin, or at the end. Quick mention of a special offer or feature, such as an impending deadline or an early-bird discount, can go in a lively starburst call-out or a "snipe" (diagonal strip across a top corner of the page). Breaking up the text like this adds visual interest and dynamic flow to a page.

"I ASKED FRANKIE TO REDUCE YOUR REPORT TO THREE OR FOUR BULLET POINTS."

PLAN FOR YOUR READERS' PRIORITIES

Graphic designers talk a lot about the "hierarchy of information", and for good reason. Your design needs to communicate the levels of importance you place on different parts of your document — always with your readers' needs in mind. While you may think that everything is vital, there is a real limit to what your readers can absorb in one sitting. A transparent design that guides them to the most relevant information is well worth planning for.

Knowing your readers and their priorities, as well as your own, will help you figure out what information needs to stand out visually from the rest. Use cues to help your reader decide whether to read your entire piece or just skim the highlights. While you want to devote plenty of space to the most prominent issues, you don't want to weigh down your piece with too much information.

Placement, length, and overall design are crucial to your message. You are the gatekeeper who decides what to say, in what sequence, and in what style. While each reader of your piece will interpret it a bit differently, you should show, for example, what you believe to be the hottest news or clincher information by presenting it upfront. This might mean your newsletter's main story, the upper half of your website's home page, your press release headline, or the single-page executive summary of your funding request or special report.

Emphasizing key words or phrases also can draw attention to your main points. Try using special type (like **boldface**, underlining, and *italics*), color, a standout font, or an interesting indentation or alignment. But don't get too fancy! Above all, make sure your piece is easy for your reader to follow.

KEEP YOUR BRAND IN MIND

As you no doubt have been realizing since the first chapter of this book, branding is a complex process that will likely take a while. Be sure to involve a good graphic designer in your efforts. Branding gets to the core of your organization's identity, attitude, image, mission, and place in the world—all with a clear sense of whom you are trying to reach. Your brand affects absolutely everything about your organization and its presentation includes not only your writing, but also your look: logo, color scheme, fonts, even the type of paper you use.

Your visual strategy must be appropriate to your readers and work well with your chosen tone (see Chapter 15, "Make sure it *sounds* right," for more). Consistency is key here, so strive for continuity and coherence in all of your documents, whether printed or online.

For example, handwriting or handprinting fonts such as **Comic Sans** or **Chalkboard** help communicate a fun, accessible, and light-hearted tone, perhaps an experimental and youthful outlook. More traditional fonts such as **Arial** or **Helvetica** give the impression of a more conventional attitude, an organization that employs tried-and-true methods.

Choose your colors carefully, as they too influence your readers' attitudes and behaviors. While colors mean different things in different contexts, your knowledge of your readers' lives (addressed in Chapter B, "Engage your specific readers") will help guide you. Light and dark shades of color also carry different connotations.

EXAMPLE

In mainstream North American culture, red, orange, and yellow are usually considered "warm" colors. They stimulate strong emotions and speak of energy, activity, optimism, enthusiasm, happiness, and creativity. They also can draw a lot of attention if used sparingly.

On the other side of the spectrum, blue, purple, and green are often called the "cool" colors. They evoke feelings of calm, relaxation, trust, belonging, control, mental clarity, and balance. Often, contrasting a warm color with a cool color can be pleasing to the eye.

Designers are also quite familiar with how pink, gold, silver, brown, white, black, and grey convey different messages to the viewer.

USE PHOTOS OR OTHER GRAPHICS STRATEGICALLY

Figure out how you can best complement and bolster your words with photos, charts, graphs, icons, tables, symbols, diagrams, calendars, simple equations, or other visuals. As they say, a picture is worth a thousand words. I would qualify that statement a bit by saying, "a good picture, used well, is worth a thousand words."

Images can add credibility to your text. They might also help explain a concept or help tell your story in a way that words alone cannot.

> **EXAMPLE**
>
> One highly effective use of explanatory graphics is the visual equivalent of "social math," in which you express data in terms of something that your readers can easily relate to (a concept described further in Chapter 3, "Reflect your true numbers"). *Penn & Teller's B.S.* on Showtime did an excellent job of this in an episode on the "war on drugs." Penn and Teller illustrated the dramatic decrease in the street price of heroin between 1970 and 2004 by using donuts to represent the volume and purity of the drug. They showed that a user could buy half a donut's worth of the drug for $40 in 1970, but could buy a tower of 25 full bakery boxes of donuts' worth of the drug for the same $40 (adjusted for inflation) in 2004.

Remember: Your visuals need to serve a purpose other than filling space. Don't just stick them in as an afterthought. Take your time and plan for them to be fully integrated into your message. And remember that the size, definition, and placement you choose will indicate each image's relative importance.

Photos of people should depict them advancing your mission or benefiting from your product or service. Feature people who actually have been involved in your work, or who at least look similar to your intended readers. Close-ups and faces work particularly well. Pay attention to the lighting, focus, and framing of the shots you use.

If you decide to show individual people, consider also showing their context. Your organization is dealing with community issues — not simply private or isolated ones — and your visuals should show those larger public settings or trends.

And, of course, take photos at special events and ongoing programs. You never know when they will come in handy in newsletters, brochures, websites, presentations, and funding requests. Another idea is to have your clients or other stakeholders photograph their own work, so they can share their perspectives.

Bonus Tip

Think about downloading times whenever you consider using complicated graphics in your online materials.

Beware the tendency to rely on the same few people to act as the symbolic faces or voices for your organization. Be honest about the diversity you currently embody and any expected future developments. Only irreverent satires can easily get away with false diversity. For instance, in the adult cartoon show, *South Park*, the only African-American child character is wryly named Token.

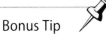

Bonus Tip

Photos with captions are also particularly useful to provide to the media. Not only do correctly identified visuals make your story stand out, but reporters will also appreciate your offer of ready-to-use graphics. Add them to your website's press section, and mention that they are available whenever you contact the press.

For exclusively online use, low-resolution shots are fine. But if you want to be able to use photos anywhere, make sure to obtain them in high-resolution. To avoid possible production delays, don't forget to get signed permission to use the images of the people you depict.

Once you have good graphics, identify them with short, lively, descriptive captions that link back to your main text. In fact, this "micro-copy" provides a perfect opportunity to summarize your story or highlight your message, because readers often look at graphics before anything else.

In those captions, identify people from left to right, double-check that you have spelled all names correctly, and use the present tense of active, vivid verbs (see Chapter 11, "Focus on the verbs," for a refresher). Strive to find action shots and, by all means, avoid pointing out that anyone is posing for the camera. As always, if you feature any non-English words, translate them.

But what if you don't have access to a lot of original graphics? You can start with attractive or unusual type styles, sizes, and weights. Plenty of free or low-cost clip art and stock photo websites also exist. Just remember to always check copyrights and licenses before you use any online images. Consult the Recommended Resources section to learn more.

KEEP AN EYE OUT FOR STRONG DESIGN YOU SEE ANYWHERE

As you design your piece, keep the winds of inspiration blowing. Some places to look for new ideas include:

- Ads for products or services that are both very similar and very different from yours
- Eye-catching fabric patterns and textures
- Famous paintings or sculptures
- Outstanding formations in nature
- Unique architecture
- Your favorite movies or television shows
- Compelling photos you come across on the Internet
- Your own dreams

While you may not pick up designs that you can immediately use to improve your own document, simply exposing yourself and paying attention to different artistic elements will eventually inform your work.

You may come across creative influences in your daily mail or any magazines you regularly thumb through. Keep copies of what you like, but also jot down notes about why you like them. Start your own file of these samples (known as a "swipe file" — see Chapter 8, "Set up for efficiency") and then refer to it whenever you could use some outside ideas. Of course, I am not suggesting that you copy anyone else's work, only that you use it to feed your internal idea factory. You can also collect poor designs and use them as reminders of what to avoid. Feel free to share your thoughts with any graphic designer you work with.

GET OUTSIDE REVIEWS OF YOUR LOOK

Bear in mind that visual tastes vary (a lot). What looks great to you or your colleagues might lack luster to your intended readers. Take the time to ask for feedback, in much the way I suggested you do with your written copy in Chapter 17, "Edit the big picture." You may be surprised at what you find out.

WRITING WORKOUT

This simple exercise is good to do on a regular basis, with various pieces you are creating. Remember that each improvement you make also influences your next project.

STEP 1:   Take a look at a recent document you produced. Is it appealing to the eye? Why or why not? Ask at least three other people who are part of your intended audience — and who do not work at your organization — the same question.

STEP 2:   Use the tips in this chapter to brainstorm what you could do to make your document more attractive and effective in getting across your message. Mark it up with your ideas. If appropriate, go ahead and try out the changes. Then stash your markup in your own swipe file for future reference.

Section-at-a-Glance: Revising and Polishing: The Next Level

CHAPTER 17: EDIT THE BIG PICTURE

The time has come to separate from the part of yourself that knows what you *meant* to say when you crafted the early draft(s) of your copy. You must now pose as an editor, seeing the piece for the first time. Wearing your new hat, your first job is to scrutinize the big picture—from the perspective of one of the author's (well, your) intended readers.

Even though you are extremely close to the material, you can still spot missing pieces and other glaring problems. These often spell the difference between a quick and dirty piece and one that comes across as a little more carefully crafted.

1. Take time away before returning to your latest draft.

2. Check for content holes.

3. Don a thick skin and get some blunt feedback.

CHAPTER 18: CULTIVATE CONCISENESS

Don't you hate wading through mounds of information to find what you want?

Most people will take a pass rather than spend much time or energy trying to sort things out. In fact, the more you can use meaningful sound bites the more effective you will be as a copywriter.

1. Every word should work; delete freeloaders.

2. Include only as much detail as your readers want or need.

3. Check prepositional phrases for wordiness.

4. Short, simple words are almost always better than longer, more complicated ones.

5. Use verbs that don't need adverbs or long phrases.

6. Don't overdo it with lengthy lists or too many examples.

7. Try out a new format designed for conciseness.

8. Come up with a snappy tagline.

Section-at-a-Glance: Revising and Polishing: The Next Level

CHAPTER 19: ELIMINATE UNINTENDED, ACCIDENTAL, REPETITIVE REDUNDANCIES

You do not want to be redundant. Careless repetition is a sure-fire way to bore your readers and give them reason to question your competence and professionalism. It also needlessly bulks up your documents and makes them less of a quick, fun, essential read.

There are actually several ways you can be redundant. Kind of ironic, don't you think? Rid your piece of all of the redundancies, and the streamlining effect may amaze you. As you might have guessed, this technique is another great way to cultivate conciseness.

1. DON'T repeat yourself, using identical or similar words.

2. DON'T refer to facts and definitions with circular reasoning.

3. DON'T overdo attempts to get your point across.

4. DON'T overuse favored words or phrases.

5. But, on special occasions, you *should* repeat for emphasis.

CHAPTER 20: MAKE SURE IT *LOOKS* RIGHT

At this point, your piece is really shaping up. Your draft has gone through several rounds of painstaking writing and editing. The process may have even involved some late nights and unhealthy doses of caffeine.

I am quite certain that you would agree: Such a fine specimen deserves a great visual presentation.

1. Organize your piece into readable chunks.

2. Plan for your readers' priorities.

3. Keep your brand in mind.

4. Use photos or other graphics strategically.

5. Keep an eye out for strong design you see anywhere.

6. Get outside reviews of your look.

Section IVb — Fine-Tuning: Picky, Picky, Picky

In this section, you will learn how to:

- ✪ Sort out confusing words
- ✪ Tackle those pesky grammar and punctuation rules
- ✪ Liven up your sentence structure
- ✪ Proofread like a pro

Take a deep breath. This won't hurt a bit … in fact, it will help!

> *"If a reader keeps tripping over strange words, or bumping his head on overhanging clauses, or stubbing his toe on concealed antecedents, he tends to give up. To hell with this, he says, and he turns to something else."*
>
> — James Kilpatrick, Columnist

21 — Reach agreement on your subjects, verbs, and pronouns

Subjects, verbs, and pronouns: We use these three parts of speech all the time. But we tend not to really think about them, and that is usually fine.

However, these seemingly simple elements of our language carry rules that hold some tricky bits in store. Misuse them at your own peril. At best, you will sound unrefined. At worst, you might offend or confuse someone you care about.

But don't let grammatical constructions intimidate you. Just stay alert and you will do fine. You can always refer back to this chapter (and its partners in crime abatement, the four chapters that follow) if you need a gentle nudge in the right direction.

COORDINATE YOUR SUBJECTS AND VERBS

You already know that subjects have to agree with their verbs. For instance, it is obvious that two or more subjects joined by "and" take the plural.

EXAMPLES

1. <u>She and I</u> manage the two local offices of our eco-friendly cleaning products company.

2. Widespread knowledge of the key players and at least a superficial understanding of how the process works are two crucial expected outcomes of our public education campaign.

And if a single unit has a plural name, it still takes a singular verb.

EXAMPLE

The CEO and Executive Director of our organization is Adrienne Jimenez, a well-known advocate for global human rights.

But what if the subjects are joined by "or" or "nor"? Then you need a singular verb, unless the subjects themselves are plural.

EXAMPLES

1. Either the sales rep or the customer was wrong.

   Either this one or that one is guilty. Only one was wrong, and "one" takes a singular verb.

   But,

2. Neither the board members nor the other volunteers were happy with the decision.

   Here, both options take a plural verb.

And what happens if one thing joined by "or" or "nor" is singular and the other is plural? In that case, make the verb agree with the subject closest to it. Why? Because it sounds best.

EXAMPLES

1. Neither the consultant nor the employees produce results.

2. Neither the employees nor the consultant produces results.

How about indefinite pronouns, such as: no one, everybody, everyone, anybody, anyone, anything, each, everything, much, nobody, nothing, somebody, someone, or something? Go with singular verbs.

EXAMPLE

Original: Each of the marketing plans are in different stages of development

Suggested revision: Each of the marketing plans is in a different stage of development.

The word "none" can actually be singular or plural, depending on what you use it for. It is singular only when it means "none of it" or "no amount."

> **EXAMPLE**
>
> 1. None of the money in the cash box was stolen.
>
>   *The rest of the time it will be plural.*
>
> 2. None of the retirees have golden parachutes.

This approach may not jibe with the rule you learned a while ago in English class. These days, most grammar experts agree that "none" is closer to meaning "not any" than to the traditional "not one," and is therefore usually plural. If you do, indeed, mean "not one" go ahead and say that; it will serve to emphasize your point, as in "Not one of the retirees has a golden parachute."

But whatever you do, be sure that a sentence's main verb agrees with its subject and not with the nouns in any prepositional phrases between the verb and subject.

> **EXAMPLES**
>
> 1. The political environment at both organizations feels rather conservative.
>
> 2. The figures and charts in our financial report need to be double-checked.

Beware! Those sneaky prepositional phrases can send you down the wrong path when a relative pronoun (e.g., that, which, who, whom, whoever, or whose) comes before the verb in the phrase. In those instances, the verb inside the phrase has to agree with the subject of the phrase, while the main verb of the sentence agrees with the main subject.

> **EXAMPLE**
>
> One of our solar panels that sell the most is the "Sun Capture."

Here, "solar panels" is actually the subject of the verb "sell" within the prepositional phrase ("of our solar panels that sell the most"). The sentence's main subject ("one") agrees with the main verb ("is"). Try flipping over the sentence and you can see that:

"Of our solar panels that sell the most, one is the "Sun Capture.""

Bonus Tip

Constructions such as those in these two examples may sound a bit weird to you. That is because English speakers tend to ignore this rule. In fact, many editors and grammar authorities would let "that sells" or "are speaking" slide, even in print.

Bonus Tip

Some words began as plural in their Latin forms but are used as singular words in popular English. Examples include: agenda, erotica, insignia, and sometimes even media and data.

However, in formal or technical contexts, you will probably want to use the original forms of these words. For instance, you might write about how "the media have consolidated in recent years," or how the "climate change data point to an extremely disturbing trend."

EXAMPLE

Not one of the artists who paint in that style is speaking at the open studio tonight.

Here, "artists" agrees with "paint," while the sentence's main verb ("one") agrees with "is speaking." By the way, you may have noticed that I wrote "not one" instead of "none" here. However, if the sentence had used "none" it would have been fine to use the plural verb ("are") because of the recent change in grammatical conventions described in the tip just above.

And finally, what should you do with collective nouns or pronouns? If you are using them as one entity, use a singular verb. That is, you are not talking about individual people, but groups:

EXAMPLES

1. The staff wants a resolution to the problem.

2. Clearly, the committee has already spent significant time and energy on the project and is ready to move on.

3. The couple comes to our office regularly to seek counseling.

But…if several people are acting as individuals, they take plural verbs.

EXAMPLES

1. Different investors care about different things.

2. Fifty invited officials are boycotting the meeting.

MONITOR YOUR VERB TENSES AND MOODS

No doubt you know the general rule of thumb that says your point of reference needs to remain in the same verb tense throughout your piece.

For instance, if your story happened in the past, it should always stay in the past. And, of course, if you lead up to something going on in the present or predicted for the future, that is fine too. Then the verbs change accordingly.

But what if you also want to include something that happened before the story even started? Then you need to use the past perfect.

EXAMPLE

In recent decades, more and more people have turned [present perfect] to alternative medicine to treat their ills or prevent future ones. Ming, one of our acupuncture clinic's patients, exemplifies [simple present] the trend. She came [simple past] to our office last year, after she had visited [past perfect] at least five Western doctors who had not been able [past perfect] to even diagnose her health issue. She was [simple past] frustrated and about to give up when she decided [simple past], as a last resort, to give us a try. Since that time, Ming has experienced [present perfect] dramatic improvement and now looks [simple present] forward to a pain-free future.

The good news is that *you* decide when the action in your piece takes place: in the past, present, or future. But once you choose, you must remain true to that choice.

Sometimes this can get a bit tricky. The English language has a surprising number of different verb tenses and moods. I don't want to get too complicated here (you can refer to the Recommended Resources to explore the hairy details). Instead, let me just illustrate the complexity.

In public-benefit organizations, we often have our sights set on the future. We tend to be idealistic, dreaming of the "what if" of life. This is as it should be. After all, we are pushing the envelope to seek a better world.

But let's translate that into how we use our verbs. In a formal setting, if you are talking about hypothetical, demanded, expected, or hoped for situations that are not yet real (and may never become real), you will use what is known as the subjunctive mood. Basically, "was" becomes "were," "is" becomes "be," and many verbs drop the "s" in their conjugations. Words like "would," "could," "might," and "should" also indicate the subjunctive mood.

EXAMPLE

She really wishes the neighborhood were safer for her kids. If she were wealthier she would buy a house far away from the toxic waste dump. But that is but a fantasy. As a low-income single mother of three, she has no choice. She must work for cleaner air and water….here and now. So she is an activist.

(Note the disappearance of the subjunctive mood when reality returns.)

Bonus Tip

I suggest not worrying about the names of the specific verb tenses and moods if that is causing confusion. Instead, focus on the auxiliary verbs (forms of "to have" or "to be") that you need.

If the thing you are talking about actually is true or even might be true, use "was."

> If our salesperson was rude please accept our apologies. I can assure you that it was unintentional, and that we are committed to serving your needs. If your daughter was not completely satisfied with the service she received, please call the store manager and we will promptly address the issue.

(For much more information about how to use verbs to make your writing sparkle, see Chapter 11, "Focus on the verbs.")

MIND YOUR PRONOUNS!

Make your writing as non-sexist as possible — carefully

While almost everyone uses "they" as a reference to a single person of unknown gender in spoken English, it is not so accepted in writing (although even some grammarians are lenient about this rule). For well over a century, English speakers have tried to coin "epicene" pronouns: ones that do not assign a gender to the person they refer to. While a few gender-neutral pronouns (e.g., "xe," "ze," "zir," and "thon") have found favor in a few communities, most of us seem condemned to dance around the issue.

In short, you will always remain technically accurate if you stick to "they" when referring to a group of people and "he/she" when talking about one person.

> **EXAMPLES**
>
> 1. All of the clients reluctantly did as they were told.
>
> 2. The staff person at the soup kitchen told each client to fill his or her bowl only once.

But what if you want to reduce or eliminate the "he/she" awkwardness? The top five ways to do that are:

1) Make the sentence plural.

> **EXAMPLES**
>
> 1. The staff person at the soup kitchen told the clients to fill their bowls only once.
>
> 2. All employees and interns at our organization feel good about their jobs.

2) Replace the pronoun with an article.

> **EXAMPLE**
>
> Each museum visitor has a right to an opinion, even if we disagree with it.

3) Use the second person.

> **EXAMPLE**
>
> If you learn to write well, you will travel far along your career path.

4) Alternate between male and female pronouns throughout your document.

> **EXAMPLE**
>
> One weekend per month, our pet store co-hosts "Adopt-a-Pet Day" with the local animal rescue organization. Each person who adopts a companion animal gets a coupon for $20 off her next purchase at our store. The coupon can be used on any product in our full line of supplies, or on our pet grooming or petsitting services. New pet owners usually have a lot of questions, and our store newsletter includes an advice column for that very purpose. We have found that this model serves our marketing and social responsibility needs, while also serving our new customer and his needs.

5) Remove the pronoun altogether.

> **EXAMPLE**
>
> *Original:* When a client walks through our door she gets a welcoming smile!
>
> *Suggested revision:* Every client who walks through our door gets a welcoming smile!

Make sure the pronouns you use remain in proper pronoun "case"

To do that, check if the pronoun you want should be in the subjective case (I, he, she, we, or they) or objective case (me, him, her, us, or them).

Here, the sentence must be gramatically correct if it were only about you or only about me. It also could be substituted with "us" (and not "we"). That is because "you" and "me" are the objects of the preposition "between." They are not subjects.

Bonus Tip

Sometimes even language scholars disagree about English "rules." For instance, while they all agree that we should always use the objective case after a preposition, some debate the status of the word "than." Some consider it a preposition, as in, "Martha writes more creatively than him." More traditional experts claim that "than" is actually a conjunction and should precede a subject, as in, "Martha writes more creatively than he." Luckily, only in the most formal of settings would people think twice about this fine point. Still, to be safe, if you want to be extremely clear about your meaning go ahead and write: "Martha writes more creatively than *he does.*"

EXAMPLE

Let's not let ideological differences come between <u>you</u> and <u>me</u>!

If you remember that prepositions always come before *objects*, you will do fine. For instance, if a pronoun follows a preposition, as in "between" above, that pronoun has to be in the objective case.

Stay consistent with your point of view

That is, determine who is doing the narrating ("I," "we," or a third-person omniscient being), and how you are referring to your readers (using the direct second-person "you," or the indirect third-person "he," "she," "it," "one," or "they").

EXAMPLE

Original: Grow as a person: Be true to <u>oneself</u> and open to making changes in <u>your</u> life.

Suggested revision: Grow as a person: Be true to <u>yourself</u> and open to making changes in <u>your</u> life.

But people acting as subjects in your sentences must appear in the subjective case, and never the objective case.

EXAMPLE

On the first page of this chapter, we looked at the sentence:

<u>She</u> and <u>I</u> manage the two local offices of our eco-friendly cleaning products company.

Notice that both of the subjects of the sentence, "she" and "I," appear in the subjective case. We would never say:

<u>Me</u> and <u>her</u> manage the two local offices of our eco-friendly cleaning products company.

WRITING WORKOUT

In this exercise you will practice the finer points of subject/verb agreement. Getting this right will help your writing sound professional.

STEP 1: Consider this exercise a quiz. Choose the best option to fill in the blank, making sure that your subjects, verbs, and pronouns all agree. Then check your answers and mull over the explanations.

A. Neither the Executive Director nor the Board President _____ [is/are] at fault.

B. The organization's search for new revenue sources _____ [continue/continues].

C. We asked each staff member if _____[they/he or she] could contribute an idea to improve organizational efficiency.

D. We asked all staff members if _____ [they/he or she] could contribute ideas to improve organizational efficiency.

E. [Does/Do] _____ anybody want to attend the free workshop?

F. The organization sent the mailing to both you and _____[me/I].

G. If our business _____ [was/were] 100% energy-efficient, we [will/would] save thousands of dollars every year.

H. Each of the ten summer interns ____ [go/goes] to a different university. But none ____[are/is] graduating next year.

I. The committee that ____ [work/works] on the annual campaign _____[do/does] a great job!

J. Each one of the thrift store employees who ____ [handle/handles] customer service ____[need/needs] to attend the orientation.

K. This afternoon's workshop will be an interactive session and we encourage ____[all/you] to bring ____ [their/your] laptop with wireless capabilities.

STEP 2: Think of at least two ways to rewrite this sentence so it becomes gender-neutral:

I am waiting for a leader in our industry to make his factory a zero-waste facility, thus starting a competition to be the greenest business in the market.

STEP 3: Look through a piece you are working on. Check for any errors you may have made in your use of subjects, verbs, or pronouns. If you prefer, practice using each of the suggested constructions in this chapter by substituting your own examples.

Get a handle on your sentence structure 22

We certainly have no lack of things to be picky about.

🤔 Ask yourself: *Are you building your sentences to be not only clean, but also clear and compelling?*

In this book I have offered many ways to ratchet up the level of sophistication in your writing. I have also shared a slew of ways to clarify your meaning. But maybe you feel unsure of how to put together your sentences smoothly and persuasively. You may be repeating some of the same mistakes you have been making since grade school. Or, you could just be getting stale and would like to find ways to spice things up.

Check to make sure you are doing the things I cover in this chapter. Since you write for marketing and fundraising (and perhaps other) purposes, you will want to become adept at applying these techniques.

WHEN COMPARING TWO THINGS, NAME BOTH OF THEM

When advertisements offer "more cell phone minutes" or "cheaper prices," you need to know what they are comparing. It may be apples to apples. But it could be apples to oranges — or cucumbers. Don't make the same mistake.

EXAMPLES

1. *Original:* Investors supported our work <u>more</u> this past year.

   (More than what? If the context does not make the answer clear, you should specify it.)

   Suggested revision: Investors supported our work more this past year than in any previous year.

2. *Original:* Managers at public-benefit organizations are often <u>more community-minded</u>.

(More community-minded than whom?)

Suggested revision: Managers at public-benefit organizations are often more community-minded than those at conventionally run companies.

WHEN YOUR SENTENCE DEALS WITH AN ARRAY OF IDEAS, REWRITE

The point here is to avoid cramming too many things into one sentence. Give that poor syntactical unit a break! Use one sentence per idea. Remember that periods, semicolons, dashes, and even commas can help you manage unwieldy sentences. You will likely also find words or phrases you can simply delete (for more about how to achieve brevity, see Chapter 18, "Cultivate conciseness").

EXAMPLE

Original: Run-on or "cluttered" sentences are sentences that run on forever and ought to be chopped up because they try to pack in too many facts or opinions but the writer never stops to think about which ideas go where or how the reader will process the information, leaving him or her feeling exhausted or lost by the sentence's end, which is too long in coming and may end up being redundant.

Suggested revision: Run-on or "cluttered" sentences run on forever. They ought to be chopped up, because they try to pack in too many facts or opinions — or just plain redundancies. Unfortunately, the writer never stops to think about which ideas go where or how the reader will process the information. These problematic sentences often leave the reader feeling exhausted or lost.

This concept actually rings true for paragraphs too. That is, all sentences in a single paragraph need to be about only one topic. And remember: Short paragraphs — like short sentences — usually are more readable than their longer cousins.

WHEN YOU FIND A SENTENCE WITH A DANGLING OR MISPLACED MODIFIER, NIP IT IN THE BUD

Here we find adjectives, adverbs, prepositional phrases, and other modifiers ending up in strange places. As a rule, keep modifiers as close as you can to the words they describe or refer to (their antecedents).

You will find dangling modifiers seemingly stuck onto the beginnings or endings of sentences, simply dangling out there like dying autumn leaves. Misplaced modifiers can float anywhere in the sentence.

EXAMPLES

1. *Original:* Writing quickly, the Public Service Announcement was finished in half an hour.

   (Who or what was writing quickly? Surely the Public Service Announcement was not writing itself, although that would be great.)

   Suggested revision: Writing quickly, I finished the Public Service Announcement in half an hour.

   It is fine to put your modifier ("writing quickly") at the beginning of the sentence, but it needs to appear right next to the person or thing that is doing the writing.
   * Also, notice how the revised version states the subject ("I") and uses an active verb ("finished") instead of the passive form in the original ("was finished"). For a refresher on active vs. passive verbs, see Chapter 11, "Focus on the verbs."*

2. *Original:* The park administrator picked up his son wearing a baseball cap.

   (Who was wearing this baseball cap, anyway?)

   Suggested revision #1: Wearing a baseball cap, the park administrator picked up his son.

   Suggested revision #2: The parks administrator picked up his son, who was wearing a baseball cap.

3. *Original:* As an artist, the dualities of our existence continually inspired her.

   Suggested revision #1: The dualities of our existence continually inspired the artist in her.

   Suggested revision #2: As an artist, she continually took inspiration from the dualities of our existence.

4. *Original (the joke that saves the day in* Mary Poppins*):*

   Person A: "I know a man with a wooden leg named Smith."

   Person B: "What's the name of the other leg?"

   Suggested revision: "I know a man named Smith who has a wooden leg."

   (Admittedly, this revision strips the sentence of its humor.)

Bonus Tip

We know that readers pay most attention to the beginning and ending of any given block of text. Given this, you should place your key information in one or both of these two hot spots. Don't make it hard for your readers to pick out the juicy bits.

REIN IN VERBS THAT STRAY TOO FAR FROM THEIR SUBJECTS

As with modifiers and the words they modify, you do not want your subject and verb to become long lost friends. You are sure to mix up your meaning that way — or at least require the reader do a double-take on the sentence. Of course, that is never a good thing.

Readers need to know both the subject and the verb early in the sentence, or they may well lose patience. Avoid imitating airplane flights that take you from New York to Chicago to Phoenix, only to finally arrive in Atlanta. Fly the nonstop route between actor (subject) and the action (verb)!

> **EXAMPLE**
>
> *Original:* A consistent, secure relationship with at least one adult is, for any child, but especially for a foster child, needed.
>
> *Suggested revision:* Every child, especially a foster child, needs a consistent, secure relationship with at least one adult.

This rule becomes especially important when you use a multi-word verb phrase. Although I usually recommend writing with freestanding vivid verbs (as described in Chapter 11, "Focus on your verbs"), some strong verb phrases involve helping words. Examples include: "fall behind," "taken aback," and "measure up." When that happens, make sure that all parts of the verb phrase appear as close together as possible. Otherwise your reader may get a bit lost.

> **EXAMPLE**
>
> *Original:* We joined the decision-making team and brought our extensive expertise in renewable energy, recycling, and green construction in the southwest region to bear.
>
> *Suggested revision:* We joined the decision-making team and brought to bear our extensive expertise in renewable energy, recycling, and green construction in the southwest region.

PRESENT MULTIPLE ITEMS IN PARALLEL GRAMMATICAL FORM

As with so many good writing practices, consistency reigns supreme. If you mention two or more items in a sentence or a list, double-check that they all appear in the same form.

EXAMPLES

1. *Original:* The organization works to protect endangered species' rights and stopping environmental damage.

   Suggested revision: The organization works to protect endangered species' rights and to stop environmental damage.

2. *Original* (from a list of accomplishments and responsibilities in a resume):
   - Appraised work done for a $50-million urban revitalization grant
   - Board training: "Developing a Resource Development Strategy"
   - Managed agency's processes, procedures, and documentation
   - Synthesize and analyze research data for policy initiatives
   - Legislative and media liaison
   - Funding prospect identification and cultivation
   - Proposals for federal and state funders

   Suggested Revision:
   - Appraised work done for a $50-million urban revitalization grant
   - Led board training: "Developing a Resource Development Strategy"
   - Managed agency's processes, procedures, and documentation
   - Synthesized and analyzed research data for policy initiatives
   - Served as legislative and media liaison
   - Identified and cultivated funding prospects
   - Prepared proposals for federal and state funders

BE OPEN TO CHANGE IN GRAMMATICAL CUSTOMS

Though it might be a tough one to swallow, the truth is that the English language *does* evolve over time. This is the nature of language: Conventions are just passing through, like fashions that may stick around a while but eventually fade away.

You may have noticed that in this book I freely violate four formal rules you (or your parents) may have learned in English class. These rules—among others—have become grey areas where writers can, indeed, dare to tread. After all, rules were made to be broken, right?

Grey Rule #1: Don't split infinitives

Go ahead, give it a try. It can be freeing! But use good judgment by not doing this all the time or when there is any risk of misinterpretation. Enjoy what it feels like *to boldly go* where no one has gone before.

Travel not the road of violated rules if you are addressing more formal or traditional readers. This takes us back to the all-important question of who your readers are. Also, if you are not too comfortable with the English language for any reason, it is always best to stick with the conventional rules.

Grey Rule #2: Don't end a sentence with a preposition

If you want to sound natural, conversational, even approachable, sometimes you just have to *dive right in.*

Grey Rule #3: Don't start a sentence with a conjunction

To maintain a friendly flow, you have seen that I often begin sentences with "So," "But," or even "And." This technique can add a welcome flavor of familiarity to your pieces. But it is not the way to start out every sentence; you must choose judiciously. (By the way, did you catch the misplaced modifier—"to maintain a friendly flow"— in this paragraph? Even these can be gotten away with on occasion. But be on the lookout for the ones that cause disruption.)

Grey Rule #4: A sentence fragment is unacceptable as a sentence

Very sparingly, experiment with sentence fragments when your meaning is clear. Natural speech usually includes fragments (phrases that resemble sentences but do not actually have both a subject and verb). If you consciously use them for effect, they can jazz up your writing.

Fragments are particularly useful in writing to communicate with an audience, since they can create full stops, pregnant pauses, or rhythmic variations. They can also help set a mood: stream-of-consciousness with a barrage of questions or observations, or the chaos of a crowd scene with snippets of overheard conversations flying about. Taglines are often sentence fragments that encapsulate an idea or feeling, or even add a note of humor.

> **EXAMPLES**
>
> 1. It's always so hot in this training room. Except when it isn't.
>
> 2. AirCurrents: Bringing wind energy to our community since 1971.
>
> 3. Health. Jobs. The environment. Education. Immigration. Race relations. Prison reform. Transportation. Voting rights. Gender issues. Technology. Foreign policy. The list of important political issues seems endless.

Of course, overusing fragments will give your writing a choppy, boring, even annoying feel. You will soon run out of steam and scramble for a subject and verb to get you going again. Follow that feeling!

Also, if you use a fragment unknowingly (i.e., when you mean to use a full sentence), it is bound to show through and detract from your credibility.

EXAMPLE

Original: Facilitating a safe, open forum series, where junior and senior high school students speak with local college students about future possibilities.

Suggested revision: Every autumn, we facilitate a safe, open forum series, where junior and senior high school students speak with local college students about future possibilities.

Personally speaking

I have to admit that violating hard and fast (and kind of cherished) English composition rules from yesteryear has been a bit tough for me. I spent years doing academic writing, where little (if any) of that kind of experimentation was tolerated. But my days as a journalist have helped.

WRITING WORKOUT

In these exercises you get to act as a copyeditor by making these sentences grammatically correct, stronger, and/or more effective.

STEP 1: Take a stab at fixing up these sentences. Feel free to fill in any missing information.

A. *Original:* Recycling is better for the environment.

Suggested revision:

B. *Original:* Serving 100 young people per month, in-kind donations keep pouring in.

Suggested revision:

C. *Original:* Let's get Alicia on our walk-a-thon team, as the person most in shape.

Suggested revision:

D. *Original:* At the end of each year, we should be able to answer these questions:

- How did we achieve our mission?

- Where our investors' money went?

- What changes to implement to improve our work?

- Success stories

Suggested revision:

E. *Original:* The conservationists could only access the outlying areas in SUVs sporting sunglasses and bright Hawaiian shirts.

Suggested revision:

F. *Original list of accomplishments and responsibilities in a resume:*

- ✇ Created diversified evaluation plan for agency
- ✇ Oversaw projects initiated by Board of Directors
- ✇ Preparation and assembly of all meeting materials
- ✇ Hired and supervised all vendors and contractors
- ✇ Maintained records
- ✇ Bookkeeping, payroll, financial reports
- ✇ Budgets and expenses monitoring

Suggested revision:

G. *Original:* "One morning I shot an elephant in my pajamas. How he got into my pajamas, I'll never know. "—Groucho Marx

Suggested (much less funny) revision:

H. *Original:* Dr. Rainwater, after arriving late to the meeting and complaining about the weather, mixed several of the most important and timely agenda items up.

Suggested revision:

I. *Original:* A group of internationally known human rights activists developed this project in the late 1990s explicitly to heal the social, cultural, and economic wounds left by the widespread civil war that took the lives of tens of thousands of people that occurred in 1992-1995, at the same time as the growing epidemic of AIDS left thousands of young children grieving for the parents they had recently lost.

    Suggested revision:

J. *Original:* In our community, parents say they don't know how or where to access wellness services for their young children and service providers are unable to keep children from falling through the cracks and so early identification of hidden disabilities is far from where it should be.

    Suggested revision:

K. *Original:* He decided to head downtown to join the rally quickly.

    Suggested revision:

STEP 2: Choose a few paragraphs from a piece you have recently written. Rewrite a few sentences by intentionally violating a "grey rule" described in this chapter.

STEP 3: Consider how the changes you made in Step 2 affect the tone, flow, rhythm, or impact of your piece.

Sort out confusing words 23

The English language sports hundreds of pairs of words that sound alike, look alike, or get confused for other reasons. Some are homophones: words that have the same, or nearly the same, sound but different meanings (e.g., "ensure" and "insure" or "discreet" and "discrete"). Others are near-homophones (e.g., "conscience" and "conscious"), or deceptively similar (e.g., "woman" and "women"). Others are simply misused a lot.

If you use the wrong words, you can confuse your meaning or just look silly. Errors can also encourage your readers to question your competence. Unfortunately, most computer spell-checkers (or grammar-checkers) will not know the difference.

Bonus Tip

"Homonyms," strictly speaking, are words that have the same spelling but different meanings and different etymologies (origins). Examples are "bear" (to carry) and "bear" (the animal).

Misphrased excerpts from student science exam papers

1. Charles Darwin was a naturalist who wrote the organ of the species.
2. Three kinds of blood vessels are arteries, vanes and caterpillars.
3. The dodo is a bird that is almost decent by now.
4. The process of turning steam back into water again is called conversation.
5. A magnet is something you find crawling all over a dead cat.
6. The Earth makes one resolution every 24 hours.
7. To collect fumes of sulfur, hold a deacon over a flame in a test tube.
8. Geometry teaches us to bisex angles.
9. The pistol of a flower is its only protection against insects.
10. English sparrows and starlings eat the farmers grain and soil his corpse.
11. If conditions are not favorable, bacteria go into a period of adolescence.
12. A triangle which has an angle of 135 degrees is called an obscene triangle.
13. The hookworm larvae enters the human body through the soul.
14. When you haven't got enough iodine in your blood you get a glacier.

(www.ahajokes.com)

Ask yourself: *When was the last time confusing word pairs got you?*

Listed here are nine of the top offenders I come across in my clients' and students' writing. If you find even one that trips you up (be honest with yourself!), be sure to note it on your Personal Cheat Sheet or elsewhere. Check the Recommended Resources section for ways to track down literally hundreds of others.

AFFECT/EFFECT

"To affect" is a verb meaning "to have an influence on"

> **EXAMPLE**
>
> The million-dollar donation from the polluting factory owner did not affect the politician's vote on the Clean Air Act. *(Somehow I doubt that.)*

whereas "effect" is a noun.

> **EXAMPLE**
>
> We gave impassioned testimony at the public meeting of our local School Board. We could see an immediate effect on our image as problem-solvers.

Remember: When you *affect* a situation, you have an *effect* on it.

These two words also have a few much less common meanings. Don't let them confuse you. For example, "affect" is also a psychological term meaning feeling or emotion (a noun), especially as seen through facial expression or body language. To make matters worse, "effect" can mean "produce" or "create," as in, "I'm trying to effect a change in the way we deal with customers."

IT'S/ITS

"It is" contracts to "it's," while "its" is the possessive form of "it."

I agree: This is kind of strange. But there it is. "It" is not the name of a person, place, or thing, so it doesn't get to have an apostrophe in its possessive form.

> **EXAMPLE**
>
> I think it's an outstanding annual report; its success stories are so striking.

WHO'S/WHOSE

"Who's" is simply the contraction of "who is." "Whose," on the other hand, is the possessive form of "who."

> **EXAMPLE**
>
> Whose car are we using for the carpool? And who's going to share the driving?

Bonus Tip

Even from the early days of the United States, people have had trouble with the distinction between "it's" and "its." In Article 1, Section 10 of the U.S. Constitution we find:

"No State shall, without the Consent of the Congress, lay any Imposts or Duties on Imports or Exports, except what may be absolutely necessary for executing it's inspection Laws."

So you are not alone if this difference keeps tripping you up.

THEIR/THERE/THEY'RE

Here we actually have three words that shouldn't be, but often are, used interchangeably. They all have entirely different meanings.

"Their" is a possessive pronoun that always describes a noun.

> **EXAMPLE**
>
> All of their computers got an upgrade, thanks to a strategic alliance with a Silicon Valley manufacturer.

"There" is an adverb meaning "at/to that location."

> **EXAMPLE**
>
> Please go there and try to set up a solar power system for her house.

Finally, "they're" is the contraction of "they are."

> **EXAMPLE**
>
> They're so pleased with your work that they're giving you an award.

WHO/WHOM

Simply stated: "Who" is a subject.

> **EXAMPLE**
>
> Who is in charge of ensuring that our hotel recycles and reuses?

"Whom" is an object.

> **EXAMPLE**
>
> To whom shall I attribute this great decision?

You can tell you need an object ("whom") if a preposition precedes it. In the example above, the preposition "to" precedes "whom."

BETWEEN/AMONG

"Between" is the preposition that shows the relationship between two nouns. "Among" is used for relationships among three or more.

> **EXAMPLE**
>
> We have to choose among these four new logo designs. It's a decision that you and I must make between us.

Bonus Tip

In spoken English, the word "whom" is rarely used (except in unusual situations or by grammarians). As we become more informal and thus conversation-like in our writing, my guess is that the same will eventually be true on paper. But for now, it is best to continue to use "whom" to refer to a person as an object in a sentence — especially if you have any doubts about how strictly you should adhere to traditional formality.

Some people also use "who" and "whom" to refer to pets or corporations. Controversy swirls around such usage because those entities are formally considered objects that require "that." However, groups of people unquestionably require the word "that" (as in, "the soccer team that won the championship for our city").

But…if you are describing one-to-one relationships of pairs within a larger group, or more of a single type of relationship shared by several parties in one group, use "between."

EXAMPLE

We act as citizen diplomats: We try to maintain peaceful relationships between the countries in our region, despite our governments' official stands.

FARTHER/FURTHER

"Farther" refers to physical length or distance.

EXAMPLE

Our projects are much too centered here in the city. We should extend them farther into the rural areas.

"Further" means "to a greater degree," "additional," or "additionally." It refers to time or amount, or anything metaphorical or figurative. "Further" is more common because it has so many more possible uses.

EXAMPLES

1. This report requires further study. *(Meaning "additional study.")*

2. I need to get further along on my to-do list before I can realistically commit to helping you write thank-you notes to the investors.

FEWER/LESS

Use "fewer" with items that you can count individually.

EXAMPLE

There were twenty fewer resumes to review today than yesterday.

Use "less" with qualities, and with quantities that you cannot individually count.

EXAMPLE

At the art opening last night, I should have drunk less organic wine than I did.

THAT/WHICH

If you thought these two words were interchangeable, you will have to think again. And no, always using "which" does not make you sound more professional, educated, or impressive (despite what you may have been led to believe). "That" tells you a necessary piece of information about its antecedent (that is, the noun that comes before it).

EXAMPLE

The twenty gloves that we used for the wetland cleanup project got tattered.

Here the phrase answers an important question: Which of the many possible gloves are we talking about? The information contained in the phrase introduced by "that" is essential to the sentence's meaning.

Without knowing this, we would have no idea which gloves got tattered. The sentence would have been: "The twenty gloves got tattered."

EXAMPLE

Please put the donated food that has already spoiled into the compost bin.

The implication here is that *not all* of the donated food has already spoiled. Only the rotten items should be composted.

"Which," in contrast, signals a non-essential (but hopefully interesting or at least worthwhile) piece of information.

EXAMPLE

Please put the donated food, which has already spoiled, in the compost bin.

Here the implication is that all of the donated food has already spoiled. If you were to remove the "which" phrase in the middle we would still know what to do with the food: "Please put the donated food in the compost bin."

Here are three other ways to help you decide if you need "that" or "which":

1. If you need the phrase in question to answer "Which one(s)?", use "that." After all, you would answer, "That one!" If you don't need the phrase to answer the question, use "which."

2. If the phrase needs commas you probably need "which."

3. Imagine "by the way" following every "which."

EXAMPLE

You would be correct in saying, "Please throw away the donated food, which (by the way) has already spoiled."

On the other hand, we would not say, "The twenty gloves that (by the way) we used for the wetland cleanup project got tattered," because we need to know specifically which gloves we are discussing.

Bonus Tip

If you have been reading or listening to a lot of work created in other English-speaking countries (such as Britain, Canada, and Australia), you probably have noticed something fishy about this rule. American English swims in a different sea in its use of "that" and "which." Go figure.

Personally speaking

I have to admit the "that"/"which" confusion is so common that I often do not worry about it anymore. I correct the usage in my clients' official or formal documents, but most people do not know or could not care less about the difference. In certain cases, your choice will determine your meaning and that, of course, needs to be addressed. However, in the final analysis, I think there often are more important things in the world to focus on. My grammarian friends may disagree.

WRITING WORKOUT

This exercise offers you a few shots at handling tricky words.

A. Will the election results _____ [affect/effect] your ability to carry out your mission?

B. What _____ [affect/effect] will the election results have on your ability to carry out your mission?

C. _____[It's/Its] difficult to determine _____ [it's/its] color because _____ [it's/its] dark in here.

D. _____ [Whose/Who's] turn is it to suggest a theme for the new website?

E. _____ [Their/They're/There] going over _____[their/they're/there], where _____ [their/they're/there] going to tabulate _____[their/they're/there] revenue from tonight's special event.

F. I'm going to the film screening tonight, but I don't know with _____[who/whom] I will be sharing a cab.

G. According to my planning schedule for the affordable housing project, we should be _____ [further/farther] along in our construction process by now.

H. I'm upset because even though he worked _____ [fewer/less] hours than I did last year, he got the promotion!

I. Our community services referral list, _____ [that/which] is five years old, needs updating.

J. We need to write a vision statement _____ [that/which] clarifies what our community will look like when we succeed.

K. All of our coffee beans _____[that/which] come from co-ops in Central America are organically grown.

Nail down your punctuation 24

The first thing I would say about punctuation is this: Minimize the need for it whenever you can. It can really get in the way of effective copywriting.

The more punctuation you use, the more complicated your sentences will become. Avoid using so many phrases that your writing becomes a jumble of lines and dots. Instead, stick to shorter sentences with more punch and spunk.

That said, you will still need to use *some* punctuation. And most people have at least one lingering question about the proper way to punctuate sentences. Clearly, if you use the wrong symbols in the wrong spots, you can ruin your meaning and confuse your reader. For example: "Let's eat, Dad!" means something completely different than "Let's eat Dad!" Health professionals often deal with "disease-causing poor nutrition," but fewer see disease *causing* poor nutrition.

Unfortunately, the answers are not always so easy to come by in everyday life. And you cannot rely on popular printed materials because they are often riddled with poor punctuation as well.

If you are like most people, you often choose to stick with the punctuation you are most familiar with. It might be a bit intimidating to risk misusing a symbol you are not used to. While that system is acceptable, if you can expand your horizons a bit you can add some texture and variety to your writing.

In particular, if you usually do not write with semicolons, colons, or dashes, consider introducing them. Parentheses can also help (if used sparingly).

Because we all could use a refresher on this stuff at times, there is absolutely no need to be embarrassed. This chapter offers a quick rundown of particularly pesky punctuation I often see in my clients' work; you can find more detailed instruction in the Recommended Resources.

Speaker Introduction

Here is the piece as it was supposed to be:

"Ladies and Gentlemen, I bring you a man among men. He is out of place when among cheaters and scoundrels. He feels quite at home when surrounded by persons of integrity. He is uncomfortable when not helping others. He is perfectly satisfied when his fellow human beings are happy. He tries to make changes in order for this country to be a better place. He should leave us this evening with feelings of disgust at ineptitude and a desire to do better. I present to you Mr. John Smith."

Someone made several punctuation errors, so that the master of ceremonies found himself reading the following:

"Ladies and Gentlemen, I bring you a man. Among men, he is out of place. When among cheaters and scoundrels, he feels quite at home. When surrounded by persons of integrity, he is uncomfortable. When not helping others, he is perfectly satisfied. When his fellow human beings are happy, he tries to make changes. In order for this country to be a better place, he should leave us this evening. With feelings of disgust at ineptitude and a desire to do better, I present to you Mr. John Smith."

(Adapted from urban legend on the Internet)

COMMAS

Commas basically suggest a short pause or hesitation, like a flashing yellow traffic light.

Use commas to attach words, prepositional phrases, or dependent clauses to the beginning or end of a sentence

EXAMPLES

1. After the massive earthquake, the city's inhabitants no longer had electricity.   *(prepositional phrase)*

2. Although I am not really interested in diamonds and rubies per se, I am delighted that some jewelers are now carrying certified conflict-free gems.   *(dependent clause, which cannot stand alone)*

3. Yes, punctuation can be kind of tricky.   *(single word)*

4. I'd like to introduce you to my favorite social entrepreneur, who is standing right over there.   *(dependent clause)*

Use commas to set off non-essential phrases within a sentence, often involving "which" or "who"

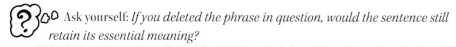 Ask yourself: *If you deleted the phrase in question, would the sentence still retain its essential meaning?*

EXAMPLES

1. The administrative assistant, who is painfully overworked, should get a raise.

2. The grantwriting seminars, which were extremely crowded, were all held during the same week.

Here, the underlined phrases are not essential, so they are set off by commas.

But think about what would happen if you wrote:
"I would like to work for a public-benefit organization that has a budget over a million dollars."

All of the info in this sentence is essential. Your meaning would be completely altered if you only wrote: "I would like to work for a public- benefit organization" and omitted the "that" phrase. Thus, you would not use a comma here.

(By the way, you can further explore the difference between "that" and "which" in Chapter 23, "Sort out confusing words.")

Use commas before a conjunction to connect two complete sentences (also known as "independent clauses")

Here, the conjunction and comma work as a team, and that team is equivalent to a semicolon. (Compare that to: "Here, the conjunction and comma work as a team; that team is equivalent to a semicolon.")

EXAMPLE

She attended the ceremony, but she was not expecting to win the Humanitarian of the Year Award.

But don't use a comma if you do not have a complete sentence on both sides of the conjunction.

EXAMPLE

She attended the ceremony but was not expecting to win the Humanitarian of the Year Award.

Bonus Tip

The phrases in these examples are not "phrases" in the grammarian's sense of the word. Because each contains a verb and a relative pronoun, they are called "subordinate clauses" (technically, relative clauses).

Use commas to separate three or more items in a list

Some punctuation conventions (such as mine in this book) require the comma before the "and" or "or" in a series of three or more items. This final comma is known as the "serial comma." Others don't use it at all. Either way is fine, as long as you are consistent throughout your document.

> **EXAMPLES**
>
> 1. We focus on planning, drafting, and editing.
>
> 2. These writing techniques apply to documents in marketing, fundraising and related fields.

If your list is long or complicated, you should consider using dashes, semicolons, or other punctuation marks to maintain clarity. See below.

DASHES

When most people say "dash" they are thinking of the line usually written as "—." Graphic designers and typesetters know this as an "em-dash," as it is roughly the length of the letter "m."

Many styles (such as the one in this book) place em-dashes directly adjacent to the words they separate. That is, they do not put spaces between them. You should decide how you want to handle em-dashes and be consistent with your choice.

Check your word processing software to see if it includes an em-dash symbol that you can type directly. You can create the low-tech version by typing two hyphens next to each other ("--").

Use dashes to emphasize a non-essential but important thought

While you can use commas or parentheses to do the same thing, dashes will make the included point stand out more.

> **EXAMPLE**
>
> We invited Janet—who is the Director—to say a few words to the board.

Use dashes to set off material already containing commas

> **EXAMPLE**
>
> My three brothers — Jim, David, and Cameron — have formed a consulting firm to help companies become more socially responsible.

Use dashes to note a break, pause, or hesitation between an introductory phrase and the featured item

This function is similar to that of a colon (see below).

> **EXAMPLE**
>
> I'm pleased to introduce a writer committed to the craft—you!

Use dashes to indicate some missing letters or words

> **EXAMPLE**
>
> The emergency phone dispatcher could only hear a few words over the cell phone: "We just ran into — pole. The airbag didn't —. Help!" But the message was clear.

Use dashes to show an emphatic or awkward pause in a sentence

> **EXAMPLES**
>
> 1. Our company will be able to sponsor an athlete in the Special Olympics with the money we raise—am I right?
>
> 2. I find their behavior totally freaky—er—I mean, "rather unusual."

Use a dash to attribute a quotation

> **EXAMPLE**
>
> "Writing is the only thing that, when I do it, I don't feel I should be doing something else."— Gloria Steinem

Use a dash to introduce an additional, closely related idea

> **EXAMPLE**
>
> Our customers shop with both their dollars and their values—both are important to them.
>
> *(A colon is also an option here.)*

HYPHENS

Don't make the mistake of confusing em-dashes with hyphens. Hyphens connect two or more words that need to stay close together to make sense. But which words get hyphenated and which ones don't? That depends somewhat on the particular orthographic (spelling) style you are using.

If you do not have an established style for your organization, edit according to a good dictionary. I suggest, however, putting together a "style guide" of standards for yourself

Bonus Tip

En-dashes (the length of the letter "n") are the not-so-well-known cousins of em-dashes. They are used to show number ranges, meaning "up to and including." Numerals, dates, money, and times all fall into this category. Examples:

❋ January–December 10 a.m. – 4 p.m.

❋ You can sponsor our work for an investment of $100–$249.

The en-dash can also show contrast between two values that would be read aloud as "to." Examples:

❋ Notre Dame beat Miami 31–30.

❋ The Supreme Court voted 5–4 to uphold the decision.

Occasionally, you will run across a few other uses.

Personally speaking

In my world, en-dashes are too much to worry about. I leave them to graphic designers to take care of.

or your organization. It will help achieve consistency on all kinds of punctuation, spelling, and related matters. Chapter 25, "Proofread—and then proofread again," goes into more detail about this.

Hyphenation goes more by convention than by strict rules, as you may have noticed. But in general, the goal is simply to make your sentences easier to read and understand. To get you started, here are some guidelines that usually apply:

Use hyphens to string together several words that comprise a single noun

EXAMPLES

1. Get-together

2. Jack-(or Jane-)of-all-trades

When two or more words or numbers go together to create a single adjective, hyphenate them

EXAMPLES

1. State-of-the-art social networking website

2. Parent-tested and parent-approved educational product

3. Well-known philanthropists in our community

4. Less-than-ideal solution to our solid waste problem

5. Atlanta-based organization

6. Thought-provoking argument

In many punctuation styles, when a word acts as an adjective it needs a hyphen. However, when the same word acts as a noun it has no such need. Again, if you don't have to abide by any particular style, choose your method and stick to it.

EXAMPLES

1. We have a *cutting-edge* approach to reducing our carbon emissions.

   But... Our approach to reducing our carbon emissions is on *the cutting edge*.

2. The *10-year-old* software system at our school needs updating.

   But... The software system at our school is *10 years old* and desperately needs updating.

You may have noticed that some people hyphenate their ethnic identities, while others do not. For instance, an African-American (adjective) person may call herself an African American (noun).

Her colleague, however, may want to emphasize the bond between both of his backgrounds and simply call himself an African-American.

DON'T hyphenate an adverb that ends in "ly" when you use it along with an adjective

> **EXAMPLE**
>
> The conference included many highly rated multi-media presentations.

Mind your prefixes and suffixes

Notice how some words with prefixes (such as: co-, pre-, de-, non-, anti-) and suffixes (such as: –like and –esque) require hyphens, while others (generally, more established terms) do not.

> **EXAMPLES**
>
> 1. "Lifelike" is not hyphenated but "ghost-like" is.
>
> 2. "Pseudo-conservative" is hyphenated but "pseudonym" is not. The same is true for "Clinton-esque" and "Rubenesque."
>
> 3. Note that the word "prefix" is not hyphenated, but when you use the prefix "pre-" before a separate word to mean "before," it will usually take a hyphen (e.g., pre-college).

Of course, when a prefix comes before a capitalized adjective, always use a hyphen (as in "non-Western medicine").

And if you are separating two hyphenated words using "and" or "or," pay close attention. If they share the same root word, but have different prefixes or suffixes, you can drop the root word from the first instance—but you have to keep both hyphens. The first one is called a "suspended," "hanging," or "dangling" hyphen.

> **EXAMPLES**
>
> 1. One way to evaluate your success is to take pre- and post-surveys.
>
> 2. This bottle cap is both child- and adult-proof.

Bonus Tip

Over time, words often evolve in their use of hyphens. Traditionally, separate words that become associated in readers' minds morph into hyphenated words. Some eventually combine to form single words.

For instance, "electronic mail" soon became "e-mail" and then finally "email."

In recent years, many formerly hyphenated words have dropped their hyphens. Some people think that hyphens often make words look messy or old-fashioned, especially on the Internet. For instance, The 2007 *Shorter Oxford English Dictionary* formally sanctioned hyphen changes in about 16,000 words. In that reference, many hyphenated words split in two, while others (as you would generally expect) combined into one.

Use hyphens to reduce ambiguity

Hyphens can help you make a clear distinction between word pairs that could otherwise be confused.

> **EXAMPLES**
>
> 1. Re-form (to form again) and reform (to improve by change)
>
> 2. Re-create (create again) and recreate (do fun or leisurely things)

If an adjective can describe two different words in a sentence, a hyphen can make sure the reader knows what is going on.

> **EXAMPLES**
>
> 1. "A disturbing news-reader" is a disturbing reader of news, but "a disturbing-news reader" is a reader of disturbing news.
>
> 2. A "man-eating shark" is a shark that eats people (or men), but a "man eating shark" is exactly what it says: a male adult human eating a shark.

Get creative with hyphens to add variety and a conversation-like feel to your pieces

Consider coining a new phrase by linking words via a string of hyphens.

> **EXAMPLES**
>
> 1. The not-so-civil disobedience
>
> 2. That sinking missed-the-deadline-now-what-do-I-do feeling
>
> 3. She prefers thoughtful, calm, inclusive discussion to we-gotta-change-the-world-right-now-or-else rhetoric.

Just apply this technique strategically, or you will sound like a breathless-always-on-the-run-and-aren't-I-clever writer.

COLONS

Use a colon to introduce and emphasize long quotations, lists, or important words

> **EXAMPLES**
>
> 1. Northrop Frye, a distinguished Canadian literary critic and literary theorist, described prose as: "Not ordinary speech, but ordinary speech on its best behavior, in its Sunday clothes, aware of an audience and with its relation to that audience prepared beforehand."

2. Our benefit concert featured several of our favorite bands from the 1980s: The Indigo Girls, Joan Jett and the Heartbreakers, Foreigner, New Edition, and Men at Work.

A colon makes the words after it stand out

EXAMPLES

1. *(without a colon)* Well-known in the field, the organization concentrates on research excellence in the key areas of objectivity and thoroughness.

2. *(with a colon)* Well-known in the field, the organization concentrates on two key excellence factors in its research: objectivity and thoroughness.

The word that comes right after the colon should be capitalized if it is a proper noun or the beginning of a complete sentence. That was the case in the previous example about the popular bands, but not in the one about objectivity and thoroughness.

SEMICOLONS

A semicolon separates one independent clause (a clause that could stand on its own as a sentence) from another in the same compound sentence. You can use a semicolon instead of a period to show a close relationship between two ideas.

EXAMPLE

We would not be able to carry out our work without individual donations; we must learn new ways to approach our wealthy supporters.

Use a semicolon before an independent clause

Look for those beginning with: however, hence, therefore, thus, indeed, accordingly, besides, consequently, then, for example, namely, and the like.

EXAMPLE

She tried to get her employer to match her tax-deductible donation; however, the company was not about to do that.

Did you notice that the word right after the semicolon requires a comma after it?

DON'T use a semicolon to separate an independent clause from a clause that starts with a conjunction (that is, it could not stand on its own)

EXAMPLE

Original: The single father of three could not pay his rent; because the factory where he had worked for twenty years suddenly closed and left him with no paycheck.

Suggested revision: The single father of three could not pay his rent, because the factory where he had worked for twenty years suddenly closed its doors and left him with no paycheck.

In this example, the word "because" is the conjunction that makes the second clause "dependent" on the first clause.

Use semicolons to separate items in a list if some items contain a comma

EXAMPLE

We invited Joe, who is the Director; Fran, who is new to the organization; and Wilma, whom I had not seen in a while.

Use semicolons in a list to separate independent clauses

EXAMPLE

A few rules to write by:
(1) Always strive for clarity; (2) Write for your reader, not for yourself; and (3) Don't let the Writer's Block Demon get the best of you.

(You may decide to use periods to separate independent clauses in a vertical list.)

APOSTROPHES

Use an apostrophe to indicate a contraction

EXAMPLE

A healthy body and a healthy environment go well together, don't you think?

Use an apostrophe to show possession

EXAMPLES

1. The Board enthusiastically endorsed the Development Director's fundraising plans.

2. Anita and Frederico's son is committed to civil rights and has just joined our staff.

DON'T use an apostrophe for a pronoun that already has a built-in possessive

EXAMPLES

1. Hers, theirs, his, whose

2. "Its" is also a word with a built-in possessive. When it includes an apostrophe, however, it becomes a contraction. (More on this in Chapter 23, "Sort out confusing words.")

In some styles, use an apostrophe to make letters, acronyms, abbreviations, and numbers plural

But never make a conventional noun plural this way! To eliminate this potential confusion, some conventions prohibit using the apostrophe for *any* plural.

EXAMPLES

1. *(in one style)* My sister received straight A's throughout her college career.

2. *(in another style)* She then went on to work for several NGOs.

QUOTATION MARKS

Place your commas, periods, and exclamation points inside your quotation marks. Semicolons and colons go outside. Question marks and exclamation points go inside if they are tied to the quoted text, and outside if tied to the larger sentence.

EXAMPLE

1. "Yes," she said. "This is a strange convention in American English. Don't ask."

2. Our professional association held an online conversation to discuss the new article by the Executive Director, "A Dollars and Sense Argument for Why We Should Green Our industry." I enjoyed the insights and perspectives. How about you and your "people"?

You can use quotation marks for actual direct quotes or exact sayings.

EXAMPLES

1. Our group met with the president of the oil company, repeating our simple message: "We demand cleaner fuel!"

2. They say, "It's better to give than to receive." I prefer to do both.

But you don't need quotation marks for a paraphrased version of quotations.

Use quotation marks to indicate letters, words, or phrases you are commenting on

EXAMPLE

The phrase "focus on our community" has so many different possible meanings. Let's try to figure out what it means within our organization.

Bonus Tip

In British English, this rule about quotation marks is reversed. Punctuation can be kind of frustrating!

Here are two of the most common misuses of quotation marks:

* Using quotation marks inappropriately to attempt to make things stand out: This can bug some people (you will never guess who happens to be one of them). Special type treatments can do this much more elegantly. I cover this in Chapter 20, "Make sure it *looks* right."

* Trying to indicate that something is alleged or so-called by stating these words *plus* using quotation marks around the word in question: Either write about the so-called poet or the "poet"— but not both. That would be overkill.

Use quotation marks for titles of short written works or parts of longer works, such as book chapters

> **EXAMPLE**
>
> In his 1729 satirical essay, "A Modest Proposal," Jonathan Swift suggests a system for combating poverty that is, to say the least, far from modest.

EXCLAMATION POINTS

Go ahead and use exclamation points, but do so sparingly. They can help you maintain a conversational tone, with ups and downs in your emphasis.

> **EXAMPLE**
>
> The $10-million (!) investment we recently negotiated will mean lots of new jobs and facility improvements to our organization.

Just remember that no one likes to be yelled at!!!!!!! Overuse of this punctuation mark, similar to the abuse of putting words in all caps, can make you look amateurish or silly. Consider mixing it up with other ways of showing emphasis, including other punctuation marks.

LATIN PHRASES

English has borrowed words from a slew of languages, with Latin as one of the most prevalent. In fact, we use Latin words and phrases so much that we even *abbreviate* them. The three to especially watch out for appear below. Note the punctuation that each abbreviation requires.

e.g., The full version is "exempli gratia," which means "for the sake of example" or "for example." Watch out for that comma that always finishes off the phrase. Many people forget that.

> **EXAMPLE**
>
> When you draft the event listing for our upcoming webinar, please don't forget to include all of the necessary details (e.g., time, speaker, and fee).

i.e., This is an abbreviation for "id est," meaning "that is." This one also has to end with a comma.

> **EXAMPLE**
>
> Our office needs new ecologically sound carpet (i.e., a type that neither contains toxins nor contributes to indoor air pollution).

, etc. Use this as your final entry in a list too long to complete. It stands for "et cetera," which translates to "and the rest," "and so on," or "and more." Precede this with a comma but never the word "and."

> **EXAMPLE**
>
> The article outlines several things you need to keep in mind when looking for a job at a socially responsible organization: your relevant skills and background, your values and motivations, your connections, your workstyle, etc.

PERIODS

Listen to William Zinsser, a great—and blunt—writing teacher, tell it like it is: "There's not much to be said about the period except that most writers don't reach it soon enough."

WRITING WORKOUT

In this exercise, you will experience how accurate punctuation can clarify meaning and clean up your sentences.

STEP 1: Punctuate each of these sentences without changing the existing word order. Feel free to change the capitalization if necessary.

    A. The accountant who is part-time needs your timesheets dont forget to include any .25s or .75s

    B. The Executive Director the father of two young children is speaking at the donor reception in the late evening but he wishes he didnt have to

    C. The foundation officer told the audience As you can see ms Mendozas grant proposal is excellent Its very fundable

    D. Our government agency is always looking for great community programs to partner with eg those working with young children the elderly or people with disabilities

    E. As a cooperative venture among three social enterprises the Community Alliance is uniquely positioned to provide a wide range of low cost wellness services to our states veterans

    F. My parents often describe themselves as non conformists at heart although they may appear mainstream with their traditional haircuts well ironed outfits and suburban home they harbor dreams of living a bohemian lifestyle

    G. I wish we could find a more detailed way to evaluate our effectiveness than simply tabulating pre and post session surveys

    H. Several state and local environmental regulations apply to this waterway so we need to clean up our act in more ways than one.

STEP 2: Try your hand at writing a few sentences about your organization using at least one well-placed exclamation point and a semicolon (feel free to punch up an existing document).

STEP 3: Then write a paragraph that creatively describes a common situation at your organization by coining at least one new hyphenated phrase. Also, highlight at least one element by using (em-)dashes.

STEP 4: Take a few moments to search for good uses of exclamation points, semicolons, hyphens, and m-dashes in the writing of a colleague or two. Jot them down on your Personal Cheat Sheet as models that relate to your specific organizational context.

STEP 5: Finally, find out if your organization has a style guide of any kind. If you do have one, familiarize yourself with it. If you need to, check out any of the established style guides listed in the Recommended Resources section; consult it for the next two weeks about any lingering punctuation questions or debates you may have.

"*What is written without effort is in general read without pleasure.*"

— Samuel Johnson

Proofread — and then proofread again. 25

LITZLER

"I'M REALLY NOT MUCH OF A PROOFREADER BUT I DID CATCH MOST OF YOUR B.S."

Great news: Your document is almost ready to roll! You have made it through a lot of editing hoops. There is just one final act: proofreading.

Going through your piece one last time to sniff out little problems will help you project a professional, polished image to the world. Whenever you are reaching out to your audience — for marketing, fundraising, or any other purpose — this last step can make the critical difference between iffy and solid.

Want to see a few famous examples of proofreading errors that got people in trouble? Here you go:

Personally speaking

I don't know how many times I have caught proofreading errors in the published material I read. Despite my best attempts, this book is also bound to have a few slip-ups. Please accept my humble apologies.

EXAMPLES

1. In January 2007, CNN ran a graphic about a show on Osama bin Laden with the title, "Where's Obama?" The show's host, Wolf Blitzer, and the network had to issue repeated apologies to Barack Obama for the slip-up.

2. In 1994, *The St. Augustine Record* boasted its centennial anniversary on the front page with the bold headline, "100 Years of Pubic Service."

3. You may think that spinach has an enormous iron content, as featured in the *Popeye* cartoons starting in 1929. But in reality, an 1870 scientific publication about spinach misplaced a decimal point, giving the vegetable ten times more iron than it actually had. German chemists discovered the mistake in 1937, and the news finally went public in the *British Medical Journal* in December 1981.

4. A 1631 version of the *Holy Bible*, often called the "The Wicked Bible," "The Adulterous Bible," or "The Sinners' Bible," left out a crucial word. One of the ten commandments it listed was: "Thou shalt commit adultery." The King of England slapped a severe fine on the book's printers, and almost all of the copies were then burned. Only a handful have survived to this day.

The lesson? Take the time to pursue the highest quality you can. High standards make your work stand out from the crowd (and help you avoid embarrassment — or worse). If you think your computer's handy-dandy spell-checker is all you need to catch your every error, think again. If only things were that simple!

Final proofreading is actually harder than it looks. You have to keep in mind dozens and dozens of grammar, spelling, and punctuation rules. And you are still bound to miss things on your first go-round.

I already mentioned this (in Chapter 17, "Edit the big picture"), but it is worth repeating. Always take a break from your writing — preferably at least 24 hours — before you proofread. You need to put some space between yourself and your piece, so your perspective can freshen up a bit. A mini-vacation will do you worlds of good.

Here are some other tips to make your proofing task less draining.

PROOFREAD MANUALLY

While your first proofing pass can be a simple computer spell-check, make sure you proofread at least once manually. I recommend printing out your piece, reading it aloud, and using a colored pen to mark your changes. Seeing your work on paper, and performing it as spoken word, can often make it much more real to you — as someone will *actually* experience it. You might even read into a tape recorder and play it back.

Read each syllable separately, and feel free to use a ruler or edge of a blank piece of paper to keep your place. After you make each correction, re-read the phrase or entire sentence to make sure it makes sense in its new form.

Please refer to the other chapters in this section ("Picky, Picky, Picky"), as you check for: subject, verb, and pronoun disagreement (Chapter 21); clumsy sentence structures (Chapter 22); confused homophones (Chapter 23), and punctuation glitches (Chapter 24). In addition, you will want to pinpoint any of these errors:

- Misused or inappropriate words or phrases
- Redundancies
- Overused words, phrases, or sentence structures
- Overly long passages
- Awkward word order
- Clichés
- Outdated language
- Simplistic or contradictory phrases
- Shifts in the narrator's point of view
- Abrupt tone changes
- Questionable spellings — especially names, places, acronyms, titles, email addresses, and URLs
- Inaccurate or questionable numbers, dates, or other facts
- Verbs mismatched with objects or prepositions (e.g., "Her dedication to environmental sustainability has *achieved* her many awards.")
- Things that just don't sound right
- Graphics without captions that contain a vivid verb in the active voice

Spelling Checker

Eye Halve a Spelling Chequer

Eye halve a spelling chequer
It came with my pea sea
It plainly marques four my revue
Miss steaks eye kin knot sea.

Eye strike a key and type a word
And weight four it two say
Weather eye am wrong oar write
It shows me strait a weigh.

As soon as a mist ache is maid
It nose bee fore two long
And eye can put the error rite
Its rarely ever wrong.

Eye have scent this massage threw it
I am shore your pleased two no
Its letter perfect in it's weigh
My chequer tolled me sew.

— Sauce unknown

(www.ahajokes.com)

◈ Improper margins, headers, footers, spacing, page numbering, etc.

◈ Inconsistent fonts or other type treatments

◈ Troublesome line, paragraph, column, or page breaks

◈ Any broken links in online writing

◈ Any other errors that jump off the page

A few other suggestions:

Read each sentence backwards. Here you are not reading for meaning but for appearance (misspellings, repeated words, font changes, etc.). You will thus ensure that you are not just seeing what you meant to write, but the actual words on the page.

Bonus Tip

Set your email program to automatically spell-check your messages before they go out. With this simple step, you can avoid tripping yourself up when you are trying to establish or maintain a professional and credible reputation. I cannot tell you how many times this trick could have helped my clients appear to be on top of things (even if they were struggling a bit). Also, be sure to skim through your messages before you send them out; sometimes even a cursory glance will show you problems or awkward segments.

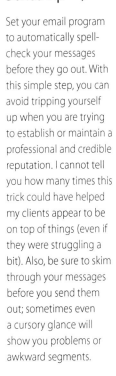

Turn your computer monitor's viewer to well over 100%. That way, the letters will attract your attention because they are much bigger than you are used to seeing them.

After manual proofing, run your piece through a spell-checker one more time. Sometimes when you correct one error you accidentally introduce a new one.

Show your work to a friend. A second pair of eyes will often catch more problems than you can alone. If you have a "style guide" (see below), you may want to share it with your friend. (You might also want to ask your helper to curb the tendency we often have to alter others' writing by simply substituting synonyms—in an effort to make it appear that we have done something.)

CHECK YOUR PIECE AGAINST YOUR ORGANIZATION'S STYLE GUIDE

If at all possible, make sure that the documents you send out maintain the same style. If your organization does not already use a certain style across the board, consider creating a style guide of your own (this has been the case for many of my clients). Check *The Chicago Manual of Style,* the *Associated Press Stylebook, The New York Times Manual of Style and Usage,* the *Modern Language Association Style Manual,* or a similar style guide to see what such a document might look like.

Your style guide will declare the standard ways your organization spells, punctuates, capitalizes, abbreviates, and/or uses common words.

EXAMPLES

- "nonprofit" *vs* "non-profit"
- "environmentally friendly" or "green" or both
- " — " or "- -"
- "twenty-two" or "22"
- "Director" or "director"
- "N.G.O.s" or "NGO's" or "N.G.O.'s" or "NGOs"
- "e-mail" or "email"
- "America" or "U.S."
- "Asian-American" or "Asian American" (for nouns)
- "we" or "the organization" or "The Organization of Perfectionists"
- "June 21" or "21 June" or "June 21st"

Sometimes people say they want "proofreading" when they really need a more in-depth copyediting session that will clear up, clean up, tighten up, brighten up, or shape up their writing. This has happened to me more than a few times. If you are asked to do this, I would recommend reviewing the earlier parts of this book — and maybe suggesting that your friend obtain a copy, too.

Then you need to consider related graphic design elements. For instance, what type treatments do you use to signify special items, such as publications you refer to, quotes you cite, or non-English words you use ("e.g." or "*e.g.*")? How should you handle headings, subheads, bullets, charts, and tables? What about your use (or avoidance) of footnotes? (See Chapter 20, "Make sure it *looks* right," for more on graphic design.)

When I am proofreading a piece, I usually put together a customized style guide. This is a list of ways the author prefers to use words, acronyms, numbers, and phrases that have multiple possibilities. I also note any special grammatical constructions.

By the way, you may think that stylistic consistency does not really matter to anyone but super-picky people. While this may be true in some cases, your image could be at stake here. It is better not to risk it.

KNOW THYSELF — BUILD YOUR PERSONAL CHEAT SHEET

Have you been keeping your own Personal Cheat Sheet? If so, that will help you steer clear of some of your most common mistakes. It will also remind you of especially important cautionary notes you have run across in this book.

But if you have not yet gotten around to putting your notes together, this would be an ideal time to go back and pull out what you have found to be most personally relevant. You may have been highlighting or dog-earing the pages, and that is fine. However, my guess is that once you have all of the information in one place, you

Personally speaking

At different times, I have tended to use an overabundance of certain types of punctuation, as well as to repeat certain words and sentence elements. You can bet that those hot-button areas have featured prominently on my Personal Cheat Sheet over the years.

will be more likely to try out my suggestions, because you will have a handy, self-customized reference guide.

DOUBLE-CHECK THE SPELLINGS OF FAMILIAR WORDS

Pay special attention to familiar words or phrases that show up a lot in your work. You can easily gloss right over them and ignore missing, incorrect, or transposed letters or words.

Cognitive psychologists tell us that when we encounter word fragments, our brains will fill in the letters that we *meant* to include, or believe should be there, but are actually missing. We also tend to skim over high-frequency words, assuming that they are always correct. We can find it hard to notice repeated letters or words when we were intending to only write them once (a phenomenon called "repetition blindness").

Some fields or institutions still require two spaces after a period. Abide by whatever convention is in place at your organization.

WHEN WRITING ON A COMPUTER, USE ONE SPACE BETWEEN SENTENCES

Back in typewriter days, we used two spaces to separate our sentences. The good news is that when you only use one space, you save precious room (and characters) in your documents. It also looks better from a graphic design point of view.

One good way to check for spacing issues after periods (or other characters) is to turn on your word processor's paragraph and spacing indicators so you can monitor for consistency more easily.

WRITING WORKOUT

This exercise will help you sharpen your eye for proofreading. Refer to your Personal Cheat Sheet and customized style guide, if you have already created them.

STEP 1:   Proofread these samples for errors. Keep in mind that you want to preserve the original writer's words and intent as much as possible, while correcting problems. Watch out: I included some tricky bits!

A. Beths Story

Beth came to The Family Agency in fear of the father of her child who has tried repeatedly to gain visitation rights regarding her young daughte. hE is still harassing them. A three year Domestic Violence Restrcturing Order against hem previously been obtained by Beth. She did not has no income.

Extreme difficult to overcome, we knew that the challenge would be daunting. beth had been born deaf, had trouble hearing: and you can communicate only in nonverbal Relay with her.

Because of the complexity of the communication system, a translator. Had to be found who knew both Realay and American sign Language to insure communication between the Fammily Agency attorney and Beth. Such translator are difficult extremely to and ffind and work with.

Beth kneads to be communicated with in order to explain the child's father's court actions, the relevant laws, and beginning to preparations for the future upcoming herring. Numerous phone calls later, we where able to finally situate a translator whom; after heari-ng about The Family Agency's work, agreed to help us out with a reduced public interest fee ($250 per hour instead of the market rate of $$70). It was far out because she rocked!

   Because of The *Family* Agency and our work of domestic violent, Beth was able to understand, participating and had a voice in decisions her regarding daughter. She didn't have to throw out the baby with the bathwater of her ex-husband.

   (Adapted from the work of the Law Center for Families, www.lcff.org)

B. About Organization X

Organization X is a leadership, development program with a cross-cultural training focus, primarily involving young people (ages 18-26) Organization W was founded in 1996 by two young adults which growed up in Chiacgo in low income, biracial family and from an early age there lives were transformed as a result of key interntional and multicultural experiences.

A primary goal of Organization X is to develop a pool of cool young leadrs of color from low-income *backgrounds* who is culturally sensitive, globally competent: and who are actively   involving in improving their communities

The core pogram of Organization X is and should be the Youth Culture Initatve. During this 10-month program; the kids met regularly met to learrn about community needs and U.S. sub — cultures through a series of innovative and stimulating activities and outings, over the 11 months, wee participate on volunteer service-learning projects in different neighborhooods overnight diversity learning retreats outside the the city environs, and sat thorough interactive workshop's which focused on cross-cultural learning, and leadership devlopment!

(Adapted from the work of World Bridges, www.world-bridges.org)

STEP 2: Proofread a document you wrote a while ago. See if you can find any errors in it now.

⌒ Section-at-a-Glance: Fine-Tuning: Picky, Picky, Picky ⌒

CHAPTER 21: REACH AGREEMENT ON YOUR SUBJECTS, VERBS, AND PRONOUNS

Subjects, verbs, and pronouns: We use these three parts of speech all the time. But we tend not to really think about them, and that is usually fine.

However, these seemingly simple elements of our language carry rules that hold some tricky bits in store. Misuse them at your own peril. At best, you will sound unrefined. At worst, you might offend or confuse someone you care about.

- Coordinate your subjects and verbs.

- Monitor your verb tenses and moods.

- Mind your pronouns!

CHAPTER 22: GET A HANDLE ON YOUR SENTENCE STRUCTURE

Maybe you feel unsure of how to put together your sentences smoothly and persuasively. You may be repeating some of the same mistakes you have been making since grade school. Or, you could just be getting stale and would like to find ways to spice things up.

Check to make sure you are doing the things I cover in this chapter. Since you write for marketing and fundraising (and perhaps other) purposes, you will want to become adept at applying these techniques.

- When comparing two things, name both of them.

- When your sentence deals with an array of ideas, rewrite.

- When you find a sentence with a dangling or misplaced modifier, nip it in the bud.

- Rein in verbs that stray too far from their subjects.

- Present multiple items in parallel grammatical form.

- Be open to change in grammatical customs.

∼Section-at-a-Glance: Fine-Tuning: Picky, Picky, Picky∼

CHAPTER 23: SORT OUT CONFUSING WORDS

The English language sports hundreds of pairs of words that sound alike, look alike, or get confused for other reasons. Some are homophones: words that have the same, or nearly the same, sound but different meanings (e.g., "ensure" and "insure" or "discreet" and "discrete"). Others are near-homophones (e.g., "conscience" and "conscious"), or deceptively similar (e.g., "woman" and "women"). Others are simply misused a lot.

Listed here are nine of the top offenders I come across:

- affect/effect
- it's/its
- who's/whose
- their/there/they're
- who/whom
- between/among
- farther/further
- fewer/ less
- that/which

CHAPTER 24: NAIL DOWN YOUR PUNCTUATION

The first thing I would say about punctuation is this: Minimize the need for it whenever you can. It can really get in the way of effective copywriting.

The more punctuation you use, the more complicated your sentences will become. Avoid using so many phrases that your writing becomes a jumble of lines and dots. Instead, stick to shorter sentences with more punch and spunk.

That said, you will still need to use *some* punctuation. Here is a list of particularly pesky punctuation I often see in my clients' work.

- Commas
- Dashes
- Hyphens
- Colons
- Semicolons
- Apostrophes
- Quotation marks
- Exclamation points
- Latin phrases
- Periods

⁓Section-at-a-Glance: Fine-Tuning: Picky, Picky, Picky⁓

CHAPTER 25: PROOFREAD — AND THEN PROOFREAD AGAIN

Great news: Your document is almost ready to roll! You have made it through a lot of editing hoops. There is just one final act: proofreading.

Going through your piece one last time to sniff out little problems will help you project a professional, polished image to the world. Whenever you are reaching out to your audience — for marketing, fundraising, or any other purpose — this last step can make the critical difference between iffy and solid.

- Proofread manually.

- Check your piece against your organization's style guide.

- Know thyself — build your Personal Cheat Sheet.

- Double-check the spellings of familiar words.

- When writing on a computer, use one space between sentences.

" *Colors fade, temples crumble, empires fall, but wise words endure.* "

— Edward Thorndike

⁓Conclusion⁓

Now that you have worked your way through this book, you are ready to go out there and start (or continue!) ***writing to make a difference***. Allow me to send you off in style.

REMINDERS FOR THE ROAD

1. Go back and revisit your Rate Your Skills Sheet (from page 11). (Recall that I recommended you write down some of your strengths and weaknesses before you read this book.)

Ask yourself: Do you feel more skilled or confident in some of those areas you have been working on? What do you still need to make progress on?

2. Pat yourself on the back! And then make a plan to continue improving. Focus on what you are already great at, and build on that. It really is true that intention and commitment are two of the most effective keys to success.

3. Take a good long look at your Personal Cheat Sheet. It should now be full of valuable reminders. If you think of important notes-to-self that you forgot to record, go back and jot down a few additional ones.

4. Don't forget the Section-at-a-Glance summaries. Those brief pieces distill the most essential information from each chapter. And feel free to share them with a colleague (or two).

5. Use the Writing Workouts and "Ask yourself" questions in this book as discussion material for staff meetings, lunch conversations, affinity

group gatherings, or exchanges on email discussion lists or blogs. Look around—you will find other writers everywhere.

WHAT'S NEXT: THE *WRITING TO MAKE A DIFFERENCE* WEBSITE

This book is only one leg of your journey toward better community-oriented copywriting. Folks in socially responsible organizations (like you) often wear more than one hat and find that being a writer is a necessary—yet perhaps quite secondary—part of the job on an ongoing basis. My website, ***www.dfmassachi.net***, will help you develop a sense of support in what I call a "writing-positive" online community. There, you can:

1. engage in lively conversations with other readers of this book;

2. discuss your writing successes and challenges;

3. ask questions of me and other online community members;

4. get feedback on a piece you are working on;

5. maybe even get to know a few of your partners in crime. If you have not yet found an ongoing writing buddy, you may find one here.

Through the website, you can also sign up for my free e-newsletter, listen to my podcast, watch a webinar, and read my blog. While you are there, notice the web-only content: additional Examples, Writing Workouts, FAQs, Recommended Resources, inspiring words from other writers, late-breaking updates, and much more. Also, look for in-depth explorations of the topics I discuss in this book.

I hope these extensive resources help guide your adventures in ***writing to make a difference***. Please drop me a line and let me know how it's going.

Bon voyage, and Happy writing!

Appendices

APPENDIX 1: Top Twenty Documents in Community-Benefit Organizations

You can apply the techniques I describe in this book to a whole range of documents you write every day. Here is a list categorizing the most common ones.

Introducing...

1. Mission statement/Vision statement
2. Brochure/Business card
3. Event announcement
4. Tip sheet/Fact sheet

Periodicals

5. Newsletter
6. Annual report
7. Special report/White paper

Mailing for Moolah

8. Case statement/Program brief
9. Fundraising appeal letter
10. Thank-you note
11. Grant proposal
12. Grant report

Cyber-Writing

13. Everyday email
14. E-newsletter
15. Website/Blog/Online post

Writing for the Press

16. Press release/Public service announcement
17. Letter to the Editor/Op-Ed

Business as *Unusual*

18. Evaluation tool
19. Internal business letter
20. Cover letter and resume

APPENDIX 2: Glossary of Buzzwords

This glossary contains terminology I use in this book that could benefit from shared definitions. Consider this my attempt to clarify my own jargon.

Benefits: The outcomes you are striving for—the great results and powerful impact that your stakeholders will get from working with you. That is, how your services or products improve the lives of people in your community and satisfy their needs and desires. Answers the question: "So what?"

Brand: Your reputation, your essence, your identity, your personality, and your promise—what your organization stands for. Answers the question: "When someone hears about your organization, what set of images, attributes, feelings, and ideas do you want them to associate with it?"

Call to action: An absolutely clear request to act, including all the details your readers need to easily and quickly respond in the way you want them to (also called "the ask"). Usually includes an implication of urgency.

Community: Group of people—as defined by you—that your organization benefits locally, regionally, nationally, or globally.

Copywriting: Persuasive writing for marketing purposes in which you educate, inspire, and activate your intended readers.

Diversity of readers: The important reality that demands that organizations be inclusive of all people across lines of race, class, ethnicity, culture, gender, age, ability, sexual orientation, education level, life experience, geography, and any other relevant parameters. Requires high levels of respect, understanding, sensitivity, and cultural competency.

Editing: Process of revising your work on multiple levels: macro-level developmental editing for content and structure; copyediting for clarity, flow, conciseness, redundancy, and accuracy; and proofreading for grammar, punctuation, typos, etc.

Evaluation: An extremely important part of any values-driven organization's work. Can include assessment of the quantity and/or quality of services rendered or changes made.

Features: Components or characteristics of the actual services or products your organization offers. Often include detailed answers to questions your most interested readers might ask (or have asked).

Framing: Wordsmithing to encourage a particular point of view and/or assign or deflect responsibility. Can involve single words, phrases, or sentences that define an issue positively or negatively, often emphasizing points with metaphors or similes.

Greenwashing: Unethical practice of portraying a product or service as significantly more environmentally sound than it actually is.

Lead: First few sentences or paragraphs of a piece of writing, enticing your reader to stay with you (sometimes spelled "lede").

Marketing: Sharing information and enthusiasm about your work with interested people who may want to exchange their involvement or support for the value you add to them and their communities.

Metaphor: Figurative language that compares by saying that one thing or concept *is* something more familiar. See *simile*.

NGO: Non-governmental organization, the internationally accepted term for non-profit or charity organization.

Partnership: Between two or more organizations a mutually beneficial arrangement with a financial and/or programmatic aspect.

Point of view: Perspective of the person telling the story. Grammatically speaking, should remain consistent throughout your piece (using first-person, second-person, or third-person pronouns).

Pull-quote: An outstanding quote or a few lines of text presented enlarged, in a special layout or type style, to draw the reader's attention.

Simile: Figurative language that compares by saying that one thing or concept *is like* or behaves in a similar manner as something more familiar. *See metaphor.*

Social math: The term used by the Advocacy Institute and Berkeley Media Studies Group to describe an especially effective technique, wherein you express numbers in terms of a social context familiar to your readers. In essence, draws comparisons to easily understood items or ideas by using vivid word pictures.

Socially responsible organization: A group or entity seeking to achieve a social benefit while remaining accountable to all involved or affected stakeholders. Term includes: nonprofits, social enterprises, green or progressive businesses, community education institutions, social ventures, public-benefit corporations, and cause marketing programs. Descriptors include: "mission-driven," "community-benefit," "community-oriented," "public-interest," "values-driven," and "values-based."

Stakeholders: Those affected by your work, including your clients, customers, members, investors, staff, volunteers, board, the natural environment, and the larger community.

Stories: Slice-of-life word snapshots that can crystallize messages for your readers. Often called "case studies" or "before-and-after stories," illustrate how people similar to your intended readers have benefited from working with your organization. Contain: memorable characters, a clear sequence, conflict, an interesting setting, and a point of view.

Strategic planning: Key process in which an organization assesses its strengths, weaknesses, and context and plans accordingly. Leads to effective marketing and fundraising.

Style guide: A reference work that standardizes your organization's writing customs. Helps achieve consistency on punctuation, spelling, capitalization, abbreviation, word usage, type styles, and related matters.

Support (of an organization): Anything from investments to purchase or patronage, to involvement by volunteers, interns, or staff members.

Sustainability: Potential to keep your work going indefinitely—financially, programmatically, and environmentally.

Swipe file: A handy collection of marketing language that other people or organizations have used successfully. Referred to for inspiration and perspective.

Testimonial: Glowing endorsement in the form of a quote from someone with direct knowledge of your organization's work.

Transparency: A core value implied in your written text, showing that your community can trust you to be clear, open, honest, and accountable for what you do and say.

Triple bottom line: A standard adopted by many socially responsible organizations, focusing on three measures of benefit: people, profits, and the planet.

APPENDIX 3: Writing for Audio

These days, your organization has lots of ways to get your voice (or voices) heard — quite literally. Not only can you still do live presentations, but you can also easily record your words—and those of colleagues, clients, or other stakeholders—and then broadcast them via your website, on blogs, and/or through radio. Examples include audio welcome messages, podcasts, web seminars, news analyses, interviews, testimonials, role-plays, and public service announcements.

The skill levels required to produce these audio pieces vary, but if you have a can-do attitude and a little time and curiosity, you will soon feel proficient and attract listeners. You might begin with an easy project and go from there. And unless you are experienced enough to speak off the top of your head, you will want to compose a script or outline.

But that script cannot be just a piece you have previously written for the page. When writing to be heard, you have to make some adjustments. Harrison Ford famously reminded George Lucas of this idea when, during the making of *Star Wars*, he exclaimed, "You can write this [crap], George, but you sure can't say it!"

Prepare yourself

- Determine the length of time you will have for your piece. Consider the medium you will use for broadcasting, as well as the likely attention span of your audience. Remember that speaking is usually slower than reading the written word, so conciseness is extremely crucial.

- If applicable, assign different roles to your "cast of characters": narrator, host, interviewee, debater, background chorus, spokesperson, presenter, actor, etc. Sometimes those who usually play background roles in work groups will welcome a chance to be the one being interviewed or giving advice. You may also want to talk to people who are unlikely to agree with you or might have an unexpected perspective.

- If there is a specific time and date that your piece will be heard, consider the context and the verb tenses you will use (present tense is usually preferable). If you are aiming for the piece to be listened to for a while, avoid details that limit its relevance.

Gather the material

- If you are doing an interview, make sure that your speakers will explain the story. That is, plan questions that will encourage your speakers to illustrate their points clearly. Put yourself in the shoes of the listener and consider what he or she would want to ask. A common broadcasters' motto says it nicely: "Take me there, make me care."

EXAMPLES

Questions that draw out vivid answers include:

- "Can you tell me a story of a time when [an observation] was true?"
- Why do you think that?
- What makes you care about that topic?
- When did you first start thinking that, and how did you come to your current conclusion?
- Can you compare that to an image or experience that listeners might be more familiar with?

- Your prepared questions should follow a logical progression, but feel free to stray from your original laundry list and go where the conversation leads. Sometimes the best material comes when you least expect it. Furthermore, as the scriptwriter, you retain creative license to play with the content and sequence later. For instance, if you allow your speaker an interesting tangent, but it leads nowhere, you can edit it out.

- Avoid having speakers continue for more than a few minutes at a time. (The human ear and mind love variety and texture.) At the same time, too many characters can be confusing and hard to follow—so stick to just a few key voices for most of the piece.

Draft it out

- Listen closely and deeply to the words of all speakers and the cadences that naturally emerge. Create a realistic, compelling, and flowing implementation of your script, interview, etc.

- Start out with a "teaser" about the general idea you want to address. If you are exploring a controversy or multiple angles of an issue, briefly mention these perspectives.

- Clearly identify all speakers, including any relevant titles or affiliations. The same goes for places, institutions, laws, or other concepts that may be unfamiliar to your listeners.

- Make sure you use everyone's comments in the right context. Help your listener make sense of the content by providing just enough, and not too much, background. If something takes too long to explain, you may need to just leave it out (however difficult that choice may be).

- If your piece is more than a few minutes long, use some narration to re-introduce your speakers and re-establish the context. Your listeners may enter your piece in the middle, or may benefit from a periodic check-in.

- While the statements you use (sound bites and conversational exchanges) are the main ingredients of your piece, consider sprinkling in some sounds other than the speakers' voices, such as sound effects or music. Encourage speakers to vary their tone of voice and emphasize key words to enhance connection to the audience.

- Simplicity is key here, where simple means elegant, not simplistic. Your listeners rarely have instant access to the written transcript, so help them keep track of important details. Keep those details, such as numbers and exact dates, to a minimum. If you do use numbers, try to compare them by using percentages, fractions, or multiples (e.g., 70% more this year, or 1/5 of last year's budget).

- The best way to listen to your work is to read it out loud—several times—at full speed, in full voice. Focus on words you want to emphasize and on which phrases might serve to perk up your listeners' ears. When you are ready to perform your script, print it out in double-space in at least 14-point font, so it is easy to read at a comfortable distance.

(If you have not already, check out Chapter 15, "Make sure it *sounds* right," which offers tips on how to make your written words roll off your reader's tongue. I also offer pointers on gathering quotes in Chapter 5, "Share stories.")

Note: Lisa Rudman, Executive Director of the National Radio Project, contributed significantly to this Appendix. Website: www.radioproject.org.

APPENDIX 4: Additional Hot Marketing Words and Phrases

A: HYPNOTIC MARKETING WORDS

This list gives you a taste of the types of words and phrases that have proven highly effective in the work of well-known copywriter Dr. Joe Vitale (a.k.a. Mr. Fire). In fact, Vitale calls them "hypnotic." Check them out, and try to incorporate them.

affordable	experience	please
always	expert	powerful
amazing	explain	practical
announcing	finally	promise
answer	fun	proven
automatically	generous	revealed
best-selling	handy	sale
beyond	hurry	share
breakthrough	ideal	simple
can't wait	imagine	smiled
caring	immediately	specialize
charm	improve	spellbinding
compelling	included	step-by-step
complete	insider	strategies
complimentary	insights	stunned
convenient	instant	successful
critical error	intuitive	suddenly
delight	iron-clad guarantee	thank you
detailed	key	the truth about
did you know...	latest hit	thrilled
discover	literally	tips
distilled wisdom	look	today
effective	love	top-notch
enjoy	mesmerize	transform
essential	now	turning point
everyday	one-stop shop	unprecedented
excited	perfect for	value

(Source: Joe Vitale, www.mrfire.com)

B: VISIONARY VOCABULARY

Review this list of community-oriented words, and see if they resonate with any of your work. The SPIN Project has identified them as particularly helpful in writing for the media.

advocate	equality	people
affirm	fairness	preserve
American	faith	pride
assist	family	principle
balance	fighting	progress
bedrock	forward	promote
benefit	harm	protect
champion	health	public
change	help	relief
community	heritage	respect
compassion	honor	responsible
confirm	hope	risk
damage	hurt	safeguard
defend	injure	strengthen
degrade	integrity	support
democracy	justice	sustain
destroy	legacy	threaten
dignity	mobilize	tolerance
diversity	nation	tradition
endanger	neighborhood	trust
energize	nourish	unity

(Source: SPIN Works! *by Robert Bray and the Independent Media Institute, available from the SPIN Project at www.spinproject.org)*

APPENDIX 5: Additional Common Metaphors and Similes

Can you freshen up these phrases or alter them in creative ways in your own writing?

all your eggs in one basket

bite the hand that feeds you

boomerang effect

break through barriers

burn your candle at both ends

cakewalk

chip on her shoulder

cooking the books

cool as a cucumber

dead as a doornail

doesn't amount to a hill of beans

dog-and-pony show

from the horse's mouth

glass ceiling

hawks and doves

hothead

hotline

in default mode

jump through hoops

let off steam

like a chicken with its head cut off

like riding a bike

look a gift horse in the mouth

looking for an itch to scratch

marching orders

mental gymnastics

moral compass

on a shoestring

on the map

plain vanilla

play hardball

price ceiling (or floor)

pushing the envelope

put out brushfires

reinvent the wheel

robbing Peter to pay Paul

seat-of-the-pants operation

set on its ear

shark-infested waters

shot in the arm

shotgun approach

smoke and mirrors

smooth sailing

split up like billiard balls

square peg in a round hole

step up to the plate

straw that broke the camel's back

tailspin

tidal wave

toothless tiger

wake up and smell the coffee

APPENDIX 6: Writing for Video

A powerful video is an incredibly useful tool for your organization. We are inundated daily by edited video, mostly on television, so most people are receptive to information and stories conveyed with moving imagery, graphics, spoken word, and music.

Video's greatest strength is its ability to make viewers sense the emotional impact of your organization's work. You can show video at events, broadcast it on television, or incorporate it into your website.

Types of videos your organization might consider producing include:

- *Fundraising videos:* shown at large fundraising events, encouraging viewers to dig deeper in their pockets when deciding to support you. They convey the emotion of your story and remind your audience why they care about your mission.

- *Outreach videos:* geared toward a broad audience that knows very little about your mission. They define the problem—and especially your proposed solution—in clear and basic terms.

- *Public Service Announcements (PSAs):* geared for broadcast television, usually running under one minute. They surprise a viewer into quickly caring about your issue. PSAs can be very elaborate or very simple, and can be a lot of fun to plan and produce.

Before you write your script, first identify your intended audience, and decide how you want them to react. A well-written script is fundamental to a successful production.

The first draft

The first draft of your script summarizes your video and helps you begin planning. It includes information about the audience, the message, and most importantly, the look and feel of the video. Video is a visual medium, so plan how you will depict abstract ideas as graphically as possible. Look at photos and other images your organization already has and plan how to feature them in your video.

Focus on the big picture: your mission. Tell the story of your organization and try to fill the viewers with the feeling that drives your work. Determine the main point of your video and write scenes that emphasize or elucidate it. One popular technique is the three-act story: describe the problem, tell how your organization addresses the problem, and show the results.

Consider your organization's best speakers and plan what you would like them to convey. Draft your script by deciding who will talk about what and when. This kind of script is not verbatim speech, but it outlines the whole story.

The script and storyboard

The script is a timeline of your video, using two columns to outline audio and video content at any given moment. First write the audio as a series of sound bites (a few seconds to two or three minutes each), and then describe the corresponding video. This brings to light which sections need special attention. Avoid planning too much video of talking heads, and fully describe each scene in as much detail as possible.

A storyboard is a further pre-visualization tool. It is a script containing a sequence of drawings of the video screen, as well as a description of what happens and what is said in each scene. Major films use very detailed storyboards to depict camera moves and background sound; doing this makes shoots more efficient.

Interviews

Testimonials can tell your success stories effectively. A first-person testimonial is especially compelling, providing an authentic "I experienced it" tale. The story of someone overcoming obstacles is a very popular format. Your organization's staff might describe what changes they have seen in peoples' lives, or why they do the work they do.

A successful interview requires good questioning. Use your script to determine what you would like each of your subjects to say, and a couple of questions you could ask to get that response. Write leading questions to elicit emotional responses, as in, "How did you feel when…" A couple of days before shooting an interview, prepare your speaker: Let her know what questions you will be asking and explain what types of stories you want to hear. Don't worry—this is not cheating!

While filming, encourage your speakers to include restatements of the questions in their answers. Ask plenty of follow-ups and explore details. Don't be afraid to come back to something or to phrase questions in several ways to get phrasing that is clear and concise. Keep a copy of your script handy.

Photos

Your organization probably already has a number of still photos that could be used to complement the spoken words available for your video. Using photos can be a great way to include historical elements that would be difficult to recreate for the camera. For example, it may not be realistic to shoot the "before" side of a "before-and-after" story. Photographs can also be given the feeling of video by adding motion effects in the editing process. In fact, a very cost-effective video can be made using only photos and voice-over.

Voice-over

Voice-over can supplement interviews, present background information, or help define a situation. You should actually write out any voice-over script twice. Use a rough draft during the editing process to keep the story moving and make other decisions, and then tweak the voice-over script to fit the edited video, bringing points together or smoothing out transitions.

A voice-over script should consist of short sentences. Read it aloud to yourself to find tongue twisters and estimate timing. Sentences should not require more than one breath to read, so avoid lists, semicolons, and long clauses. Voice-over is less engaging for the viewer than real dialogue or action, so it should be short and sweet. Writing multiple drafts helps you pare it down further. Be wary of using voice-over to introduce abstract concepts, and be sure to plan visuals to accompany what is being said.

(You can find more information on using sound in Appendix 3, "Writing for audio" and Chapter 15, "Make sure it *sounds* right.")

Conclusion

Video can get viewers emotionally involved in your organization's success. With the rise of desktop video production and the growth of online video, it has become a tool that we all can use. The process of making a video can also be a team-building exercise and a lot of fun! Telling the story of your organization can help remind your staff and volunteers why they do the good (but hard) work they do. And, of course, you'll be sharing your powerful story with the world.

(Source: *Josh Kahn, Production Director of Humanized Productions: www.humanizedproductions.com*)

APPENDIX 7: Gunning Fog Index

Try out Robert Gunning's Fog Index, one of the tests widely used to measure the readability of text. The score received correlates to the approximate grade reading level your piece demands.

STEP 1: Count the words and sentences in a representative passage of about 100 words. (If your document is long, or appears to contain varied sections, run this test on several passages.)

STEP 2: Divide the number of words by the number of sentences to give the average length of each sentence.

STEP 3: Count the number of words of three or more syllables (known as "difficult words") that are not: (a) proper names; (b) combinations of easy words (hyphenated words such as "son-in-law" and compound words, such as "newsletter"); (c) made three syllables by suffixes such as -ed, -es, or -ing; or (d) technical terms that you are certain your reader already knows.

STEP 4: Add the average sentence length (from STEP 2) to the number of difficult words per 100 words (from STEP 3).

STEP 5: Multiply the resulting sum by 0.4.

Most readers will easily digest pieces with a Fog Index score of up to seven or eight, while a score above twelve will lose most people. *The Bible* and works by William Shakespeare and Mark Twain all score about six. *Reader's Digest* has a Fog Index of between eight and nine, as do most local newspapers. *Time*, *Newsweek*, *The New York Times*, and *The Wall Street Journal* average about eleven or twelve.

Remember that the Fog Index provides a general guide, but it does not say anything about the quality of the writing or the sophistication of the thoughts behind it. Clarity is different for different audiences; let common sense be the deciding factor.

APPENDIX 8: Editing Checklist

Chapter 17, "Edit the big picture," covers some basic things that your "critics," while playing the role of your intended readers, should watch for. I have incorporated those ideas below and have added criteria that dig a bit deeper. You can copy this Checklist and attach it as a cover sheet to any document that needs editing.

AUTHOR: Fill in these two blanks:

1. The purpose of the piece is to advance my organization's brand by:

   _____

   _____

   _____

2. The piece aims to engage its specific intended readers, who are:

   _____

   _____

EDITOR: Read through this checklist, and then mark the points that ring true to you about this piece. These general comments should accompany your line edits.

☐ The piece is reader-centered, not writer-centered.

☐ The piece casts the organization or work in the best possible light and positions it as vital to the community and the intended readers.

☐ The piece includes all the information the readers need to know, but does not include unnecessary or distracting concepts.

☐ The writer makes his/her points clearly.

☐ The piece flows nicely and/or the sequence and organization make sense.

☐ The "sound" (or tone) of the piece is consistent and appropriate. It can be described as: _____

☐ The piece is easy to read and understand.

☐ The sentences and paragraphs are concise but not choppy.

☐ The piece is not abstract, but specific and intriguing.

☐ The piece is accessible to me and pulls me in.

☐ The piece starts out with a punchy opening.

☐ The writer lives up to the promise he/she makes at the beginning of the piece.

☐ The ending motivates me to act or to find out more.

☐ The three most important points (especially, benefits) I am taking away are:

    1. _____

    2. _____

    3. _____

☐ I felt _____ after reading the piece.

☐ My favorite part of the piece is: _____

_____

☐ My least favorite part is: _____

_____

☐ I want more examples or stories regarding: _____

_____

☐ I would recommend this piece to others because: _____

_____

☐ My additional specific suggestions for improvement include: _____

_____

_____

_____

_____

_____

APPENDIX 9: Additional Wordy Phrases – and Their Concise Versions

Here is a sample of common wordy phrases that can easily be tightened up. Do you see any you use regularly? If so, you might want to add the more concise versions to your Personal Cheat Sheet.

WORDY PHRASE	CONCISE VERSION
a large number of	many
as a means of; in order to; so as to	to
as per our conversation	as discussed
at a later date	later
at some point in the near future	soon
at the end of the day	finally
comes to a complete stop	stops
connect up	connect
continue on	continue
during the time that	while
exhibits the ability to; has the capability to	can
in a hasty manner	hastily
in a timely manner	quickly
in accordance with your request	as requested
in an accidental way	accidentally
is used in the place of	substitutes for
made use of	used
owing to the fact that	because
people with the responsibility of managing the program	program managers
pertaining to	about; of
place emphasis on	emphasize
should it appear that	if
take into consideration	consider
until such time as	until
with regard to	regarding; concerning; about

APPENDIX 10: How to Form and Sustain a Writing Circle

You have probably noted my recommendations throughout this book to join a writers' group (i.e., team up with at least one other writer). The group could consist of colleagues gathering at work, or of friends who want to improve their writing outside of office hours.

As with a fitness class or a jogging routine, it helps enormously to work alongside others involved in the same activity. (If you have ever tried to motivate yourself to exercise with only DVDs or music as company, you might agree with me.) A group can support you through the tough times, cheer you on at the good times, and also provide feedback to help you grow as a writer. As you hone your craft, don't you deserve to work with other writers on a regular basis?

I encourage you to use this book to guide your budding writers' group. For instance, you can read the same chapter and help each other do the Writing Workouts. You can share Personal Cheat Sheets and encourage each other to address particular challenge areas. Or you can ask each member to identify a piece of her or his own writing that exemplifies any of the 25 techniques I share.

While my website offers opportunities to join a virtual writing circle, you may prefer a face-to-face group. Try these tips to help you form and sustain it:

Stay focused and small

I recommend finding no more than five others who would also like to give this a try. By limiting the group's size, each person will have many opportunities to contribute and receive comments, and will avoid the time commitment burden of a large group.

Agree on some ground rules

Brainstorm about what each person wants to get out of the group and the time you can all devote to it. Discuss the location(s), the frequency of meetings, and the expectations of when and how people will share their work (before or during the meetings and silently or aloud). Decide the number of pages that everyone should bring to each meeting (often five to ten), or if you plan to write together while you meet. Also, define the nature of the group's facilitation (i.e., will the same person lead, or will that responsibility rotate?).

Decide how feedback will be offered

Remember that for those who believe that they "can't write," a critiquing group might be more intimidating than fun. Use the group to help all members grow in confidence, through encouragement and constructive feedback—starting with strengths and moving on to possible improvements. Remind all members that although the writing process is personal, group comments are never to be taken personally. Bear in mind that everyone has feelings and attitudes about her or his writing experience, and may want to discuss them. In the group editing sessions in my workshops, I often open with a question like, "What has your writing life been like since we last met?"

(I offer many other specifics on giving and getting feedback in Chapter 17, "Edit the big picture," and Appendix 8, "Editing checklist.")

Carefully consider all comments

Listen as objectively as possible to other members' feedback on your own work. Try to remain silent and just take notes when receiving critique. I have found that although I may not agree with everything, all comments represent the reactions of at least some of my readership and are therefore worthwhile. Take at least a day to mull over and fully appreciate all input before reworking your piece.

Remember that even during your dry spells, your contributions are very important

Especially if you do not have a writing deadline coming up, or if you want to protect yourself from writer's block, a regular commitment to reading others' work will keep you in the swing of things. Your writing group partners will appreciate your participation, and they can often offer you the understanding, ideas, and motivation to keep your pen or keyboard active.

Break out of the mold occasionally

You may sometimes find that your writing circle could use some variety. Attend a writing-related lecture or listen to a teleseminar together—and then discuss it afterward. For a change of scenery, suggest meeting at a different venue. Or invite a guest writer of another genre to share ideas about his or her craft, as cross-pollination can yield some very interesting results. Also, feel free to think up your own Writing Workouts as a group, or refer to the Recommended Resources for other helpful ideas.

APPENDIX 11: Suggested Answers to Selected Writing Workouts

Some Writing Workouts in this book ask you to rewrite or fill in blanks for specific passages or sentences. You will find my suggestions here. Keep in mind that your particular style and voice should shine through, so you will probably end up with different answers to exercises that require some creativity (and not just grammatical correctness).

CHAPTER 9

STEP 1

A. ◉ What Can We Do to Make Cafeteria Food Healthier?
 ◉ Who Will Improve Nutrition in the School Cafeteria?
 ◉ Healthier Cafeteria Food? You Bet!

B. ◉ Write a Corporate Accountability Report: Measure Your Environmental and Social Impact Today!
 ◉ Want to Know Our Environmental and Social Impacts? Read the Corporate Accountability Report!

C. ◉ 3 Steps to Greening Your Next Fix-It Project
 ◉ Build It Green: How to Use Earth-Friendly Materials
 ◉ 7 Habits of Highly Environmentally Friendly Builders
 ◉ How to Build Green: Top 10 New Ways

D. ◉ 2 Simple Steps to Buying Fair Trade
 ◉ 3,000 Fair Trade Coffee Shops: Find the One Nearest You
 ◉ 5 New Websites Make Buying Fair Trade a No-Brainer

E. ◉ Anti-Poverty Movement Gets a Booster Shot
 ◉ Poverty Takes Another Hit
 ◉ New Law Strengthens Anti-Poverty Movement
 ◉ A Shot in the Arm or a Hole in the Head? Anti-Poverty Movement Controversy

CHAPTER 11

STEP 1

A. If you decide to move forward with the plan, and request our firm's facilitation services, we will develop a bid for them.

B. As a result of recent events, community members invited us to create a neighborhood policing program.

C. Let's supplement the three traditional Rs of waste management—reduce, reuse, and recycle— with a fourth R: rethink.

D. An angry mob told our founders, local activists, to "love it or leave it."

E. Women finally won the right to vote in 1920.

F. Looters burned many precious books in the Iraq National Library and Archives in 2003.

G. We decided to ignore the unjust law.

H. When did the Europeans discover America?

STEP 2

I. The income of the average working family in our city has plummeted during the past three decades.

J. The board wants to do a CEO search, but keeps confronting barriers.

K. She compared five different electric bicycles.

L. The website article explained the new city ordinance.

M. The scientists examined each specimen with a microscope.

N. Our grantmaking emphasizes projects that encourage citizen participation and serve as models for other initiatives across the country.

O. Interestingly, even as public radio becomes more popular, funding it poses a larger challenge than ever.

STEP 3

- conclude
- attend
- stop
- invite
- encourage
- can
- discuss
- simplify
- consider

STEP 4

P. The Director plans to brief the staff on the new policy.

Q. The planned merger of the two agencies will allow them to leverage their individual strengths.

CHAPTER 12

STEP 1

A. We are working with our team to identify various marketing strategies and we will present these options to the Board.

B. For more than 15 years, our in-home educational services program has partnered with nearly 1,000 parents who have helped their children achieve academic success.

C. At my previous position I coordinated two $150-a-plate luncheons per year, and co-facilitated our strategic planning process during a major organizational leadership transition.

D. The director frequently under-budgets.

E. After losing her teenage sister in a drunk driving accident, she wanted to join a community organization that addressed alcoholism. She subsequently became Volunteer of the Year at our treatment center.

F. I accept the idea that our trucks could reduce their greenhouse gas emissions, but the steps to take to make that happen continue to elude me.

G. The boy knew he was in trouble when he looked at his father's face.

CHAPTER 14

Champions of At-Risk Youth

Organization X was founded in 1989, with a mission to rebuild the lives of severely at-risk youth and young adults. We accomplish this mission by operating four community-benefit businesses that employ and train our young clients, as they recover from homelessness, substance abuse, and related problems. Organization X uses a model focused on the specific needs and goals of the individual, supported by mentors and peers. Over several months and up to two years, we teach disadvantaged young people how to realize their potential and become economically independent members of their communities.

The Pressing Need

Disadvantaged youth in our city face significant barriers to achieving economic independence and well-being. These barriers include poverty, substance abuse, educational underachievement, lack of skills, and family instability. Youth are looking for a path to self-sufficiency: now. But it is extremely difficult for them to find paid employment-based learning opportunities that also involve the critical supportive services they need. In addition, they are looking for a place where they are valued and receive encouragement to identify and reach their own goals.

Without these opportunities and a positive experience designed for their risk factors, it will be nearly impossible for these young people to attain higher education, stable employment and, ultimately, self-sufficiency as adults. The resulting costs to society—related to public assistance benefits and incarceration alone—are enormous.

Outstanding Results

What results have we seen in the past twenty years? Compare our work to the national averages for disadvantaged adults, and you will find much higher rates of:

- Sustained employment
- Living wages
- Movement from welfare to economic independence
- Acquisition of stable housing

...and much *lower* rates of criminal activity .[1]

CHAPTER 18

STEP 1

A. The website workshop lasted for three hours.

B. The institution insisted that information based on large standardized surveys was far more accurate than stories told in the community.

C. We no longer use that letterhead, so please recycle it.

D. If the event yields leftover food, please tell us so we can rush it to the homeless shelter.

E. These copywriting tips are easy to remember, except that one.

F. The main reason is that women more easily absorb and store fat-soluble chemicals, due to their biology.

G. African NGOs are arranging a collaborative effort with their U.S. counterparts. When they begin to work together they will have to restart the decision-making process.

---

[1]   Exact statistics would go here.

CHAPTER 19

STEP 1

A. We need to find homes for these children.

B. Although our coffers are not as full as they once were, we will continue to offer scholarships. We will simply get more creative in our financing arrangements, as we remain committed to making higher education affordable.

C. We are experiencing a severe drought.

D. We continue to find socially responsible investment opportunities that we feel have great potential. Our firm is focusing on alternative energy, green chemistry, and appropriate technology stocks.

E. Children with parents in prison often must endure traumatic consequences for years.

STEP 2

- hardship
- surrounded
- unique
- principle
- custom
- beginner
- experience
- growth
- plan
- assemble
- cooperate
- above
- bits
- safe

STEP 3

Organization Builders specializes in working with community organizations. Our unique consulting firm helps you navigate the complex realities of organizational development and enhance your long-term effectiveness. We work with you to clarify your vision and mission, build capacity and infrastructure, identify your competitive advantages, manage risk, and reach out to new constituencies. Throughout our work, Organization Builders demonstrates a deep understanding of your organization's culture and context, forming a true partnership for success. Together we can deliver results by integrating business acumen with innovation and exceptional service.

CHAPTER 21

STEP 1

A. is
   (Neither one is at fault.)

B. continues
   (The verb agrees with the subject ("search").)

C. he or she
   (Each person is a single individual.)

D. they
   ("All staff members" is plural.)

E. Does
   ("Anybody" is singular.)

F. me
   (The preposition "to" needs objects: you and me. The organization sent the promotional mailing to you and to me.)

G. were; would
   (The verbs need to appear in the subjunctive mood, as the energy efficiency is not yet real.)

H. Goes; are or is
   (Each intern is an individual. "None" can be interpreted here as referring to all of the interns (plural) or "not one of them" (singular). Traditionalists would choose the singular option; most contemporary grammarians would choose the plural and not sweat it.)

I. works; does
   (The sentence refers to the committee as a single entity.)

J. handle; needs
   (The first verb, "handle," comprises part of a phrase that uses a relative pronoun: "the thrift store employees who handle customer service." The second verb, "needs," agrees with the subject of the entire sentence ("each one"). Confusing? You bet.
   If you flip the sentence around you can see it more clearly:
   Of the thrift store employees who handle customer service, each one needs to attend the orientation.)

K. you; your

(Choose to address the reader in the second person. This is generally a wise decision when copywriting, and the word "laptop" (singular) indicates that the writer intends to write the sentence in the singular.)

STEP 2

A. I am waiting for a leader in our industry to make his or her factory a zero-waste facility, thus starting a competition to be the greenest business in the market.

B. By making a single factory a zero-waste facility, a leader is our industry can start a competition to be the greenest business in the market.

CHAPTER 22

STEP 1

A. Recycling or reusing your waste is more environmentally conscious than sending it to a landfill.

B. In-kind donations keep pouring in, and we are now able to serve 100 young people per month.

C. As the most in-shape person, Alicia is our first pick for our walk-a-thon team.

D. At the end of each year, we should be able to answer these questions:

- How did we achieve our mission?

- Where did our investors' money go?

- What changes did we implement to improve our work?

- What new success stories demonstrated the difference we are making in our community?

E. The conservationists, sporting sunglasses and bright Hawaiian shirts, could only access the outlying areas in SUVs.

F. - Created diversified evaluation plan for agency
- Oversaw projects initiated by Board of Directors

- Prepared all meeting materials

- Hired and supervised all vendors and contractors

- Maintained financial, project, and related records

- Administered payroll

- Monitored and reported on projected and actual budgetary information

G. One morning I was still in my pajamas when I shot an elephant. *(Alas, it is much less funny.)*

H. After arriving late to the meeting and complaining about the weather, Dr. Rainwater mixed up several of the most important and timely agenda items.

I. A group of internationally known human rights activists developed this project in the late 1990's to heal the social, cultural, and economic wounds of the 1992-1995 civil war. While that war had claimed the lives of tens of thousands of people, a concurrent AIDS epidemic in that country left thousands of young children grieving for the parents they had recently lost.

J. In our community, parents say they don't know how or where to access wellness services for their young children. Thus, early identification of hidden disabilities in these children is far from where it should be.

K. He decided to head downtown to quickly join the rally.
or
He quickly decided to head downtown to join the rally.

CHAPTER 23

A. affect
(You need a verb here.)

B. effect
(You need a noun here.)

C. 1. It's
(The contraction form of "it" and "is")
   2. its
(The possessive form of "it")
   3. it's
(The contraction form of "it" and "is")

D. Whose
(The possessive form of "who")

E. 1. They're
(The contraction form of "they" and "are")
   2. there
(A location)
   3. they're
(The contraction form of "they" and "are")
   4. their
(The possessive form or "they")

F. whom
(You need an objective of the preposition "with.")

G. further
(This is not about physical length or distance, but is somewhat figurative.)

H. fewer

   (Individual hours can be counted.)

I. which

   (The phrase encapsulated by commas is nonessential to the sentence's meaning.)

J. that

   (The phrase beginning with "that" tells us what kind of vision statement we are talking about. It is essential to the sentence's meaning.)

K. *This is a tricky one. If we add commas to the original, and only sell organically grown coffee beans, the sentence must be:*

   All of our coffee beans, which come from co-ops in Central America, are organically grown.

   But if we do not add commas, we can restrict our statement to mean that only our Central American coffee beans are organically grown. We simply don't mention any others:

   All of our coffee beans that come from co-ops in Central America are organically grown.

CHAPTER 24

STEP 1

A. The accountant, who is part-time, needs your timesheets. Don't forget to include any .25's or .75's.

   or

   The accountant (who is part-time) needs your timesheets. Don't forget to include any .25s or .75s.

B. The Executive Director—the father of two young children—is speaking at the donor reception late this evening, but he wishes he didn't have to.

C. The foundation officer told the audience, "As you can see, Ms. Mendoza's grant proposal is excellent. It's very fundable."

   or

   The foundation officer told the audience: "As you can see, Ms. Mendoza's grant proposal is excellent; it's very fundable."

D. Our government agency is always looking for great community programs to partner with (e.g., those working with young children, the elderly, or people with disabilities).

E. As a cooperative venture among three social enterprises, the Community Alliance is uniquely positioned to provide a wide range of low-cost wellness services to our state's veterans.

F. My parents often describe themselves as "non-conformists at heart." Although they may appear mainstream—with their traditional haircuts, well-ironed outfits, and suburban home—they harbor dreams of living a bohemian lifestyle.

G. I wish we could find a more detailed way to evaluate our effectiveness than simply tabulating pre- and post-session surveys.

H. Several state and local environmental regulations apply to this waterway, so we need to "clean up our act"—in more ways than one.

CHAPTER 25

STEP 1

A. **Beth's Story**

Beth came to The Family Agency in fear of her child's father. He was still trying daily to gain visitation rights regarding their young daughter, even though Beth had previously obtained a three-year Domestic Violence Restraining Order against him. She did not have any income, had been born deaf, and could only communicate in nonverbal Relay.

Clearly, the challenge to help Beth would be daunting. We had to find a translator who knew both Relay and American Sign Language, so we could ensure that The Family Agency attorney and Beth could speak. Such translators are extremely difficult to find.

We needed to communicate with Beth to explain the child's father's court actions and the relevant laws, as well as begin to prepare for the upcoming hearing. Numerous phone calls later, we were finally able to locate a translator who, after hearing about The Family Agency's work, agreed to assist us at a reduced public-interest fee ($50 per hour, instead of the market rate of $70 per hour).

Because of The Family Agency and our work against domestic violence, Beth was finally able to understand and have a voice in decisions regarding her daughter.

B. **About Organization X**

Organization X offers a leadership development program with a cross-cultural training focus, primarily involving young people (ages 18-26). Two young adults founded the organization in 1996; they both had grown up in Chicago in a low-income, biracial family and had benefited from key life-changing international and multicultural experiences early in life.

Organization X aims to develop a pool of young leaders of color from low-income backgrounds who are culturally sensitive, globally competent, and actively involved in improving their communities. The core program is the Youth Culture Initiative. During this 10-month program, the young people meet regularly to learn about community needs and U.S. sub-cultures. Their innovative activities include volunteer service-learning projects in different neighborhoods, overnight diversity learning retreats outside the city, and interactive workshops that focus on cross-cultural learning and leadership development.

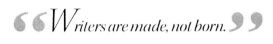

"Writers are made, not born."

— Ayn Rand

⁓Recommended Resources⁓

No single book can even hope to tell you all you need to know about ***writing to make a difference***. Although this book is a solid one-stop shop packed with the fundamental tools of the trade, you may want to dig deeper into any given topic I discuss. This section points you in the right direction to read up on the 25 techniques I share in this book. I have sifted through a veritable mountain of great works to present you with only the finest.

Here you will find more than one hundred books and websites, each categorized and briefly annotated. I have included excellent background resources, as well as resources that are specific to sections of this book. Remember that many books these days have related websites, and many websites also offer regular e-newsletters. Be sure to check for them! You can also find many more resources listed on my website, ***www.dfmassachi.net***, including references to new books, articles, websites, and other materials as they become available.

GENERAL WRITING ADVICE

Booher, Dianna. *E-Writing: 21st Century Tools for Effective Communication.* Pocket, 2001.
This is more about e-writing for communication within an organization, but also has good general information on e-writing.

Clark, Roy Peter. *Writing Tools: 50 Essential Strategies for Every Writer.* Little, Brown & Company, 2006.
A trusty toolbox of 50 concise chapters (each with an exercise at the end), written by a writing teacher at the Poynter Institute.

Forche, Carolyn, and Gerard Phillip, eds. *Writing Creative Nonfiction.* Story Press, 2001.
Familiarize yourself with this style of writing and you can begin to incorporate some of its techniques.

Hart, Jack R. *A Writer's Coach: An Editor's Guide to Words That Work.* Pantheon, 2006.
An acclaimed newspaper editor who has coached many successful writers shares his practical wisdom and insight on writing with clarity, style, and efficiency.

Plotnik, Arthur. *Spunk & Bite: A Writer's Guide to Punchier, More Engaging Language and Style.* Random House, 2005.
This updated version of Strunk & White's classic shares bolder, fresher, and more forceful techniques to draw in your readers.

Rosenthal, Lisa. *The Writing Group Book: Creating and Sustaining a Successful Writing Group.* Chicago Review Press, 2003.
Tips on forming in-person and online writing circles, contributed by real writing group participants (from many different genres).

Ross-Larson, Bruce. *Powerful Paragraphs.* Norton, 1999.
Part of the "Effective Writing Series" of advice for strong writing, with lots of examples.

Strunk, William, and E. B. White. *The Elements of Style.* Longman, 1918.
This famous classic is alst online at: *www.bartleby.com/141/index.html*

Wilbers, Stephen. *Writing for Business: Helpful, Easy-to-Apply Advice for Everyone Who Writes on the Job.* The Good Writing Press, 1993.
An oldie but goodie: a collection of short essays covering a wide range of writing issues.

Williams, Joseph M. *Style: Ten Lessons in Clarity and Grace.* Addison-Wesley Educational Publishers, 2003.
Looking for more traditional English writing instruction? Try this book.

Zinsser, William. *On Writing Well: The Classic Guide to Writing Nonfiction.* Harper-Perennial, 1998.
A classic from a well-known and bold writing teacher.

Garbl's Writing Center. *http://garbl.home.comcast.net/index.html*
A slew of general writing resources.

The Word Spy. *www.wordspy.com*
Lots of fun new words with definitions and example citations.

GENERAL COPYWRITING

Bly, Robert W. *The Online Copywriter's Handbook.* McGraw-Hill, 2002.
Although the Internet changes extremely rapidly, these concepts for online copywriting remain solid.

Camp, Lindsay. *Can I Change Your Mind? The Craft and Art of Persuasive Writing.* A&C Black, 2007.
Good info and examples about the principles and techniques of persuasive writing (by a witty, seasoned British author).

Caples, John, and Fred Hahn. *Tested Advertising Methods.* Prentice Hall, 1998.
A copywriting classic.

Gabay, J. Jonathan. *Gabay's Copywriters' Compendium: The Definitive Creative Writer's Guide.* Elsevier Ltd., 2007.
An eclectic and thorough copywriter's almanac/encyclopedia/phrase book from a well-known British copywriter.

Kranz, Jonathan. *Writing Copy for Dummies.* Wiley, 2005.
A modern, comprehensive primer on many kinds of copywriting.

Ogilvy, David. *Ogilvy on Advertising.* Vintage Books, 1983.
This copywriting classic comes from a veteran advertising wizard.

Shaw, Mark. *Copywriting: Successful Writing for Design, Advertising, and Marketing.* Laurence King, 2009.
Illustrated examples and copywriting guidance from a graphic design perspective.

Sugarman, Joseph. *The Adweek Copywriting Handbook: The Ultimate Guide to Writing Powerful Advertising and Marketing Copy from One of America's Top Copywriters.* John Wiley & Sons, 2007.
A great collection of decades of wisdom shared by a man who is often described as a copywriting legend.

CopyBlogger. *www.copyblogger.com*
A resource about online copywriting.

Flyte Blog. *www.flyteblog.com/flyte/web_copywriting/index.html*
Blog about web copywriting for small businesses.

Marketing Power: American Marketing Association. *www.marketingpower.com*
Great site for all kinds of marketing info for socially responsible organizations of all kinds; free web seminars, articles, and more.

Marketing Profs. *www.marketingprofs.com*
Membership site with expert advice on marketing concepts and strategies.

Mr. Fire. *www.mrfire.com*
The website of well-known copywriter Joe Vitale.

Online Fundraising and Nonprofit Marketing. *www.fundraising123.org*
The online fundraising website from Network for Good.

PUBLIC-INTEREST COPYWRITING

Andresen, Katya. *Robin Hood Marketing: Stealing Corporate Savvy to Sell Just Causes.* Jossey-Bass, 2006.
Written by a journalist, marketer, and nonprofit professional, this important book analyzes successful marketing campaigns and shows how to apply the principles to marketing in the public interest.

Barbato, Joseph, and Danielle S. Furlich. *Writing for a Good Cause: The Complete Guide to Crafting Proposals and Other Persuasive Pieces for Nonprofits.* Simon & Schuster, 2000.
Mostly on writing grant proposals, but includes other guidance too.

Dunlap, Louise. *Undoing the Silence: Six Tools for Social Change Writing.* New Village Press, 2007.
Advice for writing from the grassroots.

Goodman, Andy. *Why Bad Ads Happen to Good Causes: And How to Ensure It Won't Happen to Yours.* Cause Communications, 2002.
Guidance on what to do and what NOT to do in your advertising campaigns; available via download:
http://www.agoodmanonline.com/bad_ads_good_causes/index.html

Cause Marketing Network. *www.causemarketing.org*
A great place to learn about cause-related marketing.

Marketing 4 Change. *http://marketing4change.wordpress.com*
A blog on how new media and social media marketing can help tell your story; also includes a nice blogroll.

Social Edge. *www.socialedge.org/discussions/marketing-communication*
Join these online discussions on marketing and communication topics for social entrepreneurs.

CHAPTER A: CREATE AND ADVANCE YOUR BRAND

Holland, D.K. *Branding for Nonprofits: Developing Identity with Integrity.* Allworth Press, 2006.
Guidance on how to launch a great new mission-based brand or enliven an existing one, from a writer and designer.

Patterson, Sally J., and Janel M. Radtke. *Strategic Communications for Nonprofit Organizations: Seven Steps to Creating a Successful Plan.* Wiley, 2009.
This guide walks you through a deep process of communication planning.

Ries, Al, and Laura Ries. *The 22 Immutable Laws of Branding: How to Build a Product or Service into a World-Class Brand.* HarperCollins, 2002.
This marketing classic teaches branding from a traditional corporate point of view—learn from it! Make sure you get the edition that includes the 11 Immutable Laws of Internet Branding.

CHAPTER B: ENGAGE YOUR SPECIFIC READERS

Andreasen, Alan R. *Marketing Research That Won't Break the Bank: A Practical Guide to Getting the Information You Need.* Jossey-Bass, 2002.
Detailed guidance on low-cost ways to get the information you need to make smart, strategic decisions.

Gladwell, Malcolm. *The Tipping Point: How Little Things Can Make a Big Difference.* Back Bay Books, 2002.
This book explains several specific types of people who make ideas take off.

Godin, Seth. *Permission Marketing: Turning Strangers into Friends, and Friends into Customers.* Simon and Schuster, 1999.
Classic about marketing on the Internet without interrupting your reader's flow.

Ray, Paul H., and Sherry Ruth Anderson. *The Cultural Creatives: How 50 Million People Are Changing the World.* Harmony Books, 2000.
Describes the values and lifestyles of the creators of a new subculture of change; your organization is probably working with many of them!

Free Demographics. *www.freedemographics.com*
Free access to data from both the 1990 and the 2000 U.S. Census.

Public Agenda. *www.publicagenda.org*
A nonprofit, nonpartisan research organization that provides free current public opinion data.

CHAPTER 1: SPOTLIGHT YOUR MISSION REPEATEDLY

Angelica, Emil. *The Fieldstone Alliance Guide To Crafting Effective Mission and Vision Statements.* Fieldstone Alliance, 2001.
This little book will help you hammer out the right mission and vision statements for your organization.

CHAPTER 2: MAXIMIZE YOUR COLLABORATIONS

Schrage, Michael. *Shared Minds: The New Technologies of Collaboration.* Random House, 1990.
Discusses how computer technologies enhance creative collaboration across issue or approach or perspective—for marketing and other purposes.

CHAPTER 3: REFLECT YOUR TRUE NUMBERS

Paulos, John Allen. *Innumeracy: Mathematical Illiteracy and Its Consequences.* Hill and Wang, 2001.
Learn about what Americans know and don't know about numbers—and what that implies.

FrameWorks Institute. *www.frameworksinstitute.org*
A great organization that shares their communication research on social issues.

Innovation Network. *www.innonet.org*
Free evaluation instruments for social impact.

United Way's Outcome Measurement Resource Network. *www.liveunited.org/outcomes*
A solid resource of outcome measurement tools based on United Way's experiences.

CHAPTER 5: SHARE STORIES

Clarke, Cheryl. *Storytelling for Grantseekers: Telling Your Organization's Story.* Jossey-Bass, 2001.
Applies storytelling techniques to the art of crafting grant proposals; also talks about seeing a proposal in a larger context of audience relationships and packaging.

Kramer, Mark, and Wendy Call, eds. *Telling True Stories: A Nonfiction Writers' Guide from the Nieman Foundation at Harvard University.* Plume, 2007.
This excellent collection of essays covers nonfiction narrative writing from several points of view and will help you write powerful stories.

Olmstead, Robert. *Elements of the Writing Craft.* Story Press, 1997.
For the serious student of the writing craft comes this book of brief literature passages and stimulating exercises to analyze and practice techniques used by distinguished writers past and present.

CHAPTER 6: WRITE WITH READER DIVERSITY IN MIND

Lockhart, Janet, and Susan M. Shaw. *Writing for Change: Raising Awareness of Difference, Power and Discrimination.* Teaching Tolerance, 2002.
Very good resource for exploring bias in American English, with more than 50 activities; available at: *www.tolerance.org/kit/writing-change*

Maggio, Rosalie. *Talking About People: A Guide to Fair and Accurate Language.* Greenwood, 1997.
Comprehensive, explanatory dictionary of ways to use words and phrases to avoid bias.

Poynter Institute's Diversity Tip Sheets/Resources. *www.poynter.org/column.asp?id=58&aid=137951*
Updates on new ways to enhance storytelling from different perspectives.

CHAPTER 7: POWER THROUGH YOUR WRITER'S BLOCKS & CHAPTER 8: SET UP FOR EFFICIENCY

Buzan, Tony, and Barry Buzan. *The Mind Map Book: How to Use Radiant Thinking to Maximize Your Brain's Untapped Potential.* Plume, 1996.
The popularizer of the mind mapping concept explores many ways for writers and others to benefit from this non-linear thinking and planning technique.

Houston, Velina Hasu. *Writer's Block Busters: 101 Exercises to Clear the Deadwood and Make Room for Flights of Fancy.* Smith & Kraus, 2008.
This little book, written by a playwright, is great for getting your creative juices flowing by focusing on characters and scenes.

Rico, Gabriele. *Writing the Natural Way: Using Right-Brain Techniques to Release Your Expressive Power.* Tarcher, 2000.
Offers creative ways to let your inner writer out.

Rountree, Cathleen. *Writer's Mentor: A Guide to Putting Passion on Paper.* Conari Press, 2002.
Advice for those choosing a writer's life, including topics on how to get started and keep going.

Staw, Jane Anne. *Unstuck: A Supportive and Practical Guide to Working Through Writer's Block.* St. Martin's Press, 2003.
Each chapter ends with exercises you can do to help you get unstuck.

FreeMind. *http://freemind.sourceforge.net/wiki/index.php/Main_Page*
This free mindmapping software can enhance your productivity.

CHAPTER 10: SHOW, DON'T JUST TELL

Lakoff, George. *Don't Think of an Elephant: Know Your Values and Frame the Debate—The Essential Guide for Progressives.* Chelsea Green, 2004.
In-depth info on the use of framing and metaphors in political rhetoric.

Cliché finders. *www.westegg.com/cliche* and *www.clichesite.com*
Two great indexes of clichés you can freshen up and then use.

Metaphor Project. *www.metaphorproject.org*
Resources for using metaphors to frame messages of peace, justice, and ecological sustainability.

CHAPTER 12: GET CRYSTAL CLEAR

Plain Language. *www.plainlanguage.gov*
Document checklist and other info from the federal government about clarity and conciseness.

CHAPTER 13: AVOID JARGON

From the Edna McConnell Clark Foundation. *www.emcf.org/pub/otherresources.htm*
Three book-length essays about cutting jargon -- beginning in the foundation world.

CHAPTER 15: MAKE SURE IT *SOUNDS* RIGHT

History.com's Speeches Audio Gallery. *www.history.com/video.do?name=speeches*
Listen to or watch clips of famous speeches throughout history.

Vital Speeches of the Day's Virtual Library of Resources. *www.vsotd.com/Resource.php*
Recommended websites on speechwriting.

Wikisource Collection of Speeches. *http://en.wikisource.org/wiki/Wikisource:Speeches*
This site provides the text of many famous speeches.

CHAPTER 18: CULTIVATE CONCISENESS

Cone, Steve. *Powerlines: Words That Sell Brands, Grip Fans, and Sometimes Change History.* Bloomberg Press, 2008.
Here we learn about the ultimate in concise writing for brand-building: the all-powerful tagline or slogan that makes a marketing campaign sing or croak.

Fiske, Robert Hartwell. *The Dictionary of Concise Writing: More Than 10,000 Alternatives to Wordy Phrases.* Marion Street Press, 2006.
Dictionaries are not usually concise, but this one shows you how to turn verbosity into brevity—in sentences, phrases, and individual words.

Getting Attention. *www.gettingattention.org*
Offers advice on taglines and other marketing tools for the mission-minded organization.

CHAPTER 20: MAKE SURE IT *LOOKS* RIGHT

Messaris, Paul. *Visual Persuasion: The Role of Images in Advertising.* Sage Publications, 1997.
If you want a solid, illustrated academic analysis of the visual aspect of advertising, read this book.

White, Jan V. *Editing by Design: For Designers, Art Directors, and Editors—the Classic Guide to Winning Readers.* Allworth Press, 2003.
A well-illustrated design education if I ever saw one.

Williams, Robin. *The Non-Designer's Design Book: Design and Typographic Principles for the Visual Novice.* Peachpit Press, 2008.
A wonderfully concise introduction to key design principles.

Dreamstime. *www.dreamstime.com*
Free and low-cost stock images.

Everystockphoto. *www.everystockphoto.com*
Search engine of free license-specific photos.

FreeStockPhotos.com. *http://freestockphotos.com*
Photos you can use with a copyright notice; links to other free photo sites.

Green Clipart. *www.greenclipart.com*
A collection of clipart with an ecological theme.

iStockphoto. *www.istockphoto.com/index.php*
Low-cost photos, illustrations, video, and audio.

Pro Corbis. *http://pro.corbis.com*
Royalty-free images and stock photos for a fee.

SECTION IVB: FINE-TUNING: PICKY, PICKY, PICKY

Hale, Constance. *Sin and Syntax: How to Craft Wickedly Effective Prose.* Broadway Books, 2001.
Updated grammar and style "rules" and when to break them, along with traditional and non-traditional examples.

O'Connor, Patricia T. *Woe Is I: The Grammarphobe's Guide to Better English in Plain English.* Putnam, 1996.
Very readable and witty grammar book.

O'Connor, Patricia T. *Words Fail Me: What Everyone Who Writes Should Know about Writing.* Mariner Books, 2000.
Here O'Conner builds on her grammar advice to give us more thoughts on effective writing style.

Truss, Lynne. *Eats, Shoots & Leaves: The Zero Tolerance Approach to Punctuation.* Gotham Books, 2004.
This entertaining guidebook contains some British-isms but is all-around helpful to both punctuation nit-pickers and the rest of us.

Walsh, Bill. *Lapsing Into a Comma: A Curmudgeon's Guide to the Many Things That Can Go Wrong in Print—and How to Avoid Them.* McGraw-Hill, 2000.
A real-world style guide written with insider commentary by a veteran *Washington Post* copy desk chief.

Walsh, Bill. *The Elephants of Style: A Trunkload of Tips on the Big Issues and Gray Areas of Contemporary American English.* McGraw-Hill, 2004.
This manual continues in the same vein as Walsh's earlier work.

---

100 Most Often Misspelled Words in English. *www.yourdictionary.com/library/misspelled.html*
This site offers friendly advice on how to remember those tricky spellings!

Alan Cooper's Homonyms. *www.cooper.com/alan/homonym.html*
This is actually a long list of *homophones*, but who's counting?

American Copy Editors Society's Blogroll. *http://www.copydesk.org/blogroll/*
Here is a list of professional copyeditors' blogs.

Ask Oxford. *www.askoxford.com*
That's right: You can ask questions of the people who put out the famous dictionary.

Capital Community College Foundation's Guide to Grammar & Writing. *http://grammar.ccc.commnet.edu/grammar/index.htm*
Good collection of grammar guidance, interactive quizzes, and FAQs.

Common Errors in English Usage. *www.wsu.edu/~brians/errors/index.html*
An extensive alphabetical list of errors, written by a Washington State University English professor (with a personality).

English Grammar Secrets. *www.englishgrammarsecrets.com/*
This site offers many grammar lessons and interactive exercises.

Grammar Bytes! *www.chompchomp.com*
Another great online grammar site.

Grammargirl. *http://grammar.quickanddirtytips.com/*
A popular podcast on grammar.

Lynch's Guide to Grammar and Style. *http://andromeda.rutgers.edu/~jlynch/Writing/*
This extensive (and free) guide comes from an associate professor of English at Rutgers University and lists a few other good online resources.

Online Writing Lab (OWL). *http://owl.english.purdue.edu/owl/*
This well-known resource offers free writing advice from Purdue University.

Self-Study Homonym Quizzes. *http://a4esl.org/q/h/homonyms.html*
Homonym exercises written for ESL learners but helpful for anyone.

The Slot. *www.theslot.com*
Website created by Bill Walsh (see his books cited above).

POPULAR STYLE GUIDES

Associated Press. *The Associated Press Stylebook.* Basic Books, 2009.

Connolly, William, and Allan Siegal. *The New York Times Manual of Style and Usage.* Three Rivers Press, 2002.

Modern Language Association. *MLA Style Manual and Guide to Scholarly Publishing.* Modern Language Association of America, 2008.

University of Chicago Press Staff. *The Chicago Manual of Style.* University of Chicago Press, 2003.

ᴗIndexᴗ

These page references point to both literal appearances of these words and more general discussions of the broader concepts. In addition, please note that I define many of these words in Appendix 2, "Glossary of Buzzwords." Be sure to check for them!

About Writing for Community Success

In 1999, Dalya Massachi founded Writing for Community Success to help those in community-oriented organizations advance their missions and boost their impact through effective writing. Our clients quickly begin to see improvements, with no more frustratingly long learning curves.

All of our work is designed to express clients' values and vision as they engage a variety of audiences. Affordable services include:

- Interactive writing workshops
- Conference presentations and keynotes
- One-on-one writing coaching
- Customized editorial services
- Free monthly e-newsletter

Our clients are great at providing services and products to their communities, but feel they can improve the way they write about that work. They understand that poor writing can hurt their organization's reputation—and pocketbook. And they know that powerful writing will make their work stand out from the glut of information out there.

Some clients must deal with tight deadlines or staff shortfalls and could use a little extra help. Others want to grow professionally and seek fresh, objective feedback from an outside expert to help raise their writing skills to the next level.

What can you expect from working with us? Here's a quick list:

- Industry-specific guidance you cannot get from most writing teachers
- Lots of constructive feedback and encouragement
- Thorough, easy-to-understand explanations
- Great ideas and insights to make your documents educate and activate
- Customized advice for your professional level
- An interactive approach with a positive attitude and a touch of humor
- Speedy turnaround time
- Convenient availability in person, over the phone, or online
- Budget-consciousness to make your project affordable

Please see our website for more information: ***www.dfmassachi.net***.

Companion Website: www.dfmassachi.net

Interested in even more ***Writing to Make a Difference?***
Visit my website for many more resources:

- An online community for readers of this book to exchange experiences and get their questions answered

- My blog and free e-newsletter

- Articles and writing tips

- Teleseminars and webinars

- Information on upcoming book signings, workshops, and other public appearances near you

- My podcast, including audio interviews with other experts in communications for socially responsible organizations

...and much more web-only content.

Ordering Copies of This Book

This book is available either professionally printed or as an e-book. To order either, just choose one of these options:

1. Go to ***www.dfmassachi.net*** to buy online via secure credit card or e-check payment

2. From the same site, download an order form or use this one:

ITEM	PRICE	QTY	SUBTOTAL
Writing to Make a Difference: hard copy	$29.95 USD		
Writing to Make a Difference: e-book	$19.95 USD		
Sales Tax (CA residents only)	x.0975		
Shipping & Handling to U.S. Addresses (hard copy only)	$5.50 USD		
TOTAL			

Note: Bulk orders of ten or more copies will be discounted—just ask by email (orders@dfmassachi.net) or phone (510-839-1544).

Name: _____

Shipping address: _____

_____

_____

Email address: _____

Your check or money order should be payable to: "Writing for Community Success." Send it with this order form to:

Writing for Community Success
P.O. Box 5607
Berkeley, CA 94705

Thank you!

Breinigsville, PA USA
14 July 2010
241738BV00004B/2/P